"Massimo Faggioli has emerged as one of the most insightful and energetic young scholars in Catholic theology today. In this bold new book, Faggioli makes a compelling argument that the significance of Vatican II's Constitution on the Sacred Liturgy was not limited to liturgical reform; the document established a compelling ecclesiological vision that set the agenda for later conciliar documents and the postconciliar church. Faggioli lays out for us what is really at stake in the many recent assaults on the council's liturgical reform—nothing less than an assault on the entire ecclesiology of the council. This book belongs on the short list of those truly indispensable studies of the Second Vatican Council."

> Richard R. Gaillardetz
> Boston College
> Co-author of *Keys to the Council: Unlocking the Teaching of Vatican II*

"*True Reform* is a thoroughly documented analysis of *Sacrosanctum Concilium* and its reception by the Second Vatican Council itself. The document's connection with the ecclesiology of the council emerges fully. In this way, the book provides a deep understanding of the council in its liturgical dimension and its unavoidable call to reform the church in order to be more faithful to the Gospel of Jesus Christ."

> Fr. Enzo Bianchi
> Founder and prior of the ecumenical monastic Community of Bose

"This is a valuable, even groundbreaking, study for the interpretation of Vatican II. Faggioli succeeds in showing how the liturgy constitution and the subsequent liturgical reform are essential for the understanding and implementation of the council. It should be required reading for ecclesiologists and historians of the contemporary church as well as for students of the liturgy—perhaps even for members of the Roman Curia."

> John F. Baldovin, SJ
> Boston College
> Author of *Reforming the Liturgy: A Response to the Critics*

Massimo Faggioli

True Reform

Liturgy and Ecclesiology in *Sacrosanctum Concilium*

A PUEBLO BOOK

Liturgical Press   Collegeville, Minnesota
www.litpress.org

A Pueblo Book published by Liturgical Press

Cover design: Jodi Hendrickson. Cover images: Thinkstock.

Excerpts from documents of the Second Vatican Council are from *Vatican Council II: Volume 1, The Conciliar and Post Conciliar Documents*, by Austin Flannery, OP. © 1996 (Costello Publishing Company, Inc.). Used with permission.

Chapter 1 is based on the article "Quaestio Disputata: *Sacrosanctum Concilium* and the Meaning of Vatican II," published in *Theological Studies* 71, no. 2 (2010): 437–52. Used by permission.

Library of Congress Cataloging-in-Publication Data

Faggioli, Massimo.
    True reform : liturgy and ecclesiology in Sacrosanctum concilium / Massimo Faggioli.
        p.   cm.
    "A Pueblo book."
    Includes bibliographical references (p.   ) and index.
    ISBN 978-0-8146-6238-0 — ISBN 978-0-8146-6263-2 (ebook)
        1. Catholic Church—Liturgy—History—20th century.   2. Vatican Council (2nd : 1962–1965). Constitutio de sacra liturgia.   3. Liturgical reform.   I. Title.

BX1970.F34   2012
264'.02009045—dc23

                                                                    2012018096

Contents

Abbreviations

Acta Synodalia

> *Acta Synodalia Sacrosancti Concilii Oecumenici Vaticani II*, Cura et studio Archivi Concilii Oecumenici Vaticani, vols. 1–6 in 33 books (Città del Vaticano: Typis Polyglottis Vaticanis, 1970–99).

Bugnini, *The Reform of the Liturgy*

> Annibale Bugnini, *The Reform of Liturgy 1948–1975* (Collegeville, MN: Liturgical Press, 1990; English edition from the Italian: Roma, 1983).

Congar, *Journal du concile*

> Yves Congar, *Mon journal du concile*. Présenté et annoté par Éric Mahieu; avant-propos de Dominique Congar; préface de Bernard Dupuy, 2 vols. (Paris: Cerf, 2002).

Dossetti, *Chiesa eucaristica*

> Giuseppe Dossetti, *Per una "chiesa eucaristica." Rilettura della portata dottrinale della Costituzione liturgica del Vaticano II. Lezioni del 1965*, ed. Giuseppe Alberigo and Giuseppe Ruggieri (Bologna: Il Mulino, 2002).

History of Vatican II

> *History of Vatican II*, vols. 1–5, ed. Giuseppe Alberigo, English version ed. Joseph A. Komonchak (Maryknoll, NY: Orbis, 1995–2006).

Jungmann, *Kommentar*

> Josef A. Jungmann, "Kommentar zur Liturgiekonstitution," in *Das Zweite Vatikanische Konzil. Konstitutionen, Dekrete und Erklärungen lateinisch und deutsch Kommentare*, Lexikon für Theologie und Kirche, Bd. I (Freiburg i.B.: Herder, 1966), 10–109.

Kaczynski, *Kommentar*

> Reiner Kaczynski, "Theologischer Kommentar zur Konstitution über die Heilige Liturgie Sacrosanctum Concilium," in *Herders Theologischer Kommentar zum Zweiten Vatikanischen Konzil*, ed. Hans Jochen Hilberath and Peter Hünermann, vol. 2 (Freiburg i.B.: Herder, 2004), 9–227.

O'Malley, *What Happened*

> John W. O'Malley, *What Happened at Vatican II* (Cambridge, MA, and London: Belknap Press of Harvard University Press, 2008).

SC

> Second Vatican Council, Constitution on the Sacred Liturgy, *Sacrosanctum Concilium* (December 4, 1963).

Acknowledgments

I am not a specialist of liturgy, nor do I try to be. But as a historian of modern Catholicism and of Vatican II, I have tried to offer reflections to liturgists and to the faithful about the liturgical reform approved in December 1963 and implemented starting November 1964. The debate on the liturgical reform of Vatican II does not need to be more controversial than it is now, but it needs, for sure, a deeper understanding of the liturgical reform in connection with the rest of the theological reforms of Vatican II, with what happened at Vatican II, and with the historicity and inculturation as connatural dimensions of the life of the Church.

This book started as a project for my fellowship at the Jesuit Institute at Boston College in the academic year from 2008 to 2009 and is meant to be the work of a historian of the Church, and specifically of Vatican II, trying to understand and explain some aspects of the deep theological insights of the liturgical constitution, *Sacrosanctum Concilium*, at a crucial moment in the history of the reception of the council and of its most visible fruit, the liturgical reform. This research owes much to the years at the "Fondazione per le scienze religiose" in Bologna between 1996 and 2007, a particularly challenging and enriching environment, at that time led by Giuseppe Alberigo, Alberto Melloni, and Giuseppe Ruggieri. The first insights regarding the relations between the liturgical constitution of Vatican II and the rest of the council's meaning for the Catholic Church came to me through the writings on Vatican II by the founder and spiritual father of the "Bologna school," Giuseppe Dossetti—an Italian politician, canon lawyer and later priest, *peritus* at the council, and finally monk.

But even before my arrival at the "Fondazione per le scienze religiose," a personal, long friendship began with important monasteries in the history of the liturgical movement before and after Vatican II: the Monastery of Camaldoli and the ecumenical monastic community of Bose (Italy), and in more distant years, the Monastery of the Holy Cross in Chevetogne (Belgium) and the Monastery of Mar Mousa al-Habashi (St. Moses the Abyssinian) in the desert of Syria. In these places I have received an incommensurable measure of inspiration, wisdom, peace, and guidance, for which I will be forever in debt.

During these last four years I received much help in the preparation of this book, starting with Hans Christoffersen at Liturgical Press, who welcomed and encouraged this project beyond my expectations and offered my work another and much-needed spiritual home in College-ville, Minnesota. John O'Malley, SJ, has been the spark for many in-sights and the example of a theologian-historian able to comprehend the "Catholic Church" phenomenon in the context of the macro-period of Trent-Vatican II—an absolute necessity for understanding the litur-gical issue in the Catholic Church of the post–Vatican II period. Mark Massa, SJ, has given me a theological and, most of all, a personal friendship that goes beyond the time zones and has been a source of invaluable insights, ideas, and courage in addressing this issue. T. Frank Kennedy, SJ, and the Jesuit Institute provided an enviable and comfortable home for the first steps of this work, in the environment of Boston College, where theological work is not shy of engagement with the issues of our Church and at the same time is a responsible voice toward the *ecclesia*. I thank also David Schultenover, SJ, not only for publishing the first chapter of this book in *Theological Studies* in 2010 but also for offering me a partner in dialogue during these interesting times of anniversaries of Vatican II. In Italy, Andrea Grillo is a geo-graphically distant but theologically very close interpreter of Vatican II; many of the ideas here expressed owe to him many starting points and leads.

Since my arrival in St. Paul, Minnesota, at the University of St. Thomas, I could count on the friendship and advice of many colleagues in my department, especially Tom Fisch, Paul Gavryluk, Michael Hollerich, Fr. Michael Joncas, Sr. Katarina Schuth, OSF, and Victoria Young. My undergraduate students at the University of St. Thomas and my graduate students at the Saint Paul Seminary School of Divinity have revealed themselves as a much-needed voice in this debate about the reception of the theology of Vatican II, in particular of the liturgical reform. The final stages of this work were possible thanks to the precious help of my graduate research assistants at the University of St. Thomas–Saint Paul Seminary, Jeff Duresky and Ryan Langr. Lauren L. Murphy, my copy editor, was exceedingly sup-portive of my manuscript and me.

I cannot forget here other important presences of friends and colleagues in the long reflections accompanying the work on this book: among them Thomas Cattoi, Peter De Mey, Gerard Mannion, Serena Noceti, Maureen Sullivan, and the friends at the monastic communities of Bose and of Camaldoli in Italy, especially Fr. Lino Breda, Giuseppe M. Croce, and Dom Emilio Contardi.

This book on the liturgical reform and its consequences is dedicated to the women of my family and of a wider circle that has become family. Very often they have been for me wonderful teachers in the *ars celebrandi*, the art of celebrating little and big events of life: my grandmas Milena and Nives; my mother Anna; my sister Ilaria; my wife Sarah; my daughter Laura; my aunties Gioconda, Annamaria, Letizia, and Simonetta; the cousins Chiara and Elisa; my spiritual correspondent Sr. Maria Elisa in the Monastery of Ara Crucis in Faenza (Italy); my fellow *émigré* Francescaclaudia; my mother-in-law Mary; and the ever-welcoming Bostonian Ruby. This book is only a partial compensation for their support and patience.

Sacrosanctum Concilium and the Meaning of Vatican II

The issue of the hermeneutics of the liturgical constitution of Vatican II in the life of the Church is far from purely theoretical. There is no end to how much this issue has been debated in these last years, yet it is difficult to tell the debaters, aware of the stakes of the debate, apart from the theologians who deal with liturgical reform as just one issue among the issues. In this respect, the awareness of the ongoing debate on liturgy is now, fifty years after John XXIII's announcement of the council, not very different from the minimal state of awareness of most bishops and theologians regarding this issue on the eve of Vatican II.[1] Nonetheless, in 2003 the fortieth anniversary of the solemn approval of *Sacrosanctum Concilium* stirred debate about the role of liturgy in the Church of Vatican II.[2] More recently, Benedict XVI's *motu proprio Summorum Pontificum* (July 7, 2007) concerning the liturgy has revived interest in the destiny of the liturgical constitution, the first document debated and approved by Vatican II on November 22, 1963, voted by the council fathers with a majority of 2,162 to forty-six after a debate that featured 328 oral interventions on the floor of St. Peter's.

---

[1] See Rita Ferrone, *Liturgy:* Sacrosanctum Concilium (New York: Paulist Press, 2007), 19 50; Alberto Melloni, "Sacrosanctum Concilium 1963–2003. Lo spessore storico della riforma liturgica e la ricezione del Vaticano II," *Rivista liturgica* 90, no. 6 (2003): 915–30; Andrea Grillo, *La nascita della liturgia nel XX secolo. Saggio sul rapporto tra movimento liturgico e (post-)modernità* (Assisi: Cittadella, 2003).

[2] See Massimo Faggioli, "Concilio Vaticano II: bollettino bibliografico (2002–2005)," *Cristianesimo nella Storia* 26, no. 3 (2005): 743–67; Massimo Faggioli, "Vatican Council II: Bibliographical Overview 2005–2007," *Cristianesimo nella Storia* 29, no. 2 (2008): 567–610; "Vatican Council II: Bibliographical Overview 2007–2010," *Cristianesimo nella Storia* 32, no. 2 (2011): 755–91. More broadly, see Massimo Faggioli, *Vatican II: The Battle for Meaning* (Mahwah, NJ: Paulist Press, 2012).

1.1. The Nemesis of the Liturgical Reform

Although it may sound paradoxical, looking at the spectacular effects of *Sacrosanctum Concilium* in the Catholic Church during the last fifty years places the observer before a sort of tragic destiny of the liturgical constitution. In the history of the hermeneutics of Vatican II, the liturgical reform seems to have a nemesis—a kind of retribution for having overlooked the connections between the liturgical constitution and the overall hermeneutics of Vatican II. This neglect was not shared by Joseph Ratzinger whose attention to the theological and ecclesiological implications of the liturgical reform characterized some of his major works as a theologian first and as Roman pontiff later.[3]

Theologians and historians have somehow taken for granted the long history of the liturgical movement before Vatican II, the fact that Vatican II was the first council in Church history to approve a doctrinal document on liturgy, the undeniable truth that "something happened" for liturgy at Vatican II, the interconnections between the liturgical reform and the ecclesiological issue, and the patent fact that the liturgical reform of Vatican II is the last vast *reform* within the post-Tridentine Catholic Church after the reform of Church discipline between the sixteenth and seventeenth centuries. Both historians and theologians seem increasingly inclined to forget the tight associations between the liturgical debate at Vatican II, the reform of the liturgy, the striving for the *aggiornamento*, and the updating and reform of the Catholic Church. But most of all, in some interpretations of the documents of Vatican II, the fact that Vatican II has a deep, internal coherence, as John O'Malley has stressed,[4] seems to be entirely lost.

No matter what the new generations of deniers of the historical fact of "change" in the history of the Church may say, the liturgical life of the Catholic Church did, in fact, change after Vatican II and after *Sacrosanctum Concilium*, even if the *Wirkungsgeschichte*, the "history of

---

[3] See the introduction to volume 11 of the *Gesammelte Schriften*: "Als mich nach eigenem Zögern entschlossen hatte, das Projekt einer Ausgabe meiner Gesammelten Schriften anzunehmen, war für mich klar, dass dabei die Prioritätenordnung des Konzils gelten und daher der Band mit meinen Schriften zur Liturgie am Anfang stehen müsse" (Joseph Ratzinger, now Benedict XVI, "Zum Eröffnungsband meiner Schriften," in Joseph Ratzinger, *Gesammelte Schriften*, Band 11, *Theologie der Liturgie*, 2nd ed. [Freiburg i.B.: Herder, 2008], 6).

[4] For a thorough appreciation of the intertextual character of the issues at Vatican II, see O'Malley, *What Happened*, 309–12.

the effects" of the liturgical reform, both in the local churches and in global Catholicism, must still be written.[5]

The sometimes self-referential debate about Vatican II sidesteps and obscures the profound significance of *Sacrosanctum Concilium*. The interconnections between liturgy and Vatican II, seen not as a collection of documents but as a coherent reality, must emerge if we want to understand the impact of the council on global Catholicism. As Nicholas Lash observes: "the state of the liturgy is the first and fundamental test of the extent to which the programme, not merely of the decree *Sacrosanctum concilium* but of all the council's constitutions and decrees, is being achieved."[6]

What is needed today is a thorough reflection on the relationship between the liturgical constitution of Vatican II and the whole achievement of Vatican II. We must aim at understanding *whether* and *how* the liturgical debate and the resulting constitution, *Sacrosanctum Concilium*, were received by participants in Vatican II in its unfolding and final documents. In particular, it will be revealing to see how much of *Sacrosanctum Concilium* is present in Vatican II, and how much of Vatican II is present in the first constitution, *Sacrosanctum Concilium*. The real stakes are not the recovery of an aesthetics of the rites under the "reform of the liturgical reform": "serious critique of the reform— both in its formulation in the Liturgy Constitution and in the subsequent reformed liturgical books and their implementation—needs to be attended to."[7]

In the forty years after Vatican II it has become clear that forgetting the theological and ecclesiological background of the liturgical reform of Vatican II condemns *Sacrosanctum Concilium* to be quickly filed away with other documents dealing with some of the practical adjustments of the Catholic Church. More gravely, forgetting the relationship between liturgy and ecclesiologies (plural) at the council condemns

[5] For two studies of the reception of the liturgical reform, see Angel Unzueta, "L'action liturgique, expression de la Pentecôte" (about the liturgical reform in the Basque region), and Rémy Kurowski, "La messe dominicale comme creuset de la réception de la réforme liturgique en Pologne. Le cas de la diocèse de Gniezno," in *Réceptions de Vatican II. Le Concile au risque de l'histoire et des espaces humaines*, dir. Gilles Routhier (Leuven: Peeters, 2004), 91–102 and 103–29.

[6] Nicholas Lash, *Theology for Pilgrims* (Notre Dame, IN: University of Notre Dame Press, 2008), 226–28.

[7] John Baldovin, *Reforming the Liturgy: A Response to the Critics* (Collegeville, MN: Liturgical Press, 2008), 1.

Vatican II to the destiny of a council debated on the basis of a political-ideological bias. To do that overlooks the basic fact that the liturgical debate at Vatican II was the first and most radical effort of modern Catholicism to cope with the dawn of the "secular age" and the "expanding universe of unbelief."[8]

1.2. Approaches to *Sacrosanctum Concilium*

The profound ecclesiological meaning of the liturgical movement and liturgical reform has been lost. The transformation—or perhaps extinction—of the "reform movements" which led to the council (biblical, liturgical, patristical, ecumenical) as such within the Catholic Church after Vatican II[9] and the development in theology of single-field-centered theological research, and the fragmentation of theological debate and research on the council documents, have indubitably contributed to the disconnect of liturgy from ecclesiology and pastoral theology. The growing lack of mutual confidence between theologians and the official teaching of the Church has presented the field of research within Catholic theology with a specific and far-reaching task, especially concerning the relationship between liturgists and Church magisterium.[10]

One of the most insightful books on the significance of liturgy was first published in 1957, a few years before the announcement of Vatican II. Dom Cipriano Vagaggini opened his *Il senso teologico della liturgia* by underscoring two basic elements in the new understanding of liturgy on the eve of Vatican II: the need to study liturgy against the general background of sacred history and in relation to the concept of *sacramentum*.[11] How Vatican II developed showed the importance of

---

[8] See Charles Taylor, *A Secular Age* (Cambridge, MA: Harvard University Press, Belknap Press, 2007), 352–418.

[9] See Massimo Faggioli, *Breve storia dei movimenti cattolici* (Roma: Carocci, 2008); Spanish translation: *Historia y evoluciòn de los movimientos catòlicos. De León XIII a Benedicto XVI* (Madrid: PPC Editorial, 2011).

[10] See André Naud, *Le magistère incertain* (Montréal: Fides, 1987); and Francis A. Sullivan, *Magisterium: Teaching Authority in the Catholic Church* (New York: Paulist Press, 1983).

[11] See Cipriano Vagaggini, *Theological Dimensions of the Liturgy: A General Treatise on the Theology of the Liturgy* (Collegeville, MN: Liturgical Press, 1976), esp. 3–32; trans. from the fourth Italian edition of *Il senso teologico della liturgia: Saggio di*

these two ideas for the debates on the Church, *aggiornamento*, and the modern world.

An issue of *Concilium* (February 1965) devoted to *Sacrosanctum Concilium* was written before the ecclesiological debate that took place in the fall of 1964. In the editorial, Johannes Wagner stressed that "with the discussion of the schema on the liturgy the Council was from the first day dealing with its proper object: *De Ecclesia*."[12] In the opening essay about the bishop and the liturgy, Vagaggini once more demonstrated that the liturgical approach was the fullest way to give "completion and equilibrium" to the bishop, to the local Church, and to the overall theology of the Church that became prevalent after Vatican I.[13]

Vagaggini's prediction about the council fathers' grasp of the profound implications of *Sacrosanctum Concilium* turned out to be overly optimistic. After Vatican II, commentaries began interpreting the relationship between *Sacrosanctum Concilium* and *Lumen Gentium* to reframe an ecclesiological equilibrium centered far more on the outcomes of the main battlegrounds of ecclesiology (chap. 3 of *Lumen Gentium* on papacy and episcopate) than on the eucharistic ecclesiology of the liturgical constitution.

In 1967 an important volume dedicated to the liturgy in the *Unam Sanctam* series made some important points on the positioning of the liturgical constitution within the corpus of Vatican II. Yves Congar emphasized that the ecclesiology of the liturgical constitution had moved beyond Pius XII's *Mediator Dei* (1947). Congar also noted that a certain amount of time elapsed between the liturgical and the ecclesiological debates, and that there was, therefore, a difference—at least a gap in the chronology of the final approvals—between the ecclesiologies of the liturgical constitution *Sacrosanctum Concilium* and the ecclesiological constitution *Lumen Gentium*.[14] The competing ecclesiologies of

liturgia teologica generale (Rome: Paoline, 1957). See also Cipriano Vagaggini, *Liturgia e pensiero teologico recente* (Roma: S. Anselmo, 1962).

[12] See Johannes Wagner, "Preface," in *The Church and the Liturgy: Liturgy*, vol. 2 (New York, Glen Rock, NJ: Paulist Press, 1965), 3. See also Frederick R. McManus, *The Revival of the Liturgy* (New York: Herder and Herder, 1963).

[13] See Cipriano Vagaggini, "The Bishop and the Liturgy," in *The Church and the Liturgy*, 7–24, quotation at 11.

[14] See Yves Congar, "L'ecclesia ou communauté chrétienne, sujet intégral de l'action liturgique," in *La liturgie après Vatican II; bilans, études, prospective*, dir. by Jean-Pierre Jossua and Yves Congar (Paris: Cerf, 1967), 241–82.

Vatican II also emerged in Pierre-Marie Gy's essay, which stressed the need to read the liturgical constitution in light of the corpus of Vatican II in order to understand the key issues. More important, Gy rightly underscored that "the Constitution did not set a balance, but created a movement."[15] Vagaggini expressed the very same idea of the liturgical reform as a spark for the renewal of the Catholic Church and therefore for the interpretation of Vatican II under the telling heading "Leave the Door Open": "the council has wished to affirm a spirit, open a road, and so it was on its guard against an attitude that could have consisted in making a few concessions and then again hermetically sealing all doors."[16]

A similar take, but less rich in direct insights on the interpretation of Vatican II, was Josef Jungmann's commentary. Although Jungmann offered a valuable commentary on *Sacrosanctum Concilium*—that it was a beginning and not a final word—he did not develop a broader analysis of the importance of *Sacrosanctum Concilium* for what he called the "new concept of the Church" (Erneuerung des Kirchenbegriffes).[17]

While liturgists provided contributions regarding the specific significance of the liturgical constitution for the life of the Church, one of the most far-reaching interpretations of *Sacrosanctum Concilium* as the real ecclesiological kernel of the council came from an Italian canon lawyer and private *peritus* at Vatican II, Giuseppe Dossetti. On the basis of the Eucharist as "norma normans" in the life of the Church, Dossetti compared the "Eucharistic ecclesiology" of the liturgical constitution to the juridical traits of *Lumen Gentium*. Dossetti saw in *Sacrosanctum Concilium* not only a chronologically earlier ecclesiology but also its theological priority in the overall corpus of Vatican II.[18]

[15] See Pierre-Marie Gy, "Situation historique de la Constitution," in Jossua and Congar, *La liturgie après Vatican II*, 111–26, quotation 122.

[16] See Cipriano Vagaggini, "Fundamental Ideas of the Constitution," in *The Liturgy of Vatican II: A Symposium*, ed. William Baraúna, English ed. by Jovian Lang, 2 vols. (Chicago: Franciscan Herald Press, 1966), 1:95–129, quotation at 119.

[17] See Jungmann, *Kommentar*, 10–109, quotation at 16. A similar approach in Herman Schmidt, *La Costituzione sulla Sacra Liturgia. Testo, Genesi, Commento, Documentazione* (Roma: Herder, 1966).

[18] See Giuseppe Dossetti, *Per una "chiesa eucaristica". Rilettura della portata dottrinale della Costituzione liturgica del Vaticano II. Lezioni del 1965*, ed. Giuseppe Alberigo and Giuseppe Ruggieri (Bologna: Il Mulino, 2002). Dossetti is still largely unknown to English-speaking theologians, but now see Lash, *Theology for Pilgrims*,

The seventies were the age of the liturgical reform's completion: Paul VI's pontificate is still now much identified—especially by the anti–Vatican II component of Catholicism—with that era of decentralizing, pro-laity, and innovative reforms.[19] The end of Paul VI's pontificate and the election of John Paul II meant not only a new attitude toward Vatican II but also the beginning of a new indulgence toward the tiny minority of Catholic traditionalists who rejected the liturgical reform as a device for rejecting Vatican II. The traditionalists grasped better than many advocates of the council's reforms the theological principle of *lex orandi, lex credendi* for Vatican II.[20]

This development affected not just the focus of research on the liturgical renewal and the liturgical reform but also the very reception of *Sacrosanctum Concilium* by the official teaching of the Church. The achievement of the codification of canon law in 1983 did not help the liturgical constitution consolidate a new role in the life of the Church. If we follow Thomas Stubenrauch's research on the reception of Vatican II in the *Codex Iuris Canonici*, we must note that, different from the liturgical constitution, the juridical concept of *liturgia ab ecclesia* in the *Codex* overtakes the theological rationale *ecclesia a liturgia* and the overall lack of reception of Vatican II by the new *Codex*, especially concerning the liturgical ministry of the deacons and laity.[21]

Scholars have been overly confident about the coherence and consistency between the ecclesiology of the liturgical reform and the ecclesiological renewal in post–Vatican II Catholicism. In 1982

263–67, and *Giuseppe Dossetti: Studies on an Italian Catholic Reformer*, ed. Alberto Melloni (Zurich-Berlin: LIT, 2008).

[19] See Heribert Schmitz, "Tendenzen nachkonziliarer Gesetzgebung. Sichtung und Wertung," *Archiv für katholisches Kirchenrecht* 146 (1977): 381–419.

[20] *Lex orandi, lex credendi*, Latin translated as "the law of prayer is the law of belief," by Prosper of Aquitaine (390–455), in *Patrologia Latina*, 51:209–10. About the whole issue of the relationship between theology and liturgy, see Paul De Clerck, " 'Lex orandi, lex credendi': The Original Sense and Historical Avatars of an Equivocal Adage," *Studia Liturgica* 24 (1994): 178–200.

[21] See Thomas Stubenrauch, *Wer ist Träger der Liturgie? Zur Rezeption des II. Vatikanischen Konzils im Codex Iuris Canonici von 1983* (Trier: Paulinus, 2003), esp. 343–52. On the new *Codex*, see also Eugenio Corecco, "Aspetti della ricezione del Vaticano II nel codice di diritto canonico," in *Il Vaticano II e la chiesa*, ed. Giuseppe Alberigo and Jean-Pierre Jossua (Brescia: Paideia, 1985), 333–97; and Eugenio Corecco, "I presupposti culturali ed ecclesiologici del nuovo Codex," in *Il nuovo Codice di Diritto Canonico. Aspetti fondamentali della codificazione postronciliare*, ed. Silvio Ferrari (Bologna: Il Mulino, 1983), 37–68.

Franziskus Eisenbach noted the substantial continuity between the liturgical constitution and *Lumen Gentium*; moreover, he expressed regret over the lack at the council of a tighter connection between liturgy and ecclesiology, because "the liturgical Constitution could not take advantage" of the debate on *Lumen Gentium*.[22] Eisenbach's approach to the ecclesiology of the local Church according to *Sacrosanctum Concilium* 41–42 did not save him from a self-reassuring harmonization between the ecclesiology of the liturgical constitution and *Lumen Gentium*.[23]

Twenty years after the approval of *Sacrosanctum Concilium* and shortly before the Extraordinary Synod of 1985, the largely accomplished but still ongoing reform of liturgy contributed to the disappearance of any fruitful debate about the relationship between liturgy and Vatican II as such.[24] Furthermore, the emphasis on collegiality and Church reform in the theological debate in the seventies and the eighties contributed to an increasingly technical-liturgical reading of *Sacrosanctum Concilium*.[25] The indult of 1984 from the Holy See and the *motu proprio* of 1988, *Ecclesia Dei*, granted permission to celebrate "the old liturgy" of Trent. Such actions could not but weaken the theological impact of *Sacrosanctum Concilium* on the living ecclesiology of Catholicism.

The five-volume *History of Vatican II* edited by Giuseppe Alberigo and Joseph Komonchak provides new information about the key role of the liturgical debate within the council and about the dynamics in the preparatory and conciliar liturgical commissions.[26] Nevertheless, studies on *Sacrosanctum Concilium* published almost in chorus with

---

[22] See Franziskus Eisenbach, *Die Gegenwart Jesu Christi im Gottesdienst: Systematische Studien zur Liturgiekonstitution des II. Vatikanischen Konzils* (Mainz: Matthias-Grünewald-Verlag, 1982), 587.

[23] See Franz Frühmorgen, *Bischof und Bistum—Bischof und Presbyterium. Eine liturgiewissenschaftliche Studie zu den Artikeln 41 und 42 der Liturgiekonstitution des Zweiten Vatikanums* (Regensburg: Pustet, 1994).

[24] See Bugnini, *The Reform of the Liturgy*; English translation of *La riforma liturgica 1948–1975* (Rome: Centro Liturgico Vincenziano-Edizioni Liturgiche, 1983).

[25] As can be seen also in *The Reception of Vatican II*, ed. Giuseppe Alberigo, Jean-Pierre Jossua, and Joseph A. Komonchak (Washington, DC: Catholic University of America Press, 1987).

[26] See Mathijs Lamberigts, "The Liturgy Debate," in *History of Vatican II*, vol. 2: *The Formation of the Council's Identity, First Period and Intercession, October 1962–September 1963* (Maryknoll, NY: Orbis; Leuven: Peeters, 1997), 107–66; Reiner Kaczinski, "Toward the Reform of the Liturgy," in *History of Vatican II*, vol. 3: *The*

Alberigo's *History* focused on the "theological" continuity between the early twentieth-century liturgical movement and the liturgical constitution, and thus they overlooked the impact of the constitution on Vatican II as such.[27]

No really decisive contribution came from the many studies published for the fortieth anniversary of the liturgical constitution.[28] The Tübingen-based five-volume *Herders Theologischer Kommentar zum Zweiten Vatikanischen Konzil*, directed by the dogmaticians Peter Hünermann and Hans-Jochen Hilberath, made a step forward toward a new appreciation of the liturgical constitution.[29] In *Kommentar*'s volume devoted to *Sacrosanctum Concilium*, Reiner Kaczinski stressed the novelty of the liturgical constitution in the context of the history of the councils and the history of liturgy. More profound, he emphasized the function of SC 5—the centrality of the paschal *mysterium*—not only as a center of the liturgical constitution, but also as a "heart-word" (*Herzwort*) for Vatican II.[30]

But it is hard to escape the impression that many of the commentaries about *Sacrosanctum Concilium* seem to be outrun by the speed and aggressiveness—more than by the intellectual might—of the advocates of a revision of the liturgical reform of Vatican II. In the last ten years the influential calls for a "reform of the reform" of the liturgy have fueled a "political-theological" debate about the fortunes and misfortunes of the liturgical constitution and have called forth defenses of

---

Mature Council, Second Period and Intercession, September 1963–September 1964 (Maryknoll, NY: Orbis; Leuven: Peeters, 2000), 192–256.

[27] See, for example, the volume by Maria Paiano, *Liturgia e società nel Novecento. Percorsi del movimento liturgico di fronte ai processi di secolarizzazione* (Roma: Edizioni di Storia e Letteratura, 2000).

[28] See, for example, in *Liturgisches Jahrbuch* 53, no. 4 (2003): Joseph Ratzinger, "40 Jahre Konstitution über die Heilige Liturgie. Rückblick und Vorblick," 209–21; Jürgen Bärsch, " 'Von Grösstem Gewicht für die Liturgiefeier ist die Heilige Schrift' (SC 24). Zur Bedeutung der Bibel im Kontext des Gottesdienstes," 222–41; Andreas Odenthal, "Häresie der Formlosigkeit durch ein 'Konzil der Buchhalter'. Überlegungen zur Kritik an der Liturgiereform nach 40 Jahren 'Sacrosanctum Concilium,' " 242–57.

[29] See *Herders Theologischer Kommentar zum Zweiten Vatikanischen Konzil*, ed. Hans-Jochen Hilberath and Peter Hünermann, 5 vols. (Freiburg i.B.: Herder, 2004–2005).

[30] See Kaczynski, *Kommentar*, 9–227, quoting Angelus A. Häussling, "Pascha-Mysterium. Kritisches zu einem Beitrag in der dritten Auflage des Lexicon für Theologie und Kirche," *Archiv für Liturgiewissenschaft* 41 (1999): 157–65.

the historical memory of that postconciliar period,[31] rather than defenses of the deep theological implications and ecclesiological depth of *Sacrosanctum Concilium*. The political-ecclesiastical debate on the council has compelled the advocates of Vatican II to defend the liturgy. The advocates failed to emphasize that liturgy was not only the chronological starting point of Vatican II but also the theological starting point. Perhaps more important, the conviction of the importance of the liturgical renewal was the first and most undisputed common ground of the council fathers.

Somewhere between nostalgia for the pre–Vatican II era and the recognition of *Sacrosanctum Concilium*'s contribution to the liturgical life of the Catholic Church, some scholars have underscored the continuity between the encyclical *Mediator Dei* and Vatican II, and between Pius X's *motu proprio Tra le sollecitudini* (1903) and Vatican II.[32] The mix of tradition and *ressourcement* in theological discourse has generated ambiguity in the debate on Vatican II, which John O'Malley recently analyzed in his *What Happened at Vatican II*.[33]

1.3. The Agenda of the Council and the Liturgical Debate

The council that John XXIII announced was a surprise for everyone in the Catholic Church: on January 25, 1959, less than three months after his election, John XXIII opened the windows of Catholicism in order—in his very words—"to let in some fresh air." The liturgy had, however, been on the agenda of Catholicism for quite some time. The call for liturgical reform was no surprise.[34]

---

[31] See Piero Marini, *A Challenging Reform: Realizing the Vision of the Liturgical Renewal, 1963–1975*, ed. Mark R. Francis, John R. Page, Keith F. Pecklers (Collegeville, MN: Liturgical Press, 2007).

[32] See Aidan Nichols, *Looking at the Liturgy: A Critical View of Its Contemporary Form* (San Francisco: Ignatius Press, 1996); Martin Mosebach, *Häresie der Formlosigkeit. Die römische Liturgie und ihr Feind* (Neuausg., durchges. u. erw., München: Hanser, 2007; trad. it. *Eresia dell'informe. La liturgia romana e il suo nemico*, Siena: Cantagalli, 2009); Pamela Jackson, *An Abundance of Graces: Reflections on* Sacrosanctum Concilium (Chicago–Mundelein, IL: Hillenbrand Books, 2004); Pamela Jackson, "Theology of the Liturgy," in *Vatican II: Renewal within Tradition*, ed. Matthew L. Lamb and Matthew Levering (New York: Oxford University Press, 2008), 101–28.

[33] See O'Malley, *What Happened*, 300–301.

[34] See *Verso il concilio Vaticano II (1960–1962). Passaggi e problemi della preparazione conciliare*, ed. Giuseppe Alberigo and Alberto Melloni (Genova: Marietti, 1993).

The last years of Pius XII had already seen some decisions made in this respect. The novelty of the council benefited from the riches of the early twentieth-century liturgical movement, but the liturgical reform could develop its deep theological assumptions only in a council where the issue of change met clearly one of the key points of the liturgical movement: the notion of *ressourcement*.[35]

For this reason, far from being an issue of concern only to liturgists, the liturgical reform at Vatican II was clearly a path-opening debate. The choice to inaugurate the debates with the *schema De liturgia* was grounded not just on the better shape and reception of this document in comparison with the other seven *schemas* sent to the council fathers immediately before the beginning of the first session in the fall of 1962.

Interpretations of this choice by John XXIII, who underlined the propaedeutic function of the liturgical debate for the council as a whole, have been taken up again in the commentaries on *Sacrosanctum Concilium*.[36] Nevertheless, in recent years Catholic theologians and historians have been much more focused on the "technical" outcomes of the liturgical reform, and its direct effects, rather than on its profound meaning for Vatican II and for the Church. Benedict XVI's decisions have indeed promoted this feature of the post–Vatican II ecclesiological debate, boosting the impact of a political-aesthetical standpoint on liturgy and making it easier to overlook the ties between the liturgical reform and Vatican II as an agent of change or, as O'Malley insists, Vatican II as a "language event."[37]

The liturgical debate opened Vatican II and became "an event within the event" because it ignited a motion stretching beyond the

[35] See *Les Pères et la naissance de l'ecclésiologie*, dir. Marie-Anne Vannier (Paris: Cerf, 2009); Étienne Fouilloux, *Éditer les Pères de L'Église au XXe siècle* (Paris: Cerf, 1995).

[36] "Il primato della *Sacrosanctum Concilium* è ascrivibile non semplicemente alla precedenza cronologica, ma al fatto che essa è stata punto di riferimento e fonte d'ispirazione per i testi conciliari che l'hanno seguita. [. . .] L'accordo è consistito anzitutto nell'assunzione della Sacra Scrittura come norma e giudizio dell'intelligenza della liturgia e della riforma della sua prassi. La Costituzione liturgica ha in questo modo realizzato ciò che simbolicamente veniva espresso dal rito di intronizzazione dell'Evangeliario all'apertura di ogni assemblea conciliare" (Mons. Piero Marini, "Introduction" to *Concilii Vaticani II synopsis in ordinem redigens schemata cum relationibus necnon patrum orationes atque animadversiones: Constitutio de sacra liturgia Sacrosanctum Concilium*, ed. Francisco Gil Hellín [Città del Vaticano: Libreria Editrice Vaticana, 2003], x–xi).

[37] O'Malley, *What Happened*, 306.

dreams of the council leaders. Starting with the liturgy—with the liturgical debate and with the celebration of liturgy in different rites every morning in St. Peter's—helped bishops rediscover the potential of liturgy as a tool for a Church facing an increasingly secular and global world.[38] But this debate also gave voice to the drives for the reform of the Catholic Church.[39] Even in the preparatory phase, the preparatory commissions, especially the Central Commission for over-all coordination of Vatican II, debated the function of the liturgical debate and its scheduling in addressing the main issues on the agenda of Vatican II. The decision of the Council of Presidents on October 15, 1962, to reschedule the debates and put the liturgical *schema* before the other *schemas* highlights the rise of the main division within Vatican II concerning the way of addressing the issue of change; this decision was greeted with John XXIII's positive response.[40] The relationship be-tween *libro e calice* ("book and chalice"), that is, the centrality of liturgy for the theology of Angelo Roncalli (the future Pope John XXIII), had emerged already in his years as apostolic delegate in Bulgaria in the 1920s and 1930s and was one of the main points of his homily when he took possession of the Lateran Basilica shortly after his election, on November 23, 1958.[41]

At the beginning of the preparatory phase of Vatican II, it became clear even to the Roman Curia that the liturgical reform would play a major role, but they hoped it would do so as an "icebreaker" for a quick and smooth council, not as a "path-opener" for the council.[42] The history of Vatican II shows that the council debates went all but smoothly and that the debate on the liturgical constitution between October 1962 and November 1963 turned out to be much more than a pure "icebreaker."

[38] See Hermann Schmidt, *La Costituzione sulla Sacra Liturgia*.

[39] See especially *L'épiscopat et l'Église universelle*, ed. Yves Congar and Bernard Dominique Dupuy (Paris: Cerf, 1962).

[40] See Angelo Giuseppe Roncalli (John XXIII), *Pater amabilis. Agende del pontefice 1958–1963*, ed. Mauro Velati (Bologna: Istituto per le scienze religiose, 2007), 443.

[41] See Giuseppe Ruggieri, "Appunti per una teologia in papa Roncalli," in *Papa Giovanni*, ed. Giuseppe Alberigo (Roma-Bari: Laterza, 1987), 245–71.

[42] See Antonino Indelicato, *Difendere la dottrina o annunciare il Vangelo. Il dibattito nella Commissione centrale preparatoria del Vaticano II* (Genova: Marietti, 1992), 171–98; Andrea Riccardi, "The Tumultuous Opening Days of the Council," in *History of Vatican II*, vol. 2, 1–67.

The Roman Curia and the so-called minority rejected the comprehensive and programmatic reform of the liturgy laid out in the *schema* prepared by the liturgical preparatory commission, while the majority accepted the reform and long-awaited renewal of liturgy as the best possible interpretation of the "pastoral character" of the council. The outcomes of the debate and the almost-unanimous final vote on the constitution on November 22, 1963, left no doubt as to the step taken in the direction of liturgical renewal.[43]

1.4. The Liturgical Constitution: A Forgotten Hermeneutics of Vatican II?

A contribution regarding Vatican II as "constitution" for the Catholic Church came between 2005 and 2006 from Peter Hünermann, a dogmatic theologian at Tübingen, in the conclusion to the five-volume *Herders Theologischer Kommentar zum Zweiten Vatikanischen Konzil* edited by Hünermann himself and by B. J. Hilberath. Hünermann develops aspects of his lecture given at the Bologna Conference in 1996 about the "pragmatics of the conciliar texts"[44] but also includes and substantially supports Ormond Rush's suggestion about the *Hermeneutical Principles* (hermeneutics of the authors, of the texts, of the recipients) of Vatican II.[45]

In a long and audaciously reasoned essay, Hünermann designates the corpus of conciliar texts as a "constitution" for the Catholic Church.[46] In Hünermann's words:

> If one looks for an analogy along the lines of a first approach to the outline of the text of Vatican II, with the goal of characterizing the decisions

[43] See Mathijs Lamberigts, "The Liturgy Debate," in *History of Vatican II*, vol. 2, 107–66.

[44] See Peter Hünermann, "Il concilio Vaticano II come evento," in *L'evento e le decisioni. Studi sulle dinamiche del Concilio Vaticano II*, ed. Maria Teresa Fattori and Alberto Melloni (Il Mulino: Bologna, 1997), 63–92.

[45] See Ormond Rush, *Still Interpreting Vatican II: Some Hermeneutical Principles* (New York, Paulist Press, 2004). For the relationship between "letter" and "spirit" in the interpretation of *Dei Verbum*, see Ormond Rush, "*Dei Verbum* Forty Years On: Revelation, Inspiration and the Spirit," *The Australasian Catholic Record* 83, no. 4 (October 2006): 406–14.

[46] See Peter Hünermann, "Der Text: Werden—Gestalt—Bedeutung. Eine Hermeneutische Reflexion," in Hilberath and Hünermann, *Herders Theologischer Kommentar zum Zweiten Vatikanischen Konzil*, vol. 5, 5–101, esp. 11–17 and 85–87.

of the council, what results is a certain similarity with constitutional texts as drawn up by representative constitutional assemblies. This similarity is expressed in a particular way in the texts of Vatican II.[47]

For Hünermann, the identification of Vatican II as a "constitution" surely does not mean placing council texts above the Gospel: "The legitimation of a council and its authority is essentially different from that of a constitutional assembly of a modern state [. . .] for this reason the conciliar text possesses an authority essentially different from that of a constitutional text."[48] In the conclusion, Hünermann precisely states the proposal to consider the texts of Vatican II as a "constitutional text for the faith":

> The corpus of texts of this council recalls a similarity with the texts of a constitution. At the same time, there are profound differences between the two, beginning with the authority and specificity of the material of council texts. For this reason, the text of Vatican II can be prudently defined a "constitutional text of faith." If this assumption about the text of Vatican II is valid, then what follows is a whole series of problems and questions, criticisms, and also ways of interpreting Vatican II formulated without support, since they do not conform to the literary genre of the text.[49]

---

[47] "Sucht man im Sinne einer ersten Annäherung an das Profil des Textes des II. Vatikanischen Konzils nach einer Analogie, um die Beschlüsse zu charakterisieren, so ergibt sich eine gewisse Ähnlichkeit mit Verfassungstexten, die von repräsentativen verfassungsgebenden Versammlungen ausgearbeitet werden. Diese Ähnlichkeit ist bei den Texten des II. Vatikanums besonders ausgeprägt und zeigt sich lediglich in stark vermittelter, abgestufter Form auch im Blick auf das Trienter Konzil und das I. Vatikanum" (Hünermann, "Der Text: Werden—Gestalt—Bedeutung," 12). The relationship between a "constitution" and Vatican II final documents explained by Hünermann: (1) the situation of "crisis or historical necessity" (in a state as well as in the Catholic Church) that calls for a constitution; (2) the quality of the final texts as texts discussed and approved by large assemblies, representative of different if not opposite political stands; (3) a similarity in the process (committees, subcommittees, plenary assemblies); (4) the relationship between the issues at hand and the texts describing and influencing the ongoing situation; (5) the relationship between the final approval of a constitution and the act of reception of Vatican II.

[48] "Die Legitimation eines Konzils und damit seine autorität eine wesentlich andere ist als die einer verfassungsgebenden Versammlung in staatlichen Sinne. [. . .] Der Konziltext besitzt von daher eine wesentlich andere Autorität als ein Verfassungstext" (Hünermann, "Der Text: Werden—Gestalt—Bedeutung," 15–16).

[49] "Das Textcorpus dieses Konzils weist eine Ähnlichkeit mit den Texten einer verfassunggebenden Versammlung auf. Dabei ergeben sich zugleich tiefgreifende

This definition of the nature of the texts of Vatican II establishes Vatican II as a corpus of hermeneutical principles for the life of the Catholic Church that is capable of establishing what is "constitutional" and hence what is "unconstitutional" in the ecclesiology of the postconciliar Catholic Church.[50]

Sacrosanctum Concilium constitutes one of the pillars of the ecclesiology of Vatican II. The liturgical constitution presents a way to defend the ecclesiology of Vatican II on the basis of eucharistic ecclesiology, thus without making the choice between juridical and communional ecclesiology the first and last word on the Church of Vatican II.

The definition of *Sacrosanctum Concilium* as "le parent pauvre de l'herméneutique conciliaire"—"the impoverished cousin of the council's hermeneutic"—is correct because, as we have seen, its hermeneutical function has been consistently downplayed.[51] The dire need for an interpretation of Vatican II once again centered on *Sacrosanctum Concilium* is justified on the basis of a chronologically rooted relationship between the liturgical constitution—the first document voted on and approved at the council—and the whole of Vatican II. The necessity of and opportunity for a hermeneutics of the council based on *Sacrosanctum Concilium* becomes clear if we take into account that the liturgical constitution opens the way for a new balance between the "clash of ecclesiologies" at Vatican II and the gravitational center of the Church of Vatican II: Scripture and the Eucharist.

<hr />

Differenzen aus der anderen Autorität und der Eigentümlichkeit der Sache, die in den Konziltexten zur Sprache kommt. Auf Grund dieses Befund kann der Text des II. Vatikanischen Konzils vorsichtig als 'konstitutioneller Text des Glaubens' bezeichnet werden. Ist dieser *Vorbegriff* vom Text des II. Vatikanischen Konzils triftig, dann ergibt sich daraus, dass eine ganze Reihe von Problemstellungen und Anfragen, Kritiken und nicht zuletzt Auslegungsweisen in unbegründeter, weil dem Textgenus nicht entsprechender Weise an das II. Vatikanische Konzil herangetragen werden" (Hünermann, "Der Text: Werden—Gestalt—Bedeutung," 17).

[50] See Peter Hünermann, "Der Text. Eine Ergänzung zur Hermeneutik des II. Vatikanischen Konzils," *Cristianesimo nella Storia* 28, no. 2 (2007): 339–58: "Läßt man sich vom 'konstitutionellen' Charakter dieses Textcorpus überzeugen, so ergeben sich allerdings erhebliche Auswirkungen für die theologische Auslegung und die Rezeption dieser Texte" (358). See also Peter Hünermann, *Zur theologischen Arbeit am Beginn der dritten Millenniums*, in *Das Zweite Vatikanische Konzil und die Zeichen der Zeit heute* (Proceedings of the Tübingen conference of December 2005), ed. Peter Hünermann (Freiburg i.B.: Herder, 2006), 569–93.

[51] See Patrick Prétot, "La Constitution sur la liturgie: une herméneutique de la tradition liturgique," in *Vatican II et la théologie. Perspectives pour le XXIe siècle*, ed. Philippe Bordeyne and Laurent Villemin (Paris, Cerf: 2006), 17–34.

The liturgical constitution has been approached differently by the two hermeneutical and historiographical traditions of Vatican II: the pro-majority (pro-reform) and the pro-minority (nostalgic) traditions. Most pro-majority interpreters of Vatican II have looked at *Sacrosanctum Concilium* as the first reform of Vatican II, the beginning of the event, but have seemed to entrust the defense of its profound message and ramifications to liturgists. They prefer an "ecclesiological" approach—based on *Lumen Gentium* and the relationship between papacy and episcopate—for the implementation of Vatican II.

Pro-minority and essentially anti-conciliar interpreters of Vatican II did not give up the effort for a direct reinterpretation of the council and its ecclesiology, also through a downgrading of Vatican II by dismissing *Sacrosanctum Concilium* and trivializing the deep theological meaning of the liturgical reform. Despite such trivialization, some pro-minority interpreters of Vatican II seem to have a grasp of *Sacrosanctum Concilium* that is richer than the grasp of the average defender of Vatican II.

This especially is why Vatican II interpreters must attempt a more profound reading of the connections between the whole of the council and *Sacrosanctum Concilium*. Only a hermeneutic based on the liturgy and the Eucharist, as developed in the liturgical constitution, can preserve the riches of the overall ecclesiology of Vatican II without getting lost in the technicalities of a "theological jurisprudence."

It is time to make the case for a strong relationship between the liturgical constitution and the ultimate meaning of Vatican II. This relationship is not a standard defense of the post–Vatican II liturgical renewal or a criticism of the "liberalization" of the Tridentine liturgy. Nonetheless, I assert that a deeper understanding of the new conception of liturgy developed at Vatican II, and in the post–Vatican II liturgical renewal, is the first step toward seeing the profound implications and the real implementation of Vatican II and of seeing what its implementation means.

It is time to demonstrate that *Sacrosanctum Concilium* represents the early and, at the same time, the mature outcome of a council grounded in the idea that:

1. *Ressourcement* is the most powerful source of updating and reform for global Catholicism in the modern world. The anti–Vatican II "new liturgical movement" is not moved purely by nostalgia: its theological and ecclesiological consequences reach far beyond the nostalgia. The

advocates of the anti–Vatican II "new liturgical movement" are indeed right as they identify in *Sacrosanctum Concilium* the main target, since the liturgical constitution is the most radical instance of *ressourcement* and the most obviously antitraditionalist document of Vatican II. The principle of *ressourcement* affected the liturgical constitution like no other council document; it is hard to find passages in the corpus of Vatican II that are closer to the very essence of the Church and driven by the idea of *ressourcement*.

2. The liturgical reform as it was planned in the liturgical constitution aimed at the rediscovery of the centrality of Scripture and of the Eucharist. It is the most direct way to grasp Vatican II *ecclesiology*. *Sacrosanctum Concilium* is aware that "the sacred liturgy does not exhaust the entire activity of the Church" (SC 9) and that liturgy has its role in the Church as a *theologia prima*, as *locus theologicus*, and as *culmen et fons*. The liturgical constitution sponsored a new awareness within the Roman Catholic Church that *things change*. That is why the liturgical reform of Vatican II and the most recent calls for a "reform of the reform" touch the whole essence of Vatican II. Changing worship sets off a rethinking of ecclesiology in a more profound and long-lasting way than the definition of the Church in *Lumen Gentium*.

3. This eucharistic ecclesiology provides the grounds for the basic motion of Vatican II, that is, *rapprochement* inside and outside the Church. *Rapprochement*—a term used many times by the pioneer of ecumenism and liturgist Dom Lambert Beauduin[52]—is not part of the corpus of Vatican II in a material way, but it belongs fully to the aims of Vatican II. The liturgical reform of Vatican II plays a significant role in developing (during Vatican II) and performing (after Vatican II) this key feature of the council in a way that is not less important than other, better-known "*rapprochement* manifestos" of Vatican II, such as the decree on ecumenism *Unitatis Redintegratio*, the declaration *Nostra Aetate*, and the pastoral constitution *Gaudium et Spes*. The main *rapprochement* carried out by *Sacrosanctum Concilium* consists in a reconciled and unifying vision of the Church, of Christian life, of the

[52] See Raymond Loonbeek and Jacques Mortiau, *Un pionnier, Dom Lambert Beauduin (1873–1960). Liturgie et unité des chrétiens*, 2 vols. (Louvain-la-Neuve: Collège Erasme, 2001), esp. vol. 1, 907–9. See also Jacques Mortiau and Raymond Loonbeek, *Dom Lambert Beauduin visionnaire et précurseur (1873–1960). Un moine au coeur libre* (Paris: Cerf, 2005).

existential condition of the faithful in the world.[53] Far from being a purely aesthetical option, the theological starting point of the liturgical reform aimed at resetting the relationship between Christian liturgy, the spiritual needs of the faithful, and Catholic theological reading of the modern world in its historical and social dimensions.

4. *Ressourcement*, eucharistic ecclesiology, and *rapprochement* require a drive for a full implementation of Vatican II and provide an unambiguous appraisal of the issue of Vatican II's continuity and discontinuity and the role of liturgical reform in the Church of the twenty-first century. Any attempt to undermine the liturgical reform of Vatican II reveals a clearly reductionist view of Vatican II and its epoch-making changes.[54]

---

[53] See Dossetti, *Chiesa eucaristica*, 41.
[54] See *Ressourcement: A Movement for Renewal in Twentieth-Century Catholic Theology*, ed. Gabriel Flynn and Paul D. Murray (Oxford: Oxford University Press, 2012).

Chapter 2

Liturgical Reform and *Ressourcement*

2.1. The Liturgical Constitution as a Key to Understanding Vatican II

Sacrosanctum Concilium was the first *schema* to be debated and approved by Vatican II and the first one to be implemented by the Church of Vatican II, still during the council, in Advent of 1964. The liturgical debate peaked during the first period in the fall of 1962 and was already almost complete when John XXIII died; *Sacrosanctum Concilium* did not carry—different from many other key documents of Vatican II—the burden of interventions "from a higher authority," that is, Paul VI and his "red pencil."[1] On the other hand, it is fair indeed to acknowledge that Paul VI saw in the liturgical reform the pathway to the Church of Vatican II; many of the hard feelings against Paul VI nowadays come from the most fierce adversaries of the liturgy of Vatican II. Many advocates of a "new liturgical movement" are, in fact, anti–Vatican II "Pius V–Mass Catholics" moved by nostalgia, whose theological and ecclesiological consequences can reach far beyond the nostalgia for the aesthetics of Latin liturgical language and the preconciliar rite. They are, indeed, right as they identify in *Sacrosanctum Concilium* the main target, being that the liturgical constitution is arguably the most radically "ressourced" and the most plainly antitraditionalist document of Vatican II.

The liturgical reform was not only the first but also the single most important and most visible element of change made possible by

---

[1] See Jan Grootaers, "Le crayon rouge de Paul VI. Les interventions du pape dans le travail des commissions conciliaires," in *Les commissions conciliaires à Vatican II*, ed. Mathijs Lamberigts, Claude Soetens, Jan Grootaers (Leuven: KUL, 1996), 317–51; O'Malley, *What Happened*, 201–45.

Vatican II.[2] The liturgical reform was also the one that owed much more to the pre–Vatican II theological movements than the "political mechanism of Vatican II" and the uneasy balance of power between the floor of St. Peter's, the Roman Curia, and Paul VI.[3] But it was also the reform that benefited more than any other from the "atmosphere of the council," which reoriented the positioning of entire national episcopates and made much more visible the real balance between the tiny ultraconservative minority and the overwhelming majority— much more visible in the liturgical debate in St. Peter's than in the commissions.

The debate on liturgy and its final document, *Sacrosanctum Concilium*, managed to maintain the "theological lift" of the liturgical movement into the rest of Vatican II. The liturgical constitution not simply extended the reforms of Pius X and Pius XII[4] but also developed theologically the insights of the liturgical movement that had flourished, along with the *ressourcement* and the rediscovery of patristic theology well before the pontificates of Pius X and Pius XII.[5] The very idea of *ressourcement* constitutes the distinctiveness of the liturgical reform of Vatican II in comparison to the reforms of the liturgy promoted by the popes of the pre–Vatican II period, which had focused only on the idea of the "active participation" of the faithful: "ressourcing the liturgy" lead to the reform, while mere "active participation" did not require a comprehensive reform of the liturgy.

The common knowledge about the liturgical movement limits its success to the issues of the vernacular language and of the faithful's active participation in liturgy, but the force of the liturgical movement had a voice in and an impact on Vatican II that was far more impor-

---

[2] See Mark S. Massa, *The American Catholic Revolution: How the Sixties Changed the Church Forever* (New York: Oxford University Press, 2010), esp. 15–28.

[3] See Philippe Levillain, *La mécanique politique de Vatican II: la majorité et l'unanimité dans un concile* (Paris: Beauchesne, 1975).

[4] See Rita Ferrone, *Liturgy:* Sacrosanctum Concilium (New York: Paulist Press, 2007), 8–11.

[5] A clear continuity between the liturgical reform of Vatican II and the theological and political agenda of early twentieth-century popes is the reading shared— despite their opposite ideological standpoints—by Pamela Jackson, *An Abundance of Graces: Reflections on* Sacrosanctum Concilium (Chicago–Mundelein, IL: Hillenbrand Books, 2004); Maria Paiano, *Liturgia e società nel Novecento. Percorsi del movimento liturgico di fronte ai processi di secolarizzazione* (Roma: Ed. di Storia e Letteratura, 2000).

tant, profound, and direct than the other movements' effect on the council debate and agenda.[6] It can be said that undermining the liturgy of Vatican II is like drying up one of the theological sources of the council. Together with the constitution on revelation, *Dei Verbum*, the liturgical constitution received from the preconciliar movements of renewal the principle of *ressourcement* like no other council documents did; it is hard to find passages in the corpus of Vatican II that are closer to the very essence of the Church and driven by the idea of *ressourcement*.[7]

Far from being an invention of Vatican II, *ressourcement* had been an intellectual undertaking that provided an invaluable contribution to the experience of renewal started in early twentieth-century Catholicism with the biblical movement, the patristic revival, the ecumenical movement, and the liturgical movement: "The very word *source* assumed an emblematic value with the publication of the first volumes of the collection 'Sources Chrétiennes,' starting in 1942."[8] In those same decades in Europe, and especially among the Russian Orthodox theologian *émigrés* in France, *ressourcement* became the basis for the renewal of the Orthodox theology of the diaspora in the twentieth century.[9] It was not an accident that the eucharistic ecclesiology of the

---

[6] See Étienne Fouilloux, "The Antepreparatory Phase: The Slow Emergence from Inertia (January 1959–October 1962)," in *History of Vatican II*, vol. 1: *Announcing and Preparing Vatican Council II: Toward a New Era in Catholicism* (Maryknoll, NY: Orbis; Leuven: Peeters, 1995), 55–166; O'Malley, *What Happened*, 74–77.

[7] See Dossetti, *Chiesa eucaristica*, 35. "*Ressourcement*" was a neologism coined by the French poet Charles Péguy at the beginning of the twentieth century, as Congar reminded: "Peguy [. . .] in the Cahiers de la Quinzaine (Mar. 1, 1904) had the idea but not yet the word. [. . .] For Péguy this meant going back to the sources of life—to a new release of energies" (*Vraie et fausse reforme dans l'Église* [Paris: Cerf, 1950], 43 and 623; English translation: *True and False Reform in the Church*, trans. Paul Philibert [Collegeville, MN: Liturgical Press, 2011], 39). About *ressourcement* in the ecclesiological debate at Vatican II, see Daniele Gianotti, *I Padri della Chiesa al Concilio Vaticano II. La teologia patristica nella "Lumen Gentium"* (Bologna: EDB, 2010).

[8] Gianotti, *I Padri della Chiesa al Concilio Vaticano II*, 35. See also Étienne Fouilloux, "Mouvements théologico-spirituels et concile (1959–1962)," in *À la veille du Concile Vatican II: vota et réactions en Europe et dans le catholicisme oriental*, ed. Mathijs Lamberigts and Claude Soetens (Leuven: KU Leuven, 1992), 185–99. For the intellectual history of *ressourcement*, see Gianotti, *I Padri della Chiesa al Concilio Vaticano II*, 25–114.

[9] See, for example, Alix Kniazeff, *L'Institut Saint-Serge. De l'Academie d'autrefois au rayonnement d'aujourd'hui* (Paris: Beauchesne, 1974).

post–Vatican II period retrieved many of its insights from Orthodox theology. Also, for Vatican II *ressourcement* was one of the most decisive keywords for twentieth-century theology: it embodied the need for theology to go back to the old sources of the undivided Church in order to fulfill its aspiration of a new unity within the Church—a unity between the Church and the modern world, and between Christians and all of humankind.

2.2. Liturgical Movement and *Ressourcement*

This intertwined *ressourcement* in *Sacrosanctum Concilium*—return to the sources of Christianity and return to liturgy as source, as "font"—is visible at a glance by the balance between biblical quotations (twenty-three footnotes out of forty-two), fathers of the Church (six footnotes: Augustine, Ignatius of Antioch, Cyprian, Cyril of Alexandria), and canons from the Council of Trent (five footnotes: sessions 13, 21, 23, 24). The fact that Pius XII's decisions on liturgy are implicitly received in the constitution does not obscure the fact that *Sacrosanctum Concilium* is the most ressourced and the least dependent on recent papal teaching for its inner balance and core concepts.

Sacrosanctum Concilium set out the principles for a general reform of the liturgy, calling for a "general restoration" (*generalem instaurationem*). The first paragraph of SC 21 affirms:

> In order that the Christian people may more certainly derive an abundance of graces from the sacred liturgy, holy Mother Church desires to undertake with great care a general restoration of the liturgy itself. For the liturgy is made up of unchangeable elements divinely instituted, and of elements subject to change. These latter not only may be changed but ought to be changed with the passage of time, if they have suffered from the intrusion of anything out of harmony with the inner nature of the liturgy or have become less suitable.

In order to understand the deep meaning of this passage, it is essential to analyze its background, that is, the critical contribution of *ressourcement* in the liturgical movement and, from there, the role of the liturgical debate in Vatican II.[10]

---

[10] See Keith F. Pecklers, *The Unread Vision: The Liturgical Movement in the United States of America, 1926–1955* (Collegeville, MN: Liturgical Press, 1998). For an assessment of the theological tendencies of the liturgical movement, see also

This passage is made difficult because the twentieth-century Catholic liturgical movement somehow has been dismissed and also because of the generation gap between precouncil, Vatican II, and post–Vatican II Catholicism. The liturgical movement in some way has been disavowed by contemporary Catholicism, being analyzed in the last years by many Church historians as an agent of the ideological reaction of the Catholic Church against secularization and liberalism instigated by the liberal States in Europe.[11] The main allegation brought against the liturgical movement is, in brief, that it prepared the liturgical reform not on the basis of a profound theological rationale (*ressourcement, rapprochement,* renewal) but on the mere basis of the need to "reconquer" a Christian society on the verge of falling into the hands of secularization and modernity after the shock of the French Revolution and the liberal culture of the nineteenth and twentieth centuries.[12]

At the same time and from the opposite bank, the liturgical movement has become the main target of the traditionalist Catholic groups and their "conspiracy mind-set."[13] In this sense, it is unquestionable that the adversaries of Vatican II picked the best target for their attempt to set the watch back to a pre–Vatican II Catholicism. If it is true that "ressourcement is skeptical of the present because of what it has discovered in the past,"[14] the advocates for an anti–Vatican II "new liturgical movement" reject the radical consequences of *ressourcement*: the recent past of late medieval and Tridentine Christendom seems to some Catholics far more "Roman *and* Catholic" than the headwaters of the Christian tradition. It is thus time to reframe the debate about the liturgical reform in order to understand the relations between the liturgical movement and the debate on liturgy at Vatican II—being

---

Étienne Fouilloux, *Une Église en quête de liberté: la pensée catholique française entre modernisme et Vatican II (1914–1962)* (Paris: Desclée de Brouwer, 1998), 223.

[11] On the other hand, an example of this ideological reaction of the Catholic Church is the language of the new English translation of the Roman Missal, in use since the First Sunday of Advent 2011.

[12] See Paiano, *Liturgia e società nel Novecento*; Daniele Menozzi, *Sacro cuore: un culto tra devozione interiore e restaurazione cristiana della società* (Roma: Viella, 2001).

[13] See Denis Crouan, *The Liturgy after Vatican II: Collapsing or Resurgent?* (San Francisco: Ignatius, 2001); Didier Bonneterre, *The Liturgical Movement: From Dom Guéranger to Annibale Bugnini, or, The Trojan Horse in the City of God* (Kansas City, MO: Angelus Press, 2002); László Dobszay, *The Bugnini-Liturgy and the Reform of the Reform* (Front Royal, VA: Catholic Church Music Associates, 2003).

[14] O'Malley, *What Happened*, 40.

part of a bigger issue, that is, the relationship between "reform movements" and Vatican II.[15]

The liturgical movement surely shared some features with the nineteenth-century and post-Revolution Catholic "restoration movements" in Europe and connected the need for the liturgical renewal and the search for the purity of Catholic liturgy (against devotionalism) with some issues of conservative or "traditional" Catholicism.[16] But it also connected with the spirituality of renewal and represented the most successful, coherent, and cross-cultural contribution to the preparation for Vatican II.[17] The fact that the liturgical movement had moved from the need for a new appeal to the faithful against the growing secularization does not relieve historians and theologians of the attempt to understand the theological roots and the cultural impact of this movement.[18]

The mostly European (France, Belgium, Germany) but also North American theologians and monks active in the liturgical movement were moved from the "conservationist" and, at the same time, "revolutionary" assumption that the reform of the liturgy required a return

---

[15] See Étienne Fouilloux, "I movimenti di riforma nel pensiero cattolica del XIX e XX secolo," in *I movimenti nella storia del cristianesimo. Caratteristiche, variazioni, continuità*, ed. Giuseppe Alberigo and Massimo Faggioli, *Cristianesimo nella Storia* 24, no. 3 (2003): 659–76; Massimo Faggioli, *Breve storia dei movimenti cattolici* (Roma: Carocci, 2008; Spanish translation: *Historia y evolución de los movimientos católicos. De León XIII a Benedicto XVI* [Madrid: PPC, 2011]); Massimo Faggioli, "Council Vatican II between Documents and Spirit: The Case of the 'New Catholic Movements,'" in *After Vatican II: Trajectories and Hermeneutics*, ed. James Heft and John W. O'Malley (Grand Rapids, MI: Eerdmans, 2012).

[16] See Paul B. Marx, *Virgil Michel and the Liturgical Movement* (Collegeville, MN: Liturgical Press, 1957); Franco Brovelli, *Per uno studio de "L'année liturgique" di P. Guéranger. Contributo alla storia del movimento liturgico* (Roma: C. L.V.-Edizioni liturgiche, 1981); *The Spirit of Solesmes: Dom Prosper Guéranger (1805–75), Abbess Cécile Bruyère (1845–1909), Dom Paul Delatte (1848–1937)*, selected, edited, and introduced by Mary David Totah (Kent: Burns & Oates; Petersham, MA: St. Bede's Publications, 1997).

[17] See Étienne Fouilloux, "Le due vie della pietà cattolica nel XX secolo," in *Chiesa e papato nel mondo contemporaneo*, ed. Giuseppe Alberigo and Andrea Riccardi (Roma-Bari: Laterza, 1990), 287–353; Bernard Botte, *From Silence to Participation: An Insider's View of Liturgical Renewal*, trans. John Sullivan (Washington, DC: Pastoral Press, 1988); original French: *Le Mouvement liturgique: temoignage et souvenirs* (Paris, 1973).

[18] See Jozef Lamberts, "L'évolution de la notion de 'participation active' dans le Mouvement liturgique du XXe siècle," *La Maison-Dieu* 241 (2005): 77–120.

to the very headwaters of the Christian tradition: the closer to the sources, the purer the water. The year 1942 is a watershed with the beginning of the series of the volumes of the Sources Chrétiennes in France.[19] *Ressourcement* wanted to give back to the fathers of the Church the influence that they had had in the education of the leadership of Catholicism, that was lost in favor of neoscholastic theology, and that also had become suspect of "modernistic" heresy at the beginning of the twentieth century.[20] In this sense, Catholic theology between the postwar period and Vatican II became the point of convergence of more than one "going back to the sources." The biblical and patristic movements shared with the liturgical movement the thought that "it was proper to the patristic age to form a tight connection between liturgy, theology and mysticism."[21] It was clear that "the biblical renewal, the liturgical renewal, the spiritual renewal, the apostolic renewal *do question* the scholastic method of Christian thought."[22]

This going back to the sources was foundational for the future renewal of the Church. Already in 1952 Karl Rahner affirmed that "the research on the primitive times of Christianity is not only necessary for the justification of the actual dogmatic theology but also for its development."[23] Only a shortsighted vision can indeed overlook the "radical" sides of this movement from a theological standpoint.[24] The original "conservativism" of the liturgical movement pushed the quest

[19] See Étienne Fouilloux, *La Collection "Sources chrétiennes". Editer les Pères de l'Eglise au XXe siècle* (Paris: Cerf, 1995).

[20] About this shift in theology between the nineteenth and twentieth centuries, see also Avery Dulles, *Models of Revelation* (New York: Doubleday, 1983), 36–67.

[21] Fouilloux, *La Collection*, 35: "le propre de l'âge patristique [est] que liturgie, théologie, mystique s'y compénètrent intimement." See also Brian E. Daley, "The *Nouvelle Théologie* and the Patristic Renewal: Sources, Symbols, and the Science of Theology," *International Journal of Systematic Theology* 7 (2005): 362–82.

[22] From the letter (February 16, 1946) of Henri Brouillard, SJ, to Father Chevignard, OP, in Fouilloux, *La Collection*, 117: "le renouveau biblique, le renouveau liturgique, le renouveau spirituel, le renouveau d'évangelisme apostolique, *met en cause* le mode scolastique de la pensée chrétienne."

[23] See Karl Rahner, "Zur Theologie der Buße bei Tertullian," in *Abhandlungen über Theologie und Kirche* (Festschrift für Karl Adam), ed. Marcel Reding (Düsseldorf, 1952), 139–67.

[24] See Andrea Grillo, "40 anni prima e 40 anni dopo 'Sacrosanctum Concilium'. Una 'considerazione inattuale' sulla attualità del movimento liturgico," *Ecclesia Orans* 21 (2004): 269–300.

for the sources of the liturgy further back than the theological boundaries of modern Catholicism, defined by John O'Malley as "Trent and all that."[25] The early liturgical movement had clearly in mind the idea that the "Tridentine paradigm" was a real touchstone.[26] This idea has not become less important for the comprehension and the evaluation of the Church reforms in the nineteenth and twentieth centuries, especially of the liturgical reform of Vatican II.[27] From the point of view of the liturgical reform and the legacy of Trent, Vatican II is really a paradigmatic event. Also, taking into account the ecclesiological criticism of Congar directed to the liturgical movements,[28] it is fair to say that the *ressourcement* of the liturgical movement went as far as it took to rediscover—beyond the much asserted uniqueness and singleness of the Roman Rite in modern Catholicism—a forgotten "liturgical pluralism." The coexistence of different liturgical rites within Western Catholicism had been erased not only by the changing of the confessional landscape in Europe and in the Mediterranean between the sixteenth and nineteenth centuries but also by the very "Roman way" to enforce the Council of Trent in Europe's Christendom and in a Catholic Church hardened and impoverished by the theology of polemics and apologetics armed against the Reformation.[29]

Ressourcement searched for a way to restore a theological discourse free from baroque theology. By doing this, *ressourcement* crossed with

[25] See John W. O'Malley, *Trent and All That: Renaming Catholicism in the Early Modern Era* (Cambridge, MA: Harvard University Press, 2000).

[26] See Paolo Prodi, *Il paradigma tridentino. Un'epoca della storia della Chiesa* (Brescia: Morcelliana, 2010).

[27] See Jungmann, *Kommentar*, 10; Pierre-Marie Gy, "Situation historique de la Constitution," in *La liturgie après Vatican II. Bilan, études, prospective*, ed. Jean-Pierre Jossua and Yves Congar (Paris: Cerf, 1967), 111–26: "Si, du point de vue ecclésiastique, Vatican II est en quelque sorte symétrique et complémentaire de Vatican I, du point de vue de la théologie de la liturgie et des sacrements (et de l'attitude générale envers une réforme liturgique) c'est avec Trente que la comparaison s'impose" (120–21).

[28] "En général, les mouvements liturgiques ne se sont pas assez donné la base *ecclésiologique* qu'ils devraient avoir. Dans le cas, la question théologique fondamentale, qui n'a pas été abordée: quel est le sujet de l'action liturgique!" (Congar, *Journal du concile*, vol. 1, 146–47 [entry of October 24, 1962]).

[29] See the chapter "Renouveau" ("Renewal") in Henri de Lubac, *Catholicisme: les aspects sociaux du dogme* (Paris: Cerf, 1938), 247–51; English translation: *Catholicism: A Study of Dogma in Relation to the Corporate Destiny of Mankind* (New York: New American Library, 1964), 166–72.

the liturgical movement, helping it in the rediscovery of the christo-logical dimension of the sacraments and thus the purification of the liturgy from formalistic and empty "rubricism." The crossing of ressourcement with the liturgical movement produced a new type of theological reflection, distant from the way traditional dogmatic theology approached the subject of liturgy–sacraments–Church. The farewell to neoscholastic and apologetic theology involved an overall reset of methodology, tools, and aims of theological studies. Along with the notion of collective salvation, *ressourcement* meant the redis-covery of the notion of "history" for the theological disciplines.[30] The liturgical movement managed to use and develop, for and along with *ressourcement*, the historical-critical method that had been harshly condemned by the antimodernist repression and, accordingly, banned from Catholic biblical scholarship from the first decade of twentieth century on.[31]

Quite remarkably, the theology of *ressourcement* and the liturgical movement had survived and flourished in the first half of the twentieth century, that is, in the most critical period for the encounter between Catholic theology and modern scientific methods. A certain continuity of activity of the liturgical movement, thanks to its monastic roots and despite the generational turnover, helped the intellectual milieu engaged in the liturgical renewal keep up the issues on one side and maintain good relations with the Holy See on the other. Under the umbrella and the shield of the *liturgical renewal* and its push for "active participation," the core intellectual issues of the *liturgical movement* could survive. At the end of Pius XII's pontificate, the "entrepreneurs" of theological *ressourcement* managed to appeal to cardinals and bishops in Europe and in the Roman Curia (Cardinals Maurice Feltin, Achille Liénart, Ignace Tappouni, and Eugène Tisserant and Bishops Jean-Julien Weber and Michele Pellegrino).[32] Some years later this impor-tant part of the leadership of European Catholicism would become part of the core theological driving force of Vatican II.

---

[30] See Fouilloux, *La Collection*, 115.

[31] See François Laplanche, *La crise de l'origine: la science catholique des Évangiles et l'histoire au XXe siècle* (Paris: Albin Michel, 2006); Bernard Montagnes, *Father Marie-Joseph Lagrange: Founder of Modern Catholic Bible Study* (New York: Paulist Press, 2006); original French: *Marie-Joseph Lagrange. Une biographie critique* (Paris: Cerf, 2005).

[32] See Fouilloux, *La Collection*, 193–96.

The 1955 reform of Holy Week was a sign of the liturgical movement's good relationship with the Roman Curia and the quiet yet attentive acceptance by the Holy See of some points from the liturgical movement's agenda.[33] In light of this fact, the relationship between the liturgical movement, Vatican II, and liturgical reform is indeed very telling about the issue of "change" and "continuity-discontinuity" in twentieth-century Catholicism. As a matter of fact, among the pre–Vatican II "reform movements," the liturgical revival was the one that had been weakened the least by Pius XII's doctrinal policing against the so-called new theology.[34] In a diplomatic message for the Department of State of the *République Française* (le Quai d'Orsay), the ambassador of France to the Holy See, Jacques Maritain, wrote that the aim of Pius XII's encyclical *Mediator Dei* (November 20, 1947) was "to satisfy the need for 'renewal' manifested in pastoral theology and liturgy and at the same time to prevent theoretical and practical errors that, before the eyes of the Holy See, mingle with this renewal."[35]

Pre–Vatican II liturgical adjustments were just a minor amendment in comparison to the depths of the theological postulation of the liturgical movement. If we look at the final outcome of the liturgical debate at Vatican II, it becomes clear that the liturgical constitution was the only council document that could maintain the framework and the insights of the preparatory *schema*, on the basis of a pluri-decennial experience of the liturgical movement—another reason for the choice of liturgy as the first *schema* to be debated at Vatican II:

> Although the Constitution was reviewed by four appointed "courts"— the central commission, the subcommission for changes, the council itself, and the conciliar commission—no substantial changes were made in the text that emerged from the preparatory commission on January 13, 1962, and was approved by Cardinal Gaetano Cicognani on February 1, 1962.[36]

[33] For the pre–Vatican II history of the liturgical movement (1947–60), see Kaczynski, *Kommentar*, 24–44.

[34] See, for example, the telling testimony of Yves Congar, *Journal d'un théologien: 1946–1956*, ed. Étienne Fouilloux (Paris: Cerf, 2001), 116–17; Gianotti, *I Padri della Chiesa al Concilio Vaticano II*, 71–114.

[35] Quoted by Fouilloux, *Une Église en quête de liberté*, 271: "Son but est de donner satisfaction au besoin de 'renouveau' qui s'est manifesté en matière de pastorale et de liturgie et de prévenir en même temps les erreurs théoriques et pratiques qui, aux yeux du Saint-Siège, se mêlent à ce renouveau."

[36] Bugnini, *The Reform of the Liturgy*, 27.

It is certainly true that the liturgical reform of Vatican II implied and meant more than *ressourcement*, but *ressourcement* remained the core yet concealed force of liturgical reform. The "theological dissemination" of *ressourcement* into Vatican II remained largely intact—even if unidentifiable for many fathers—during the liturgical debate of 1962–63 and struggled to disseminate in other documents. But it is true that *Sacrosanctum Concilium* represents an exception in the corpus of Vatican II, for it is founded on a significantly vast number of biblical and patristic quotations (Augustine, Ignatius of Antioch, Cyril of Alexandria), matched by a relatively few number of quotations from the teaching of the Catholic Church, the most recent quotations being taken from the Council of Trent (sessions 22 and 23). Pius X is quoted twice in the text, and no quotation is devoted to Pius XII's teaching; nevertheless, some passages are implicitly taken from *Mediator Dei*.

In order to understand *Sacrosanctum Concilium*, the relationship between the text of the liturgical constitution and the "theology in act" of Vatican II must not be forgotten. At the beginning of the council in October 1962, it became evident that John XXIII considered the celebration of liturgy every morning in St. Peter's an essential part of the proceedings of the *aula*, although some important leaders of the *aula* (Cardinals Leo Jozef Suenens and Giovanni Battista Montini) asked the pope to cancel the Mass from the daily agenda of the council. On the contrary, John XXIII stood firm in his decision to proceed along the *Ordo Concilii* and to stress the importance of the ceremony of the intronization of the gospels in St. Peter's. While it is known that as a young priest Angelo Giuseppe Roncalli was suspected of being a "modernist," during his long episcopate—as a Vatican diplomat and later as patriarch of Venice—Roncalli had not been a member of the liturgical movement, but he had always emphasized the importance of Church history in his education and the centrality of the liturgy in his spiritual life.[37] Roncalli was far from conceiving of the "liturgical experiments" performed and advocated by the theologians of the movement, but it was no accident that in May 1959 John XXIII, the new pope, "discreetly" donated five million Italian lire to the association

---

[37] See Angelo Giuseppe Roncalli (Giovanni XXIII), *Nelle mani di Dio a servizio dell'uomo. Diari della giovinezza e della prima maturità 1905–1925*, ed. Lucia Butturini (Bologna: Fondazione per le scienze religiose, 2008); Angelo Giuseppe Roncalli (Giovanni XXIII), *Tener da conto. Le agendine di Bulgaria 1925–1934*, ed. Massimo Faggioli (Bologna: Fondazione per le scienze religiose, 2008), viii–x.

working on the series of the fathers of the Church, Sources Chrétiennes.[38]

Despite the pitiless analysis of the opening ceremony given by a theologian like Congar and a liturgist like Jungmann,[39] the significance of "beginning with liturgy" is clear.[40] In the words of John XXIII at the end of the first period (December 8, 1962):

> It was no accident that the first *schema* to be considered was the one dealing with the sacred liturgy. The liturgy has to do with man's relationship with God. This relationship is of the utmost importance. It must be based on the solid foundation of revelation and apostolic teaching, so as to contribute to man's spiritual good; and that, with a broadness of vision which avoids the superficiality and haste often characterizing relationships among men.[41]

It was no accident also that the liturgical preparatory commission of Vatican II adopted a quite particular method for the drafting of the text, refusing to oppose the doctrinal sphere and pastoral approach.[42] It was no accident that Yves Congar found the text prepared by the liturgical preparatory commission in August 1962 "quite at the level of the *ressourcement*."[43] The debate on the liturgical constitution prepared the theological terms for the following debates on the floor of St. Peter's in the first session of the fall of 1962: the battle for the *De fontibus revelationis* and ecumenism in the preparatory *schema De ecclesiae unitate*. No surprise that in the preparatory liturgical commission the major experts of the liturgical movement had worked at the international

---

[38] See Fouilloux, *La Collection*, 219.

[39] See Andrea Riccardi, "The Tumultuous Opening Days of the Council," in *History of Vatican II*, vol. 2: *The Formation of the Council's Identity, First Period and Intercession, October 1962–September 1963* (Maryknoll, NY: Orbis; Leuven: Peeters, 1997), 11–13.

[40] See Johannes Wagner, *Mein Weg zur Liturgiereform, 1936–1986. Erinnerungen* (Freiburg i.B.: Herder, 1993), 66.

[41] Quoted in Bugnini, *The Reform of the Liturgy*, 33. See also the December 8, 1962, address of John XXIII in *Acta Synodalia*, vol. 1, bk. 4, 645, and the December 4, 1963, address of Paul VI in *Acta Synodalia*, vol. 2, bk. 6, 565.

[42] See Levillain, *La mécanique politique de Vatican II*, 73–75.

[43] See Congar, *Journal du concile*, vol. 1, 99 (entry of August 5–6, 1962): "Le texte sur la liturgie est bon; il est beaucoup plus au niveau du ressourcement actuel."

level: Vagaggini, Capelle, Botte, Chavasse, Jounel, Jungmann, and Martimort.[44]

In the eyes of bishops and theologians at Vatican II, the liturgical debate not only was perceived as a highly symbolic way to open a council devoted to *aggiornamento* but also held a position that was pedagogical and strategic at the same time. Being that the liturgy was the summit of the activity of the whole Church, it was expected to break the ground for other theological and institutional issues strictly connected with the idea of *ressourcement* for the reform of the Church and the ecumenical dialogue. In his letters to the monastery of St. Anne in Jerusalem, Fr. Pierre Duprey (active at Vatican II as theologian and translator for the Orthodox observers and delegates to the council) wrote:

> When the time comes for the debate on the episcopacy, and we hope that it will be after the debate on liturgy, we will have already a precedent and it will not be possible to go back. [. . .] It will come time to introduce, through the Secretariat for extraordinary affairs, other projects about the reform of the Roman Curia.[45]

2.3. Liturgy, *Ressourcement*, and Ecumenism

Paragraph 7 of the liturgical constitution was a turning point. It represents the connection—*through liturgy*—between *ressourcement* on one side and a less "ecclesiocentric," thus more ecumenical, ecclesiology of Vatican II on the other side: "The liturgy, then, is rightly seen as an exercise of the priestly office of Jesus Christ" (SC 7). The conception of

---

[44] See Bugnini, *The Reform of the Liturgy*; Maria Paiano, "Il rinnovamento della liturgia: dai movimenti alla chiesa universale," in *Verso il concilio Vaticano II (1960–1962). Passaggi e problemi della preparazione conciliare*, ed. Giuseppe Alberigo and Alberto Melloni (Genova: Marietti, 1993), 67–140, esp. 78–84. About Jungmann and the liturgical movement in Germany, see also Rudolf Pacik, "Josef Andreas Jungmann, SJ (1889–1975)," in *Gottesdients als Feld theologischer Wissenschaft im 20. Jahrhundert. Deutschsprachige Liturgiewissenschaft in Einzelporträts*, ed. Benedikt Kranemann and Klaus Raschzok (Münster: Aschendorff, 2011), 1:538–55.

[45] "Lorsque la discussion du *de episcopatu* viendra et on espère que ce sera après la liturgie, il y aura déjà un précédent et on ne pourra pas aller en arrière. [. . .] Il sera temps alors de déposer auprès des affaires extraordinaires, d'autres projets portant sur la réforme de la curie" (entry of October 23, 1962). See Pierre Duprey files, in Archive of the John XXIII Foundation for Religious Studies in Bologna, www.fscire.it.

liturgy as an exercise of the priestly office of Christ, as sanctification of human beings and worship of God, and as liturgy performed by means of sensible signs was made possible by a debate that perceived sensibly—although not theologically in its "unintended consequences"[46]—the intrinsic link between liturgy, *ressourcement*, and ecumenism.

From the beginning of the debate some fathers, and especially the bishops from Eastern Catholic Churches, pointed out that an "ecumenical council" could not address the issue of the reform of the Roman Rite only.[47] As a matter of fact, Vatican II was the first council that issued a document about the renewal of a "particular" rite like the Roman Rite that should have been debated and issued by a synod of the Latin Church chaired by the bishop of Rome.[48] But this "occupation" of Vatican II by the Roman Rite was counterbalanced by the celebrations in St. Peter's in other rites, from the Eastern traditions especially, and by the profound impact they had on many of the fathers' ideas of global Catholicism and of ecumenism.[49]

The ecumenical significance of *Sacrosanctum Concilium* in the corpus and in the event of Vatican II is made clear by the fact that the opening lines of the liturgical constitution state the aims of the whole of Vatican II:

> The sacred Council has set out to impart an ever-increasing vigor to the Christian life of the faithful; to adapt more closely to the needs of our age those institutions which are subject to change; to foster whatever can promote union among all who believe in Christ; to strengthen whatever can help to call all mankind into the Church's fold. (SC 1)

[46] See John O'Malley, "Vatican II: Did Anything Happen?," in *Vatican II: Did Anything Happen?*, ed. David Schultenover (New York: Continuum, 2007), 52–91, esp. 58–64.

[47] See Jungmann, *Kommentar*, 16.

[48] See Kaczynski, *Kommentar*, 57.

[49] Many diaries and private journals of council fathers and theologians at Vatican II testify to the profound impact of the non-Roman liturgies on their understanding of the Catholicity of the Church; see Riccardi, "The Tumultuous Opening Days of the Council," in *History of Vatican II*, vol. 2, 67; and Reiner Kaczinsky, "Toward the Reform of the Liturgy," in *History of Vatican II*, vol. 3: *The Mature Council, Second Period and Intercession, September 1963–September 1964* (Maryknoll, NY: Orbis; Leuven: Peeters, 2000), 221–22.

Thanks to the reassurances given during the preparatory phase (1959–60) that Vatican II would not be a council aimed at a mechanical, leader-driven, top-down "reunification" of the Churches into the Roman Catholic Church, like some other councils that failed at this intent in the Middle Ages (like the second council of Lyon in 1274 and the council of Ferrara-Florence in 1439),[50] paragraph 1 of *Sacrosanctum Concilium* clearly affirms that Vatican II aims to "foster whatever can promote union among all who believe in Christ" (SC 1). In that respect, *Sacrosanctum Concilium* received some of the most important contributions of *ressourcement* and of the liturgical movement, thus opening the way for the "ecumenical spirit of Vatican II" some weeks before the debate on "the sources of Revelation" (*Dei Verhum*), which in November 1962 put the ecumenical issue as such at the center of Vatican II.[51]

In the central passage of paragraph 2 "the real nature of the true Church" is defined:

> The Church is essentially both human and divine, visible but endowed with invisible realities, zealous in action and dedicated to contemplation, present in the world, but as a pilgrim, so constituted that in her the human is directed toward and subordinated to the divine, the visible to the invisible, action to contemplation, and this present world to that city yet to come, the object of our quest. (SC 2)

The definition of the Church as "both human and divine" clearly represented for Vatican II a step toward a more ecumenical concept of the Church, centered in the mystery of Christ far more than in the Counter-Reformation idea of the Catholic Church as the *societas perfecta*—a "perfect institution."[52] The sacramental dimension of the Church as the *Ursakrament* is very telling of the deep connection between the renewal of liturgy and the ecclesiology of Vatican II:

---

[50] See Claude Soetens, "The Ecumenical Commitment of the Catholic Church," in *History of Vatican II*, vol. 3, 257–345.

[51] See Giuseppe Ruggieri, "The First Doctrinal Clash," in *History of Vatican II*, vol. 2, 233–66; Riccardo Burigana, *La Bibbia nel concilio. La redazione della costituzione "Dei Verbum" del Vaticano II* (Bologna: Il Mulino, 1998).

[52] For the classical, papal-centered model of Church, see Robert Bellarmine, *Disputationes de Controversiis Christianae Fidei adversus hujus temporis Haereticos* (Ingolstadt, 1586).

33

ressourcement was an essential intellectual move that made possible both and that enabled Catholic theology to develop its understanding of ecumenism.[53]

The contribution to the ecumenical dialogue and to the rediscovery of plurality within the Church, made possible through a *ressourcement*-based concept of liturgy, was clear from the very beginning of Vatican II. On one side the "liturgical way" in the language of Vatican II represented for the Catholic Church a new start, very different from the dogmatic theological approach to the issues of ecclesiology, ecumenism, and the modern world.[54] Liturgy seemed to provide for the encounter between Christians of different Churches a new and at the same time old language, shaped by the first millennium and thus ecumenically shared and far less polemical than dogmatic theology and canon law. On the other side, the direct experience of other liturgical traditions gave the council fathers a much-needed basic knowledge of the variety of legitimate rites within the Catholic Church. The eucharistic celebrations performed in St. Peter's in different Catholic rites during Vatican II displayed the inner diversity within the Catholic Church and made the approach to the dialogue with Christians from other traditions, especially with the Eastern Orthodox Churches, much more possible.[55] John XXIII was particularly aware of the importance of the diversity of liturgical rites in the Catholic Church when, on April 19, 1961, he celebrated Mass in the Greek Rite and in the Greek language at the liturgy for episcopal consecration of Msgr. Acacio Coussa, whom he appointed official for the Roman Curia Congregation for the Eastern Churches. John XXIII was the first pope who celebrated in a liturgical rite different from the Roman Rite.[56]

[53] See Otto Semmelroth, *Die Kirche als Ursakrament* (Frankfurt am Main: Knecht, 1953); English translation: *Church and Sacrament*, trans. Emily Schossberger (Notre Dame, IN: Fides Publishers, 1965).

[54] See the three "issues under the issues" identified by O'Malley: (1) the possibility of change in the Catholic Church; (2) the relationship between center and periphery; (3) Vatican II, a language-event (O'Malley, *What Happened*, 290–313).

[55] See Andrea Riccardi, "The Tumultuous Opening Days of the Council," in *History of Vatican II*, vol. 2, 67; Neophytos Edelby, *Il Vaticano II nel diario di un vescovo arabo*, ed. Riccardo Cannelli (Cinisello Balsamo: San Paolo, 1996), 77–78.

[56] See Giovanni Caprile, *Il Concilio Vaticano II. Cronache del concilio Vaticano II edite da "La Civiltà Cattolica,"* vols. 1–5 (Rome, 1966–69), 1:2, 81.

Yves Congar noted that "the way the Eastern Churches talk to the council is a liturgical way";[57] not surprisingly, the council adopted the same liturgical way *to talk with herself and about herself* as well as to talk to the other Churches. The new attitude of the Catholic Church was presented by the new role of liturgy in the council as an event:[58] "The examples of the Oriental liturgies [celebrated at Vatican II] will have a great influence on the council more than the speeches, since these liturgies are a demonstration of the adaptation of the liturgy to the people."[59]

As early as November 1962 it became clear to the leaders of the ecumenical milieu at Vatican II that liturgy was the main way to steer a new dialogue between the ancient Eastern Orthodox theological tradition and the official "Latin theology."

Pierre Duprey wrote in those days:

> Latin Theology has given us a good *Intellectus fidei*, but it ignores completely the great catechetical tradition of the Greek Fathers of the Church. We do not have the right to monopolize the universal faith into a particular theology. The Eastern tradition sees especially the economy of salvation received in the liturgy and not elaborated in an abstract way.[60]

In his report to the *aula* on November 19, 1962, about the *schema* on the revelation, Bishop De Smedt (of the Secretariat for Christian Unity) affirmed that the liturgical way, together with a more biblical language

[57] "Messe de rite oriental. C'est aussi, pour l'Orient, une façon de parler au concile. Une fois de plus, il parle par sa liturgie" (Congar, *Journal du Concile*, vol. 1, 145 [entry of October 24, 1962]).

[58] About the liturgical character of Vatican II, see the last yet pioneering article by Giuseppe Alberigo, "Sinodo come liturgia?," *Cristianesimo nella Storia* 28 (January 2007): 1–39.

[59] "Messe de rite maronite. Cet exemple des liturgies orientales influera sur le concile plus que les discours, il est par lui-même démonstration d'une adaptation de la liturgie au peuple" (Congar, *Journal du Concile*, vol. 1, 182 [entry of November 5, 1962]).

[60] "C'est de la théologie latine qui a procuré un bel Intellectus fidei mais ignore complètement toute la grande tradition catéchiste des pères grecs. On n'a pas le droit de monopoliser la foi universelle dans une théologie particulière. La tradition oriental voit surtout l'économie du salut reçu dans la liturgie et non pas formulée abstraitement" (entry of November 18, 1962, Pierre Duprey files, in Archive of the John XXIII Foundation for Religious Studies in Bologna, www.fscire.it).

and a theology founded on patristic texts, was the only way for the council to present the doctrine ecumenically: "The biblical and patristic way to speak prevents difficulties, misunderstandings, and prejudices."[61]

One of the most important contributions to the ecumenical language of Vatican II was the clear decision to accept the idea that Catholicism could legitimately and necessarily *change*. Despite the clash between historicism and Catholicism and some decades after the merciless repression of "modernists"—whose classmates in seminary were now sitting at Vatican II as council fathers—Vatican II adopted a liturgical reform in which "sound tradition [may] be retained, and yet the way remain open to legitimate progress" (SC 23).

Liturgical *ressourcement* at Vatican II also meant the ripening of the ecumenical language of Catholicism and a powerful blow to every nostalgia of "Uniatism"—toward the failed experience of Uniatism in Eastern Europe as well as toward the dreams of a possible new Uniatism with some fractions of European Protestantism.[62] Whereas Uniatism tried, from the fifteenth through the twentieth centuries, to build a new and fictitious institutional unity between Eastern and Western Christianity through a kind of "liturgical-ecclesiological engineering,"[63] the twentieth-century liturgical movement and *ressourcement* aimed at meeting the other Christian denominations at the very sources of Christianity and at rediscovering the original unity of the

---

[61] Bishop de Smedt, in *Acta Synodalia*, vol. 1, bk. 3, 184–87, quotation at 185 (November 19, 1962). See also Ruggieri, "The First Doctrinal Clash," in *History of Vatican II*, vol. 2, 258–59.

[62] See Étienne Fouilloux, *Les catholiques et l'unité chrétienne du XIXe au XXe siècle: itinéraires européens d'expression française* (Paris: Centurion, 1982); Mauro Velati, *Una difficile transizione. Il cattolicesimo tra unionismo ed ecumenismo (1952–1964)* (Bologna: Il Mulino, 1996); Joseph Famerée, "Les méthodes en oecumenisme: des Conversations de Malines à Vatican II (1921–1962)," *Irénikon* (April 2005): 491–520.

[63] For an important example of the use of liturgy in the "Uniatist" approach in twentieth-century Catholicism, see Cyrille Korolevskij, *Liturgie en langue vivante: orient et occident* (Paris: Éditions du Cerf, 1955); Cyrille Korolevskij (Cyril Korolevsky), *Living Languages in Catholic Worship: An Historical Inquiry*, trans. Donald Attwater (Westminster, MD: Newman Press, 1957). About the incredibly rich personality of Cyrille Korolevskij, see the monumental edition of his autobiography in Cyrille Korolevskij, *Kniga bytija moego (Le livre de ma vie). Mémoires autobiographiques, texte établi, édité et annoté par Giuseppe M. Croce*. Avant-propos du cardinal Jean-Louis Tauran, préface de Étienne Fouilloux, 5 vols. (Città del Vaticano: Archivio Segreto Vaticano, 2007).

Christian faith. Through a liturgy purified from the burden of the doctrinal clashes of the second millennium and from devotional sectarianism, Vatican II determined that "devotions should be so drawn up that they harmonize with the liturgical seasons, accord with the sacred liturgy, are in some way derived from it, and lead the people to it, since in fact the liturgy by its very nature is far superior to any of them" (SC 13).

The new concept of the Church as "people of God" and of the laity in its full liturgical ability started with the recognition that the rites' revision was necessary in order to favor the "devout and active participation by the faithful" (SC 50):

> "For this purpose the rites are to be simplified, due care being taken to preserve their substance. Parts which with the passage of time came to be duplicated, or were added with little advantage, are to be omitted. Other parts which suffered loss through accidents of history are to be restored to the vigor they had in the days of the holy Fathers, as may seem useful or necessary.
>
> The treasures of the Bible are to be opened up more lavishly so that a richer fare may be provided for the faithful at the table of God's word. (SC 50–51)

It is hard to overlook the importance of these core issues of *Sacrosanctum Concilium* for the ecumenical dimension of Vatican II: the new liturgical dignity of the laity that was closer to Martin Luther's assumption of a "common priesthood of all believers"; the recognition that elements of liturgy had suffered "loss through accidents of history" and that therefore the Church had to heal those injuries; the new centrality of the Bible in the liturgical life of the Catholic Church; the acknowledgment of the importance of historicity in the readings, so that "the accounts of the martyrdoms or lives of the saints are to be made historically accurate. [. . .] They are to be purged of whatever smacks of mythology or accords ill with Christian piety" (SC 92–93).

2.4. Liturgy, *Ressourcement*, and Mission

The opening of the liturgical constitution states that one of the aims of the council is clearly mission: Vatican II desires "to strengthen whatever can help to call all mankind into the Church's fold. Accordingly, it sees particularly cogent reasons for undertaking the reform and promotion of the liturgy" (SC 1). The correlation between *ressource-ment*, liturgical renewal, and the missionary aim of the "new liturgy" is made clear by stating that "the rites should be distinguished by a noble simplicity. They should be short, clear, and free from useless repetitions. They should be within the people's powers of comprehension, and normally should not require much explanation" (SC 34).

The liturgical renewal was aimed at restoring the Church thanks to the fontal role of Eucharist for a spiritual renewal of Catholicism and a more ecumenical Church. But the liturgical renewal—in the pre–Vatican II liturgical movement and at Vatican II alike—was also aimed at finding a new language for a missionary dialogue with the modern world. The end of Christendom and of the "Constantine Era"[64]—something both theologians and leadership of Vatican II were well aware of—meant also the end of a common religious language in the cultural landscape of the modern world and even within Western civilization. Vatican II saw in the reform of the liturgy, renewed through *ressourcement*, a powerful tool for the Church's missionary identity and activities. Behind this new discovery of the rites and their untranslatability it is to see a religious anthropology that had perceived the dire need of a new language for Catholicism. In a way, *Sacrosanctum Concilium* represents the reversal of Charles Journet's judgment about Origen in a polemics about the relationship between patristic renewal and Thomism: "the ontology must come before every symbolic."[65]

The most radical *ressourcement* in *Sacrosanctum Concilium* is the option to get back to liturgy as *the* language in which the Church expresses and communicates within herself and with the world: less legalism, a new and more symbolic relationship with human cultures.[66] In other words, the liturgical renewal needs *ressourcement*, but

[64] See Robert Rouquette, *La fin d'une chrétienté. Chroniques, I* (Paris: Cerf, 1968); Marie-Dominique Chenu, "La fin de l'ére constantinienne," in *Un concile pour notre temps* (Paris: Cerf, 1961), 59–87.

[65] "Une ontologie doit précéder toute symbolique" (Charles Journet, quoted in Fouilloux, *La Collection*, 126). See Charles Journet, *The Theology of the Church* (San Francisco: Ignatius Press, 2004); and Guy Boissard, *Charles Journet, 1891–1975* (Paris: Salvator, 2008). About the new paradigm for Catholic theology between the nineteenth and twentieth centuries, see Dulles, *Models of Revelation*, 36–67.

[66] For the relationship between Church and cultures, see the intervention by Cardinal Giacomo Lercaro, on December 6, 1962, in *Acta Synodalia*, vol. 1, bk. 4, 327–30; see Giuseppe Ruggieri, "Beyond an Ecclesiology of Polemics: The Debate on the Church," in *History of Vatican II*, vol. 2, 345–46.

liturgy itself is the main source to which the Church needs to return in order to understand its essence and its mission. Cardinal Maurice Feltin (archbishop of Paris) reminded the council fathers not only that the Latin language had become an obstacle for evangelization but also that since the earliest times the liturgy had been the locus par excellence of catechesis.[67] The Patriarch of Antioch of the Melkytes, Maximos IV Saigh, speaking in French (an absolute exception at Vatican II), reminded the council fathers that the need to go back to the sources did not mean "giving a quasi-absolute value to the Latin," given that the Church has come through the use of Aramaic, Greek, Latin: "In the Eastern Churches, on the contrary, we never had the problem of the liturgical language: every language is a liturgical language. [. . .] Latin is a dead language, but the Church is alive."[68]

The connection between liturgical renewal and the new missionary character of the Church had been developed already before the beginning of Vatican II, in the liturgical milieus and conferences of the late 1950s.[69] The blunt acknowledgment that the Church is missionary in the Western World and in the "missionary countries" alike had already been articulated by European theologians and sociologists in the 1940s.[70] But at Vatican II this assumption became common language.[71]

From the beginning of the debate in October 1962 many council fathers, and especially missionary bishops, also supported the liturgical *schema* because of its missionary dimension.[72] The bishops from

[67] See Cardinal Maurice Feltin (archbishop of Paris), speech of October 23, 1962, in *Acta Synodalia*, vol. 1, bk. 1, 368.

[68] Patriarch Maximos IV Saigh (Antioch of the Melkyte), speech of October 24, 1962, in *Acta Synodalia*, vol. 1, bk. 1, 378.

[69] See Kaczynski, *Kommentar*, 42–44.

[70] See the famous essay by Henri Godin and Yvan Daniel, *La France, pays de mission?* (Paris: Cerf, 1943); and the pioneering works of Fernand Boulard, *An Introduction to Religious Sociology: Pioneer Work in France*, preface by Gabriel Le Bras (London: Darton, Longman and Todd, 1960); original ed. *Premiers itinéraires en sociologie religieuse* (Paris: Éditions ouvrières, 1954).

[71] See the intervention of Bishop Joseph Emmanuel Descuffi (Izmir–Smyrna, Turkey) in *Acta Synodalia*, vol. 1, bk. 1, 416 (October 24, 1962).

[72] See the interventions of Cardinals Josef Frings (Cologne, Germany), Giacomo Lercaro (Bologna, Italy), Raul Silva Henrìquez (Santiago, Chile), Laurean Rugambwa (Bukoba, Tanganyika), Alberto Devoto (Goya, Argentina), Hermann Volk (Mainz, Germany), Juan Landàzuri Ricketts (Lima, Chile), Maximos IV Saigh (Antioch, Syria): *Acta Synodalia*, vol. 1, bk. 1, 309, 311–13, 323, 333, 524, 355–56, 375, 377

African and Asian Churches were pleased by the fact that the *schema* gave an opportunity to non-Western cultures to celebrate the liturgy according to their own aesthetical tradition and sensibility.[73] About the use of vernacular, the Chilean bishops reminded the council fathers that the early Church did not keep using the Hebrew and Greek languages, since they were not understood anymore.[74] The bishops from Africa significantly asked that the adjective "Western" would be removed from a passage ("Eastern and Western rites"; SC 24) that classified the Christian traditions along the East–West axis and did not take into account the hopes of Africa for a cultural and theological emancipation.[75] The Indian bishops took a positive position with regard to the proposed *schema* for similar reasons.[76]

The new links among liturgical renewal, ecclesiology, and the missionary Church are quite clear if we analyze the leap from the encyclical *Mediator Dei* and the ecclesiological constitution *Lumen Gentium* on one side to *Sacrosanctum Concilium* on the other side. The former documents present a quite similar view of the ecclesiology of the people of God's participation to the celebration of sacraments, while the liturgical constitution develops an ecclesiology of sacraments typical of the *ecclesia congregata*, quite different from the hierarchical priesthood of *Mediator Dei*:[77]

> Accordingly, just as Christ was sent by the Father so also he sent the apostles, filled with the Holy Spirit. This he did so that they might

---

(October 22, 1962). See Mathijs Lamberigts, "The Liturgy Debate," in *History of Vatican II*, vol. 3, 107–66, esp. 115–46.

[73] See Cardinal Rugambwa (Bukoba, Tanganyika) in *Acta Synodalia*, vol. 1, bk. 1, 333–34; Cardinal Paul Tatsuo Doi (Tokyo, Japan) in *Acta Synodalia*, vol. 1, bk. 1, 323; and Bishop Yoshigoro Taguchi (Osaka, Japan) in *Acta Synodalia*, vol. 1, bk. 2, 630–31 (November 12, 1962).

[74] See *Acta Synodalia*, vol. 1, bk. 1, 324 (October 22, 1962).

[75] See *Acta Synodalia*, vol. 1, bk. 1, 420 (October 24, 1962).

[76] See Paul Pulikkan, *Indian Church at Vatican II: A Historico-Theological Study of the Indian Participation in the Second Vatican Council* (Trichur, India: Maryamatha Publications, 2001), 210–20.

[77] See Yves Congar, "L'ecclesia ou communauté chrétienne, sujet intégral de l'action liturgique," in *La liturgie après Vatican II; bilans, études, prospective*, ed. Jean-Pierre Jossua and Yves Congar (Paris: Cerf, 1967), 241–82; English translation: "The Ecclesia or Christian Community as a Whole Celebrates the Liturgy," in Yves Congar, *At the Heart of Christian Worship: Liturgical Essays of Yves Congar*, trans. and ed. Paul Philibert (Collegeville, MN: Liturgical Press, 2010), 15–68.

preach the Gospel to every creature and proclaim that the Son of God by his death and resurrection had freed us from the power of Satan and from death, and brought us into the Kingdom of his Father. But he also willed that the work of salvation which they preached should be set in train through the sacrifice and sacraments, around which the entire liturgical life revolves. Thus by Baptism men are grafted into the paschal mystery of Christ: they die with him, are buried with him, and rise with him. They receive the spirit of adoption as sons "in which we cry, Abba, Father" (Rom. 8:15) and thus become true adorers such as the Father seeks. In like manner as often as they eat the Supper of the Lord they proclaim the death of the Lord until he comes. (SC 6)

This new idea of liturgy as a tool for a missionary Church led to wording in paragraph 36, about the use of Latin, that is careful yet open to development: "The use of the Latin language, with due respect to particular law, is to be preserved in the Latin rites. But since the use of the vernacular, whether in the Mass, the administration of the sacraments, or in other parts of the liturgy, may frequently be of great advantage to the people, a wider use may be made of it" (SC 36.1–2). At the same time, it was clear that Latin had become a relic for the vast majority of Catholics and that SC 36 would soon have to be interpreted in a broad way to make more room for the vernacular languages. Already in October 1962 Yves Congar noted, "It is true that the wound inflicted to the Latin will be enlarged inevitably; already now young priests, also among us [Dominicans], do not know Latin well enough to follow the Liturgy of the Hours properly, and they do not seem to be aware of the grave professional obligation that they have to learn Latin."[78] Congar's long-term view of the Church helped him understand the impossibility of going back to a Latin-speaking Catholic Church.

Ressourcement brought about a new awareness of the multifaceted nature of Catholicism. Therefore, the need for a mission-based idea of liturgy is at the root of paragraph 37: "Even in the liturgy the Church does not wish to impose a rigid uniformity in matters which do not involve the faith or the good of the whole community. Rather does she respect and foster the qualities and talents of the various races and nations" (SC 37). Paragraphs 38, 39, and 41—about the adaptations of the Roman Rite, the duties of individual bishops and, at the time, of

---

[78] Congar, *Journal du concile*, 154 (entry of October 27, 1962).

the yet-to-be-created national bishops' conferences for the liturgical life of their Churches—made clear that not only the bishops from Asia and Africa but also the other bishops had at heart the link between liturgical renewal and mission. Paragraph 64 on the catechumenate and paragraph 123 on sacred art enlightened the role of liturgy and liturgical education in "post-Christendom Catholicism."

This basic new role of liturgy resounded in other Vatican II documents dealing with the missionary activity of the Church, but with very different degrees of reception. On one side, in *Apostolicam Actuositatem*[79] and in *Ad Gentes*[80] liturgy is perceived as a source of the strength in apostolic work and a crucial moment of the catechumenate, and in *Presbyterorum Ordinis*[81] liturgy is framed between the service of priest to the community and the mere act of "hearing" by the people, while "the one-sided cultic character of the Catholic priesthood has been absorbed into wider apostolic ministry."[82] On the other hand, in other

---

[79] "Participators in the function of Christ, priest, prophet and king, the laity have an active part of their own in the life and action of the Church. [. . .] Nourished by their active participation in the liturgical life of their community, they engage zealously in its apostolic works" (*Apostolicam Actuositatem* 10).

[80] "Those who have received from God the gift of faith in Christ, through the Church, should be admitted with liturgical rites to the catechumenate which is not a mere exposition of dogmatic truths and norms of morality, but a period of formation in the whole Christian life, an apprenticeship of sufficient duration, during which the disciples will be joined to Christ their teacher. The catechumens should be properly initiated into the mystery of salvation and the practice of the evangelical virtues, and they should be introduced into the life of faith, liturgy and charity of the People of God by successive sacred rites" (*Ad Gentes* 14).

[81] "Thus the ministry of the Word is exercised in many different ways according to the needs of the hearers and the spiritual gifts of preachers. In non-Christian territories or societies people are led by the proclamation of the Gospel to faith and by the saving sacraments. In the Christian community itself on the other hand, especially for those who seem to have little understanding or belief underlying their practice, the preaching of the Word is required for the sacramental ministry itself, since the sacraments are sacraments of faith, drawing their origin and nourishment from the Word. This is of paramount importance in the case of the liturgy of the Word within the celebration of Mass where there is an inseparable union of the proclamation of the Lord's death and resurrection, the response of its hearers and the offering itself by which Christ confirmed the new covenant in his blood" (*Presbyterorum Ordinis* 4).

[82] Friedrich Wulf, "Commentary on the Decree: Articles 1–6," in *Commentary on the Documents of Vatican II*, ed. Herbert Vorgrimler, vol. 4 (New York: Herder and Herder, 1967–69), 224.

Vatican II documents liturgy is treated as only a mirroring of the attitude of the Church toward the modern world and different cultures in *Gaudium et Spes*,[83] and liturgical studies are at the bottom of the list of the theological disciplines seminarians are encouraged to study.[84]

The fact that the liturgical constitution does not provide a definition of liturgy is not to be read as an omission but as an option to approach liturgy in a rather different way. Andrea Grillo has fittingly affirmed that *Sacrosanctum Concilium* "will answer [to the encyclical *Mediator Dei*] with a change of style, not through a theoretical and definitive style, but narratively and, in a way, 'patristically.'"[85] After a carefully worded "non-definitive definition" of liturgy in paragraph 7,[86] *Sacrosanctum Concilium* 10 states that "the liturgy is the summit toward which the activity of the Church is directed; it is also the fount from which all her power flows" (SC 10). This sentence, which has become for many Catholics the *summa* of the liturgical renewal debated and started at Vatican II, condenses in a few words the principle of the reform and its theological roots.

Casting aside the linguistic and aesthetic directions of the reform and its local implementations for a moment,[87] the early link between the pre–Vatican II push for an active participation of the faithful and the concept of liturgy as "summit and fount" contributed enormously to shaping the role of the liturgical constitution at Vatican II. The sum of the implementation of the *actuosa participatio* (Pius X) on one side and the theological push for *ressourcement* on the other did not intend

[83] "Similarly the Church has existed through the centuries in varying circumstances and has utilized the resources of different cultures in its preaching to spread and explain the message of Christ, to examine and understand it more deeply, and to express it more perfectly in the liturgy and in various aspects of the life of the faithful" (*Gaudium et Spes* 58).

[84] See *Optatam Totius*, 8. See Peter A. Kwasniewski, "Education and Liturgy: Thoughts on the Fortieth Anniversary of the Closing of Vatican II," *The Downside Review* (April 2006): 135–48.

[85] See Andrea Grillo, *La nascita della liturgia nel XX secolo. Saggio sul rapporto tra movimento liturgico e (post-) modernità* (Assisi: Cittadella, 2003), 131: "significativamente *Sacrosanctum Concilium* darà una risposta [to the encyclical *Mediator Dei*] cambiando registro, non parlando più teoricamente e definitoriamente, ma narrativamente e in qualche modo 'patristicamente.'" See also Gianotti, *I Padri della Chiesa al Concilio Vaticano II*, 421–26.

[86] See Jungmann, *Kommentar*, 21–23.

[87] See, for example, Ralf van Bühren, *Kunst und Kirche im 20. Jahrhundert. Die Rezeption des Zweiten Vatikanischen Konzils* (Schoening: Paderborn, 2008), 215–51.

just to call each and every faithful back to the Church for the celebration of liturgy but also began the reframing of the whole concept of Church:

> The fundamental principle of the liturgical reform was the participation of the whole assembly in the sacred action, a principle derived from ancient liturgical practice. Restoring the dignity of the first part of the Mass, the Liturgy of the Word, was similarly derived. And so forth. The application of such principle to the present, the *aggiornamento*, was a consequence, not the starting point.[88]

The history of the text of *Sacrosanctum Concilium* is extremely telling. Paragraph 10 is preceded by paragraph 7, which places Christ at the very center of the liturgy:

> Christ is always present in his Church, especially in her liturgical celebrations. He is present in the Sacrifice of the Mass not only in the person of his minister, "the same now offering, through the ministry of priests, who formerly offered himself on the cross," but especially in the eucharistic species. By his power he is present in the sacraments so that when a man baptizes it is really Christ himself who baptizes. He is present in his word, since it is he himself who speaks when the holy scriptures are read in the Church.

Paragraph 7 affirms that liturgy is an action not of individuals but of the whole Church. A phrase about the presence of Christ in the reading of the Scripture was added in the second session (October 1963): "He is present in the Sacrifice of the Mass not only in the person of his minister, 'the same now offering, through the ministry of priests, who formerly offered himself on the cross,' but especially in the eucharistic species" (SC 7).

The first sentence of paragraph 10—"Nevertheless the liturgy is the summit toward which the activity of the Church is directed; it is also the fount from which all her power flows" (*attamen liturgia est culmen ad quo actio ecclesiae tendit et simul fons unde omnis eius virtus emanat*)— was moved from paragraph 9 and given a new wording, with "summit" instead of "center." The change gave this passage much more

---

[88] See O'Malley, *What Happened*, 301.

importance, as it was now located in paragraph 10, which deals specifically with the eucharistic sacrifice as fount of life for the Church.[89]

The well-known passage in paragraph 10 affirms that the whole liturgy is "summit" and "fount." This passage was reformulated thanks to the conciliar commission (and especially the French liturgist Henri Jenny) that rejected the attempt of the central preparatory commission to limit the concepts of "summit" and "fount" only to the sacrifice[90] and thus rebutted the criticism of some council fathers who did not realize that the same statement was to be found in the encyclical *Mediator Dei* of Pius XII, the encyclical *Mirae Caritatis* of Leo XIII, and the *Catechism* of the Council of Trent.[91]

During the liturgical debate, the liturgical commission and the leaders of the reformers managed to rally an overwhelmingly large number of fathers around the issues proposed by the majority. The focus on the liturgy as "summit and fount" and on the Eucharist helped the conciliar majority to combine the issue of pastorality and the thrust toward a *ressourcement* of the Catholic Church in search of the "Christian origins" effectively narrated by the patristic language of the constitution. Paragraph 6 narratively links the paschal mystery of Christ with the early history of Christianity: baptism, supper of the Lord, and Pentecost, "when the Church appeared before the world."

The reception of this patristic language by other council documents proves difficult, especially in the fragile balance of power between pope and bishops engineered by the ecclesiological constitution of Vatican II, *Lumen Gentium*. After affirming that "though they differ essentially and not only in degree, the common priesthood of the faithful and the ministerial or hierarchical priesthood are none the less ordered one to another" (LG 10), *Lumen Gentium* adopts a narrative to explain that "the faithful are appointed by their baptismal character to Christian religious worship. [. . .] Taking part in the eucharistic sacrifice, the source and summit of the Christian life, they offer the divine

<hr/>

[89] As it was emphasized by the report of Bishop Joseph Martin to the *aula* of St. Peter's (November 29, 1962); *Acta Synodalia*, vol. 1, bk. 3, 706.

[90] See Jungmann, *Kommentar*, 24–25.

[91] See Bugnini, *The Reform of the Liturgy*, 34. For example, the apostolic delegate in Washington, DC, Bishop Egidio Vagnozzi, declared that only God is "*culmen and fons*" of Christian life and therefore proposed that the constitution should be left to the conciliar commission *De fide*; see Congar, *Journal du concile*, vol. 1, 140 (entry of October 22, 1962); and *Acta Synodalia*, vol. 1, bk. 1, 325–26.

victim to God and themselves along with it" (LG 11). Nevertheless, it is true that *Sacrosanctum Concilium* was at the beginning of a crucial move of Catholic theology during Vatican II in the direction of a *ressourcement* broadly understood.

2.5. Bible, Fathers, and History:
The Sources of the Liturgical Reform

The level of knowledge of the history and theology of the liturgy by the average council father at Vatican II was far from exceptional at the beginning of the council. It is well known, however, that the council was defined by many council fathers as a sort of "coming back to school."[92] The results of this renewed learning by the bishops gathered in St. Peter's are evident in the liturgical constitution of Vatican II. On the other side, especially in the conservative wing of Vatican II, the attempt to push back the reformers was motivated by a presupposed yet antihistorical changelessness of the Roman Rite. One of the prominent leaders of the most active conservative group at Vatican II, the Coetus Internationalis Patrum, Saboia Bandeira de Mello (bishop of Palmas, Brazil), dared to state that the Roman Rite should not be changed because it dated back directly to the apostle Peter.[93] The bishop of Agrigento (Italy) affirmed that Latin should remain the language of the rite because all the saints (he mentioned St. Charles Borromeo, St. Francis de Sales, and St. Alphonsus de Liguori) had "opted" for the Latin tradition.[94]

Together with some leading members of the Roman Curia, a small part of the Anglophone and southern European bishops was vehemently opposed to any adaptation and reform of the liturgy.[95] But the vast majority of European, American, and African bishops embraced

---

[92] One of them was the bishop of Vittorio Veneto (Italy), Albino Luciani (future Pope John Paul I, 1978); see Massimo Faggioli, "Per un 'centrismo conciliare': Albino Luciani e il concilio Vaticano II," in *Albino Luciani dal Veneto al mondo*, ed. Giovanni Vian (Roma: Viella, 2010), 355–83.

[93] "Ritus romanus ab ipso S. Petro Apostolo in suis fundamentis exaratus est" (Bishop C. Saboia Bandeira de Mello [Palma, Brazil] in *Acta Synodalia*, vol. 1, bk. 2, 117 [November 5, 1962]).

[94] Bishop Giovanni Battista Peruzzo in *Acta Synodalia*, vol. 1, bk. 1, 594–97 (October 29, 1962).

[95] See, for example, the speeches of Cardinal William Godfrey (Westminster; *Acta Synodalia*, vol. 1, bk. 1, 373–75 [October 23, 1962]), Cardinal James McIntyre

the need for a liturgical reform along the lines traced by the liturgists active at Vatican II.[96] As the secretary of the liturgical commission recalled some years after Vatican II, "The men who took part in those study meetings will never forget the effort to find solutions that would strike a balance between past and future, between the call of tradition and pastoral needs."[97]

If we consider the raging debate about the eventual outcome of *Sacrosanctum Concilium* fifty years after its implementation and the attempt to undermine its legitimacy, it is worth remembering that the liturgical reform was far from being a partisan reform, and in the liturgy debate the council easily reached the "moral unanimity" that Paul VI later tried to reach for every final document of Vatican II. The fact that it was not a partisan reform is evident not just in the aims of the reform but also in the sources of the reform. The liturgical reform of Vatican II developed a singularly "conservative" approach to the liturgy in order to restore the simplicity and the splendor of the rites on the basis of a more biblical set of readings and a patristic concept of celebration. In the words of Henri de Lubac, "Let us abide by the sources of the Fathers."[98]

At the beginning of the council debate on the draft of the liturgical constitution, the liturgical commission underscored that the preservation of the liturgical patrimony of the Church was its main goal. On October 22, 1962, the secretary of the commission, the Franciscan Ferdinando Antonelli (of the Roman Congregation of Rites), explained that five principles guided the liturgical renewal: (1) concern to preserve the Church's liturgical patrimony, (2) elaboration of principles to guide a general renewal of the liturgy, (3) derivation of doctrinally grounded practical and rubrical norms, (4) concern that the clergy be better educated and more deeply imbued with the spirit of the liturgy,

---

(Los Angeles; *Acta Synodalia*, vol. 1, bk. 2, 108–9), Cardinal Bacci (*Acta Synodalia*, vol. 1, bk. 1, 408–9), Cardinal Enrico Dante (*Acta Synodalia*, vol. 1, bk. 1, 331).

[96] Two examples of speeches in favor of the vernacular coming from non-Western Catholic Churches are by Bishop Louis La Ravoire Morrow (Krishnagar; *Acta Synodalia*, vol. 1, bk. 1, 467–69) and Bishop Frans Simons (Indore; *Acta Synodalia*, vol. 1, bk. 1, 586–87). About the issue of the vernacular in the debate, see Lamberigts, "The Liturgy Debate," in *History of Vatican II*, vol. 3, 117–25.

[97] Bugnini, *The Reform of the Liturgy*, 18.

[98] De Lubac, *Catholicism*, 35.

and (5) desire to lead the faithful into more active participation in the liturgy.[99]

The issue of the relationship between "sound tradition" and "legitimate progress," and therefore the issue of the sources of the liturgical reform, was the focus of a great number of amendments proposed and discussed during the first session of Vatican II. The vast majority of the amendments proposed by the council fathers were aware of the need for *aggiornamento*:

> Signs and rites are likely to become incrusted by time, that is, to grow old and outmoded. They may therefore need to be revised and updated, so that the expression of the Church's worship may reflect the perennial youthfulness of the Church itself. This kind of change is vitally necessary for a living organism [. . .] tradition consists not in restoring what others have done, but in rediscovering the spirit that brought those things into existence.[100]

Paragraph 23 of the liturgical constitution expresses this pivotal goal of the liturgy debate, foreshadowing the general aim of Vatican II:

> In order that sound tradition be retained, and yet the way remain open to legitimate progress, a careful investigation—theological, historical, and pastoral—should always be made into each part of the liturgy which is to be revised. Furthermore the general laws governing the structure and meaning of the liturgy must be studied in conjunction with the experience derived from recent liturgical reforms and from the indults granted to various places.
>
> Finally, there must be no innovations unless the good of the Church genuinely and certainly requires them, and care must be taken that any new forms adopted should in some way grow organically from forms already existing.

The "theological, historical, and pastoral" investigation was to be pursued along the lines of a more general reorientation of the center of gravity in the Catholic Church. The liturgical constitution builds the path toward the liturgical reform not on the basis of a set of texts or traditions to be followed but on the centrality of baptism and Eucha-

---

[99] See *Acta Synodalia*, vol. 1, bk. 1, 307–9; and Lamberigts, "The Liturgy Debate," in *History of Vatican II*, vol. 2, 109.

[100] Bugnini, *The Reform of the Liturgy*, 44.

rist for the understanding of the Church, especially in the ecumenical context after Vatican II, and in dialogue with the ecclesiology of Orthodox Churches. There is no particular "cultural option" made during the liturgy debate and subsequently worded in the final text of the liturgical constitution, and even less a recently alleged "preferential option for the primitive."[101] Together with a certain balance between the Latin fathers and the Greek fathers of the Church in the liturgical constitution (different from the ecclesiological constitution),[102] the only theological option is to be found in the Church's liturgy on baptism and Eucharist and on the role of Christ in the liturgical celebration.

Liturgy was not untouched by this major theological development, sowed in the first half of the twentieth century and harvested at Vatican II. Already in his fundamental book, *Theological Dimensions of the Liturgy* (1957), Dom Cipriano Vagaggini talked about the "concept of unity of the two Testaments and of sacred history."[103] The "operational principles" of the liturgical *renewal*—language, Word of God, catechetical instruction, singing, and liturgical *reform* as general mobilization of the entire Church—shape the effort of giving back liturgy its role in the life of the Church faithfully complying with the centrality of baptism and Eucharist. The background for the operational principles of language and Word of God was the Bible as the

---

[101] See Romanus Cessario, "The Sacraments of the Church," in *Vatican II: Renewal within Tradition*, ed. Matthew L. Lamb and Matthew Levering (Oxford and New York: Oxford University Press, 2008), 133.

[102] In SC there are two quotations each from Ignatius of Antioch and Augustine of Hippo, and one each for Cyprian of Carthage and Cyril of Alexandria. For a comparison with *Lumen Gentium*, see Gianotti, *I Padri della chiesa al concilio*, 436–37.

[103] Cipriano Vagaggini, *Il senso teologico della liturgia. Saggio di liturgia teologica generale* (Roma: Edizioni Paoline, 1957); English translation: *Theological Dimension of the Liturgy: A General Treatise on the Theology of the Liturgy* (Collegeville, MN: Liturgical Press, 1976), 456. The publication in 1957 of *Il senso teologico della liturgia* by Vagaggini was a milestone (and an important editorial success), as it provided the Catholic liturgical movement with theological foundations impossible to ignore; see Olivier Rousseau, *Storia del movimento liturgico. Lineamenti storici dagli inizi del secolo XIX fino ad oggi* (Roma: Paoline, 1961), 344–45. Testimony of his fidelity to the great Tradition of the Church was his *votum* for the preparatory phase of the council; see Enrico Galavotti, "Verso una nuova era liturgica. Appunti sul contributo di Cipriano Vagaggini al concilio Vaticano II," in *Teologia in un regime di simboli. Scritti in onore di Cipriano Vagaggini (1909–1999)*, ed. Matteo Ferrari and Giordano Remondi (Camaldoli: Edizioni Camaldoli, 2011), 65–66.

first source to return to. The editorial success and the cultural penetration among the European elites of the new Jerusalem Bible in the mid-1950s had shown the thirst for the Word of God in the Catholic Church.[104] After the famous book by Jules Isaac, *Jésus et Israël*,[105] the new wave of studies on the Jewishness of Jesus and the research about the relationship between Jews and Christians in the early Church built a complex kernel of connections between the rediscovery of the historical dimension of the Church, the need to read the early texts of Christianity in light of the history of religions, and the urgency to become more aware of the religious and historical rooting of Christianity and of its anti-Semitic elements.[106]

It is thus impossible to underestimate the importance of the indivisibility of *Sacrosanctum Concilium* and *Dei Verbum* in evaluating the contribution of the liturgical constitution to the Church of Vatican II.[107] More than 50 percent of the footnotes are quotations from the Bible— one of the highest rates of biblical quotations among the documents of Vatican II.[108] Paragraph 35 of the liturgical constitution—"In sacred celebrations a more ample, more varied, and more suitable reading from sacred scripture should be restored"—finds a necessary prolepsis in paragraph 5: "The wonderful works of God among the people of the Old Testament were but a prelude to the work of Christ Our Lord in redeeming mankind and giving perfect glory to God."

The fathers of the Church were the second major source of the *ressourcement* for the liturgical reform, that is, a period of the Church history when there was a legitimate variety of liturgical rites and

[104] See Fouilloux, *Une Église en quête de liberté*, 220–27; Laplanche, *La crise de l'origine*, 358–61.

[105] Jules Isaac, *Jésus et Israël* (Paris: Albin Michel, 1948). Jules Isaac, victim of the anti-Semitic laws of the Vichy regime, was one of the key persons who met John XXIII during the preparation of Vatican II; see José Oscar Beozzo, "The External Climate," in *History of Vatican II*, vol. 1, 393–97; see also Angelo Giuseppe Roncalli (Giovanni XXIII), *Pater amabilis. Agende del pontificato 1958–1963*, ed. Mauro Velati (Bologna: Fondazione per le scienze religiose, 2007), 127. About Jules Isaac, see André Kaspi, *Jules Isaac ou la passion de la verité* (Paris: Plon, 2002).

[106] See *The Catholic Church and the Jewish People: Recent Reflections from Rome*, ed. Philip A. Cunningham, Norbert J. Hofmann, Joseph Sievers (New York: Fordham University Press, 2007).

[107] See Dossetti, *Chiesa eucaristica*, 95.

[108] For the recurrences and concordances in the corpus of Vatican II, see Philippe Delhaye, Michel Gueret, and Paul Tombeur, *Concilium Vaticanum II: Concordance, Index, Listes de fréquences, Tables comparatives* (Louvain, 1974).

eucharistic prayers. Through recourse to Hippolytus of Rome (235 CE) and the *Traditio Apostolica*[109] and the synod of Hippo when Augustine was a presbyter (393 CE), Vatican II communicates a model of Church in which the criteria for the liturgical order is the orthodoxy of prayer and not its uniformity to a standard.[110] This very principle of catholicity, according to which "even in the liturgy the Church does not wish to impose a rigid uniformity in matters which do not involve the faith or the good of the whole community" (SC 37), was implicitly based in Benedict XV's and Pius XII's emphases on the need of a unity and not of a uniformity in everything.[111]

A further example taken from the fathers of the Church was the episcopal character of liturgy; the importance of liturgical life in the local, diocesan Church; and the unity of the local Church with its bishop and ministers. The ecclesiology of the liturgical constitution embodies the rediscovery of the ecclesiology of the monarchic episcopate in accordance with the model of the fathers of the Church, and not only according to the more modern—at least on a Church history timeline—Tridentine model of bishop. If it is true that the end of the episcopal monarchy in the Catholic dioceses and the beginning of a more collegial Catholicism is to be attributed to Vatican II, the liturgical constitution marked the start of this huge institutional and theological change in four centuries of "practical ecclesiology."[112] Although contradictory in their postconciliar enforcement, paragraphs 36.3 and 36.4 of *Sacrosanctum Concilium* signify not only the approval of the most recent meaning of the bishops' conferences in Europe and in the

---

[109] For the role of liturgy in the *Traditio Apostolica*, see Bernard Botte, *La tradition apostolique de Saint Hippolyte: essai de reconstitution*, ed. Albert Gerhards and Sabine Felbecker (Münster: Aschendorf, 1989).

[110] See Kaczynski, *Kommentar*, 112–13.

[111] "The Church of Christ, the faithful depository of the teaching of Divine Wisdom, cannot and does not think of deprecating or disdaining the particular characteristics which each people, with jealous and intelligible pride, cherishes and retains as a precious heritage. Her aim is a supernatural union in all-embracing love, deeply felt and practiced, and not the unity which is exclusively external and superficial and by that very fact weak" (Pius XII, encyclical *Summi Pontificatus* [October 20, 1939], par. 44).

[112] See Hubert Jedin, *Il tipo ideale di vescovo secondo la riforma cattolica* (Brescia: Morcelliana, 1985); Giuseppe Alberigo, "L'episcopato nel cattolicesimo post-tridentino," *Cristianesimo nella Storia* 6 (1985): 71–91; Joseph Bergin, "L'Europe des Évêques au temps de la réforme catholique," *Bibliothèque de l'Ecole des Chartes* 154 (1996): 509–31.

Americas but most of all the attempt to bind their nineteenth- and twentieth-century experiences with the venerable tradition of local councils and synods in the ancient and undivided Church.[113]

Among the sources of *Sacrosanctum Concilium*, Ignatius of Antioch's Christology plays a particularly central role: Christ as body and spirit, "Christ who enters, with his body, very directly in the dimensions of time and space, and lives a historical life."[114] In this sense, the liturgical constitution draws from history as an important source for the liturgical reform, thus embodying what has been called "the return to the historical dimension, duty for Catholic theology."[115] If it is true that the postconciliar reception of paragraph 3 makes evident that the liturgical constitution should have been the object of a Synod of the Latin Church—and not of an ecumenical council[116]—the historical awareness of the mind of the liturgical reform made possible the rediscovery of the plurality of liturgical form in the tradition of the Catholic Church (SC 37) and the legitimacy of the push to scale back the role of the Holy See as unique legislator in liturgical matters in favor of a more active role of bishops' conferences and diocesan bishops.[117]

2.6. Tradition and *Ressourcement* in the Liturgical Reform

The choice to "start with liturgy" marked the beginning and the peak of the *ressourcement* at Vatican II. It is a legitimate question whether *Sacrosanctum Concilium* was also the early end of *ressourcement* at the council. Soon after the completion of the liturgy debate (and after the death of John XXIII), Vatican II became more and more taken up with the very complex effort of institutional modernization of the Catholic Church. But it is clear that the most "radical" document of Vatican II chose *ressourcement* because the council was aware of the liturgical crisis already developing in pre–Vatican II Catholicism. The liturgical crisis was not the effect but the cause of *Sacrosanctum*

---

[113] See Hermann Josef Sieben, *Die Konzilsidee der alten Kirche* (Paderborn: Schöningh, 1979).

[114] Dossetti, *Chiesa eucaristica*, 51.

[115] Laplanche, *La crise de l'origine*, 491.

[116] See Kaczynski, *Kommentar*, 57.

[117] The term *Summus pontifex* is only at paragraph 112 on sacred music; *Sedes apostolica* is instead at paragraphs 13, 22, 36, 40, 44, 55, 63, 87.

Concilium and its *ressourcement*. The "radicalism" of *ressourcement* was not simply a renewed attention to the sources but the costly effort to say—once again, but this time differently—in which sense liturgy is the source.[118]

However lacking in theological depth the preparation of the debate might have been before Vatican II,[119] the council leaders proclaimed, by setting the liturgy as the first test for Vatican II, the need to get "back to the sources" of the Church. Notwithstanding the fact that centering the Church on the Eucharist was perhaps more instinctive than strategic—since the majority of the council fathers still held a devotional concept of liturgy[120]—the "liturgical way" embodied some of the main goals of the council according to John XXIII.

Vatican II was supposed to show the concern of the Catholic Church for its ability to update its message in the modern world. The ressourcing of the liturgy, its language and its pastoral character, had among its consequences the abandonment of the "language of condemnations" and the severance of every tie between liturgy, spirituality, and the legacy of Tridentine ideology: the battle for Christendom, the political crusades of the nineteenth and twentieth centuries, the civil religion of anti-Communism, and "Cold War devotionalism."[121] *Ressourcement* and liturgical reform were, in this respect, also a first step in abandoning the heavy legacy of the culture of the Western hemisphere, in this particular case, moving beyond the forms of piety typical of the political culture of ultramontane Catholicism after the French Revolution.

The first language of Church turned out to be once again—as in the very beginning of the history of the Christian faith—the liturgy. The other "markers of belonging"—ideology, citizenship, cultural background—seemed to be relegated to a lower place. The liturgical debate

---

[118] See Grillo, *La nascita della liturgia nel XX secolo*, 125–26.

[119] See the sharp assessment by Yves Congar: "*pas de théologie à la base de la question!* En général, les mouvements liturgiques ne se sont pas assez donné la base *ecclésiologique* qu'ils devraient avoir" (*Journal du Concile*, vol. 1, 146–47 [entry of October 24, 1962]).

[120] See Kaczynski, *Kommentar*, 74. A group of fathers expressed their satisfaction with the lack of any dogmatic definition, the intention of the *schema* being to renew liturgical life as such, casting aside the theological debates on it; see *Acta Synodalia*, vol. 1, bk. 1, 367, 373, 400–401, 441.

[121] About this, see James P. McCartin, *Prayers of the Faithful: The Shifting Spiritual Life of American Catholics* (Cambridge, MA: Harvard University Press, 2010).

was the first and most effective way "to use the medicine of mercy rather than the weapons of severity," to quote John XXIII's words from the opening speech of the council, *Gaudet Mater Ecclesia*.[122] A few days later, the *Message to the World* (October 20, 1962) "proved an adumbration of the council's future direction."[123] The liturgical debate continued and confirmed that direction. *Ressourcement* also meant that belonging to the Church implied adhering not simply to formal boundaries such as juridical norms or sociological parameters but to a liturgical concept of Church.

The end of the Counter-Reformation and the shift to the post-Tridentine and post-ultramontane era was not rhetorically declared on the floor of St. Peter's; rather, it was profoundly signified by this new fundamental theological orientation. It was through the focus on the liturgy and its spiritual role that the Catholic Church at Vatican II moved from the age of antiliberal and anti-Communist ideological mobilization to the era of Karl Rahner's "world-church" (*Weltkirche*).

The continuities between the formulas used by Leo XIII, Pius X, and Pius XII and the text of the liturgical constitution have to be framed in the context of the liturgical debate at Vatican II, as it is clear that a "fundamentalist" or literalist approach to Vatican II's final documents does not help understand the mind of the council fathers. Given a certain continuity in concepts and ideas grounding the liturgical renewal launched by Vatican II, the discontinuity between Leo XIII's and Pius XII's statements on the liturgy and the concept of liturgy as a search for the origins of Christian faith is to be found in the theological context of the debate in St. Peter's. The value of the shift operated by *Sacrosanctum Concilium* is clear if we consider that the *ressourcement* of Vatican II can be understood only together with the new approach to the biblical texts affirmed by *Dei Verbum* and in connection with the ecumenical tone of the council expressed in *Lumen Gentium*.[124] *Sacrosanctum Concilium* was never supposed to be a legal document to be read by itself, that is, out of the hermeneutical context of the other

---

[122] See Giuseppe Alberigo, "Dal bastone alla misericordia. Il magistero nel cattolicesimo contemporaneo (1830–1980)," *Cristianesimo nella Storia* 2 (1981): 487–521.

[123] O'Malley, *What Happened*, 99.

[124] See Giacomo Lercaro, "Liturgia ed ecumenismo," in Giacomo Lercaro, *Per la forza dello Spirito. Discorsi conciliari del card. Giacomo Lercaro*, ed. Istituto per le Scienze Religiose (Bologna: EDB, 1984), 85–102.

council documents, especially *Dei Verbum* and *Lumen Gentium*, where the principle of patristic *ressourcement* is very evident.[125]

The need for a liturgical renewal went far beyond small alterations, and a restoration-like reform was clearly emphasized from the very beginning of the debate. The council fathers did not address directly the issue of *ressourcement*, as the reform of liturgy had to be focused on the pastoral approach rather than on historical reasoning.[126] *Ressourcement* in the liturgical constitution and at Vatican II in general was not a historical or theological assessment of their doctrine in a systematic way but a "listening to" the fathers.[127] The *ressourcement* of the liturgical reform was clear in the mind of one of its theologians, Cipriano Vagaggini, who was an admirer of Thomas Aquinas and of monastic theology, without espousing the baroque neoscholastic theology of more recent times.[128]

The Thomistic character of the liturgical reform was clear in the consideration of the Eucharist as the main way for the announcement of the Gospel, here matched by the need for a deeper inculturation of the Gospel with every particular culture; the issue of the inculturation of the liturgy became one of the first signs of the *ressourcement* in the liturgical reform.[129] Cardinal Montini of Milan (later Paul VI) pointed out that liturgy "was instituted for men and not men for liturgy."[130] Many bishops underscored the pastoral aims of the liturgical reform, and especially the need for the use of the vernacular language in the liturgy, since the sacraments were instituted for the Christian people.[131]

[125] See Gianotti, *I Padri della Chiesa al Concilio*, 414.

[126] See Cardinal William Godfrey (Westminster), in *Acta Synodalia*, vol. 1, bk. 1, 374 (October 23, 1962).

[127] See Gianotti, *I Padri della Chiesa al Concilio*, 419.

[128] See Andrea Grillo, "Il pensiero di Cipriano Vagaggini, tra eredità tomista e confronto con la modernità. Profilo e fortuna di un grande liturgista," in *Cipriano Vagaggini. L'intelligenza della liturgia. Rivista Liturgica* 3 (maggio–giugno 2009): 362–84.

[129] See Archbishop Gilbert Ramanantoanina (Fianarantsoa, Madagascar), in *Acta Synodalia*, vol. 1, bk. 1, 419–20 (October 24, 1962); and Yoshigoro Taguchi (Osaka, Japan), in *Acta Synodalia*, vol. 1, bk. 2, 651 (November 13, 1962).

[130] "Liturgia nempe pro hominibus est instituta, non homines pro liturgia" (*Acta Synodalia*, vol. 1, bk. 1, 315 [October 22, 1962]).

[131] See Cardinal Paul-Émile Léger (Montréal), in *Acta Synodalia*, vol. 1, bk. 1, 371 (October 23, 1962).

The need for adaptation and the use of vernacular languages in the liturgy became the source of the first clash between the majority and minority on the issue of reform: on one side the reformers (Maximos IV, Feltin, Léger) pushing an open-ended agenda in favor of vernacular language; on the other side the opponents of the reform (Ernesto Ruffini, James McIntyre, Alfredo Ottaviani, Enrico Dante) willing to reassign the *schema* from the too-independent liturgical commission to the Curia-leaning theological commission presided over by Cardinal Ottaviani. This split showed that the radical but at the same time disguised *ressourcement* approach had many enemies, mostly in the so-called conciliar minority; they did not share the option to go back to the "sources" in order to rediscover the riches of liturgy and the undivided Christianity, as they preferred a mediated approach through the more recent theological "traditions" of the Roman, Latin, Western Catholic Church.[132]

However important "change" and "reform" were for Vatican II, *ressourcement* was at the very center of Vatican II as one of most pervasive and powerful theological drives of the liturgical reform, as well as of contemporary Catholicism.[133] One of the reasons for the coherence of the theological foundation of *Sacrosanctum Concilium* around *ressourcement* has to be found in the fact that one of the major splits in the theological *avant garde* that made Vatican II possible, that is, the division within the *nouvelle théologie* between "neo-Augustinians" (Daniélou, de Lubac, Ratzinger, von Balthasar) and "neo-Thomists" (Chenu, Congar, Rahner, Lonergan, Schillebeeckx), appeared only later in the unfolding of the council and after Vatican II.[134]

The starting point for Vatican II was indeed a ressourced, "non-restorationist" revival of the liturgical practice and its central role in the life of the Church. Far from being presented in the appearance of a mere "revanche" toward a secularist world, the new, "ressourced liturgy" was meant to reset the cultural and ideological garment of

---

[132] Being aware of the differences between *ressourcement* and recourse to the "Tradition," see Yves Congar, *Tradition and Traditions: An Historical and a Theological Essay* (New York: Macmillan, 1967).

[133] See Jungmann, *Kommentar*, 10; Kaczynski, *Kommentar*, 24–42.

[134] See Joseph Komonchak, "Augustine, Aquinas, or the Gospel *sine glossa*? Divisions over *Gaudium et Spes*," in *Unfinished Journey: The Church 40 Years after Vatican II*, ed. John Wilkins (London: Continuum, 2004), 102–18. See also Massimo Faggioli, *Vatican II: The Battle for Meaning* (Mahwah, NJ: Paulist Press, 2012).

Catholicism in the modern world in order to start over from the core essence of Christianity, closer to the ancient liturgical traditions of the Eastern Churches and of the Roman Church.[135]

During the drafting of the *schema*, the preparatory commission had in mind these theological priorities: a great attention to the preservation of the liturgical patrimony of the Church; the need for guidelines preparing a broad renewal of liturgy; the elaboration of rites grounded on solid doctrinal principles; and the effort toward the faithful's active participation in the liturgy. In the summer of 1962 the liturgical *schema* looked the most mature and far-reaching of all the *schemas* prepared by the commissions between 1960 and the spring of 1962. Despite the tensions of the beginning of Vatican II, the liturgical *schema* reached across the already clearly defined aisle. Its decisiveness and the far-sightedness of its consequence were matched by its open-ended reform approach.

[135] See Marcel Metzger, "L'attention aux traditions dans le mouvement liturgique occidental," in *Les mouvements liturgiques. Corrélations entre pratiques et recherches*, ed. Carlo Braga and Alessandro Pistoia (Roma: CLV, 2004), 255–76, esp. 261–64.

Chapter 3

Liturgical Reform and Ecclesiology

The combination of liturgical reform and ecclesiological renewal in the Catholic Church represents the beating heart of *Sacrosanctum Concilium*. Since liturgical reform is part of the ecclesiology of Vatican II, to undermine this reform is the surest possible way to undo Vatican II and its ecclesiology. Thus, it is clear that the liturgical reform visibly articulates the ecclesiology of Vatican II, since the ecclesiological outcomes—the *ecclesiologies*, plural—of Vatican II are more ambiguous than the liturgical reform.

3.1. Between *Mystici Corporis* and *Lumen Gentium*

At the eve of Vatican II, something had already happened for Catholic ecclesiology, not only concerning theologians, but also in the official teaching of the Church. During the pontificate of Pius XII a major change was introduced by his encyclical *Mystici Corporis* (1943), "the first significant shift in ecclesiology since the Counter-Reformation."[1]

The encyclical rediscovered a biblical category for the definition of the Church. Pius XII "defined the Church of Jesus Christ as the Mystical Body of Christ, and stated that the Mystical Body is identical with the Roman Catholic Church."[2] But that change of language and imagery for the definition of the Church was not inclusive of the developments in Catholic ecclesiology in the nineteenth and twentieth centuries. The encyclical tried to harmonize the idea of a "mystical body" with the societal concept elaborated by Robert Bellarmine after

---

[1] See Richard P. McBrien, *The Church: The Evolution of Catholicism* (New York: HarperOne, 2008), 122; see also Antonio Acerbi, *Due ecclesiologie. Ecclesiologia giuridica ed ecclesiologia di comunione nella Lumen gentium* (Bologna: EDB, 1975), 40–48; and Richard R. Gaillardetz, *Ecclesiology for a Global Church: A People Called and Sent* (Maryknoll, NY: Orbis Books, 2008), 106.

[2] Avery Dulles, *Models of the Church* (New York: Image Books, Doubleday, 2002), 44.

the Council of Trent. At the same time, *Mystici Corporis* "insisted on the role of the Holy Spirit in the Church and thus on the balance that was needed to hold between the hierarchical structures and the charismatic gifts of the Spirit."[3] It was a significant step forward from a concept of the Church expressed in juridical terms, but *Mystici Corporis* continued to identify the Mystical Body of Christ with the Roman Catholic Church, since membership in the Church was restricted to those who were baptized, professed the true faith, and were in communion with the pope.[4]

The ecclesiological shift of *Mystici Corporis* was followed four years later by the liturgical encyclical of Pius XII. *Mediator Dei* (1947) represented the first magisterial document presenting a systematic liturgical doctrine, and it opened the door to some issues put forward by the liturgical movement: vernacular language, participation of the lay faithful, and liturgical spirituality.[5] Very soon the connections between the liturgical renewal and the ecclesiological shift of *Mystici Corporis* became apparent. Between 1950 and Vatican II a very important series of ecclesiological studies went beyond these adjustments and cast new light on the Church as a theological subject: episcopate, sacramentality, and the Church as sacrament.[6]

We cannot say that during the preparation of Vatican II the connection between ecclesiology and liturgy was evident. In the *vota* on liturgy, the dominant attitude was "the desire for liturgical reform extended to more than a mere adjustment of the rubrics; the issue was rather the participation of the laity, and the concern was therefore pastoral and apostolic."[7] Neither was the liturgy-ecclesiology connection

---

[3] O'Malley, *What Happened*, 85.

[4] About Robert Bellarmine's (1542–1621) definition of the Church, defined in terms that are visible, organizational, and institutional, see Dulles, *Models of the Church*, 7–38.

[5] See Herman Schmidt, *La costituzione sulla Sacra Liturgia: testo - genesi - commento - documentazione* (Roma: Herder, 1966), 86–87.

[6] See, for example, Bernard Botte, *Études sur le sacrement de l'ordre* (Paris: Cerf, 1957); *Le Concile et les Conciles. Contribution à l'histoire de la vie conciliaire de l'Église* (Chevetogne-Paris: Cerf, 1960); Karl Rahner and Joseph Ratzinger, *Episkopat und Primat* (Freiburg-Basel-Wien: Herder, 1961); *L'épiscopat et l'Église universelle*, ed. Yves Congar and Bernard-Dominique Dupuy (Paris: Cerf, 1962); Jean Colson, *L'épiscopat catholique. Collégialité et primauté dans les trois premiers siècles de l'Église* (Paris: Cerf, 1963).

[7] Étienne Fouilloux, "The Antepreparatory Phase: The Slow Emergence from Inertia (January 1959–October 1962)," in *History of Vatican II*, vol. 1: *Announcing and*

evident in the preparatory *schema* on the Church, since the issues of the "visible Church," the relationship between Church and State, and the problem *de membris Ecclesiae* were still the most relevant issues.[8]

But the composition of the first subcommission of the preparatory commission on the liturgy had some members who would prove decisive in shaping the ecclesiology of the first part of the liturgical constitution.[9] The contribution of the Italian liturgical scholar and Camaldolese monk Cipriano Vagaggini proved particularly important already during the preparatory phase (May 1961).[10] Vagaggini was in charge of the drafting of the *proemium* and of the first chapter, in which the renewal of the liturgy was put in the context of the *aggiornamento* of the Church: "the criteria of the renewal are the conservation of the *sana traditio* and the opening to a valid development."[11]

The connection between liturgical reform and ecclesiological renewal became apparent during the first debate on the liturgy at Vatican II in October 1962, when fierce opposition arose from the ones who opposed the proposal of giving to episcopal conferences "rights" in the process of adaptation and implementation of the liturgical reform.[12] This example is telling of the relationship between *Sacrosanctum Concilium* and *Lumen Gentium*: the ecclesiological development that led to the institution of episcopal conferences originated from the liturgical debate and the plan for the liturgical life of the Church after Vatican II.

Preparing Vatican Council II: Toward a New Era in Catholicism (Maryknoll, NY: Orbis; Leuven: Peeters, 1995), 120.

[8] See Joseph A. Komonchak, "The Struggle for the Council during the Preparation of Vatican II (1960–1962)," in *History of Vatican II*, vol. 1, 285–301.

[9] The secretary of the first subcommission ("The mystery of the sacred liturgy and its relations to the life of the Church") was Cipriano Vagaggini, and among the members were Henri Jenny, Josef Andreas Jungmann, and Herman Schmidt; see Bugnini, *The Reform of the Liturgy*, 15.

[10] See Enrico Galavotti, "Verso una nuova era liturgica. Appunti sul contributo di Cipriano Vagaggini al concilio Vaticano II," in *Teologia in un regime di simboli. Scritti in onore di Cipriano Vagaggini (1909–1999)*, ed. Matteo Ferrari and Giordano Remondi (Camaldoli: Edizioni Camaldoli, 2011), 56–93.

[11] Maria Paiano, "Il rinnovamento della liturgia: dai movimenti alla chiesa universale," in *Verso il concilio Vaticano II (1960–1962). Passaggi e problemi della preparazione conciliare*, ed. Giuseppe Alberigo and Alberto Melloni (Genova: Marietti, 1993), 67–140, at 121.

[12] Mathijs Lamberigts, "The Liturgy Debate," in *History of Vatican II*, vol. 2: *The Formation of the Council's Identity, First Period and Intercession, October 1962–September 1963* (Maryknoll, NY: Orbis; Leuven: Peeters, 1997), 117–25.

That is why it is possible to see the importance of the ecclesiology of the liturgical reform on the basis of the gap between the accomplished and coherent ecclesiology of the liturgical constitution and the *ecclesiologies* of *Lumen Gentium* and *Gaudium et Spes* and of the decrees *Christus Dominus, Unitatis Redintegratio,* and *Apostolicam Actuositatem.*[13]

The ecclesiological debates of Vatican II were made possible through the opening made by *Mystici Corporis* as well as by the development of ecclesiological studies, but the final result of the *ecclesiologies* of Vatican II seems too complex in its balance—between the juridical-societal images on one side and the communional-sacramental dimensions on the other—to be reduced to a simple step forward from Pius XII's *Mystici Corporis* in the direction of a clear-cut *ecclesiology* of Vatican II.[14] In the words of Avery Dulles, "Vatican II in *Lumen Gentium* reaffirms the idea that the Church is the Body of Christ, but it slightly retrenches from two positions taken by *Mystici Corporis*. It distinguishes between the Church as hierarchical society and as Body of Christ, and it asserts that the two are related to each other in a way comparable to the human and divine natures of Christ."[15]

It has been said that "Vatican II stopped halfway."[16] The liturgical constitution *Sacrosanctum Concilium* represents the first half of this way, not just chronologically, since it was the first constitution of Vatican II to be approved, but also theologically. *Sacrosanctum Concilium* managed to develop in the most coherent and consistent way the ecclesiology of the preconciliar era pointing toward a sacramental concept of the Church.[17] The later developments of the ecclesiological debate at

[13] About this issue, see Acerbi, *Due ecclesiologie*; Dulles, *Models of the Church*; Hervé Marie Legrand, "Lo sviluppo di chiese soggetto: un'istanza del Vaticano II. Fondamenti teologici e riflessioni," in *L'ecclesiologia del Vaticano II: dinamismi e prospettive,* ed. Giuseppe Alberigo (Bologna: EDB, 1981), 129–63; Joseph A. Komonchak, "The Significance of Vatican II for Ecclesiology," in *The Gift of the Church: A Textbook on Ecclesiology,* ed. Peter Phan (Collegeville, MN: Liturgical Press, 2000), 69–91.

[14] See *The Reception of Vatican II,* ed. Giuseppe Alberigo, Jean-Pierre Jossua, and Joseph A. Komonchak (Washington, DC: Catholic University of America Press, 1987).

[15] Dulles, *Models of the Church,* 48.

[16] Angel Antón, "Postconciliar Ecclesiology: Expectations, Results, and Prospects for the Future," in *Vatican II: Assessment and Perspectives; Twenty-Five Years After, 1962–1987,* ed. René Latourelle, 3 vols. (New York: Paulist Press, 1988–89), 1:423.

[17] See Otto Semmelroth, *Die Kirche als Ursakrament* (Frankfurt a.M.: J. Knecht, 1953); Henri de Lubac, *Méditation sur l'église* (Paris: Aubier, 1953); Paul Broutin, *Mysterium Ecclesiae* (Paris: L'Orante, 1947).

Vatican II leave the impression of an interruption of this theological stream in favor of a rehabilitation of the juridical dimension of the Church, in the delusional attempt to balance Vatican I with Vatican II.[18]

It is true that Vatican II received from more than one council document (*Lumen Gentium, Gaudium et Spes,* and *Christus Dominus*) the most important contributions for its very ecclesiological balance;[19] it is also true that *Sacrosanctum Concilium* built its ecclesiological framework differently. The critics of Vatican II often aim at the liturgical reform, blaming *Sacrosanctum Concilium* for theological and cultural options made after Vatican II that had very little to do with the ecclesiology of the liturgical constitution. The core of the ecclesiological debate at Vatican II was about the constitution on the Church, *Lumen Gentium,* and took place in October and November 1963, when the text of the liturgical constitution was fixed and essentially ready for final approval. But it is undeniable that the liturgy debate was founded on a distinct image of the Church and that the liturgies (in rites different from the Roman) celebrated in St. Peter's contributed greatly to the development of a truly catholic, that is, "universal," ecclesiology in the council fathers of Vatican II.[20]

Many of the bishops and theologians active in the first session of Vatican II had the clear impression that the liturgy debate was the first step toward the formulation of an ecclesiology not detached from some institutional changes. But already in the meetings of the liturgical preparatory commission of April 1961 the issue of the adaptation of the liturgy was connected to a deep understanding of the renewed, and at the same time ancient, structure of the Catholic Church with the bishops (and not Rome) at the center of the regulating mechanism

[18] For Karl Rahner's (and German theologians') contribution to the sacramental ecclesiology of Vatican II, see Günther Wassilowsky, *Universales Heilssakrament Kirche: Karl Rahner's Beitrag zur Ekklesiologie des II. Vatikanums* (Innsbruck, Wien: Tyrolia, 2001).

[19] See Pierre-Marie Gy, "Situation historique," in *La liturgie après Vatican II. Bilans, etudes, prospective,* ed. Jean-Pierre Jossua and Yves Congar (Paris: Cerf, 1967), 111–26.

[20] For some examples of the impression on the fathers, see Auguste Jauffrès, *Carnets conciliaires* (Aubenas sur-Ardèche, 1992), 148; *Carnets conciliare de l'évêque de Namur A.-M. Charue,* ed. Leo Declerck and Claude Soetens (Louvain-la-Neuve: Peeters, 2000), 214; *Carnets conciliaires de Mgr Gérard Philips secrétaire adjoint de la Commission doctrinale,* ed. Karim Schelkens (Leuven: Peeters, 2006), 129; Yves Congar, *Journal du concile,* vol. 2, 132–33. For the ecclesiological significance of the celebration in St. Peter's in non-Roman liturgical rites, see Daniele Gianotti, *I Padri della Chiesa al concilio Vaticano II. La teologia patristica nella "Lumen gentium"* (Bologna: EDB, 2010), 415.

of liturgy. The preparatory text of the liturgical commission came from one of the American members of the commission, John Quasten,[21] who stressed the importance of giving back to the individual bishops and the gathering of bishops of a region the authority in liturgical matters.[22]

[21] John Quasten (1900–1987) was a German-born patrologue who had to leave Germany in 1937 because the Nazi regime withdrew his *venia legendi* at the University of Münster, and—thanks to the intercession of Cardinal Pacelli—in 1938 he was offered an extraordinary (in 1941, ordinary) position at the Catholic University of America in Washington, DC, in ancient Church history, patrology, and Christian archaeology. From 1945 to 1949 Quasten was dean of the department of theology, and in 1960 he received the Cardinal Spellman Award of the Catholic Theological Association of America for his theological work. In 1964 Paul VI appointed him consultant of the Consilium ad exsequendam. See Patrick Granfield, "John Quasten: A Biographical Essay," in *Kyriakon. Festschrift Johannes Quasten*, ed. Patrick Granfield and Josef A. Jungmann, 2 vols. (Münster: Aschendorff, 1970), 2:921–23; Norbert M. Borengässer, s.v. "John Quasten," in *Biographisch-Bibliographisches Kirchenlexikon*, vol. 15 (1999), 1187–92, http://www.bautz.de/bbkl/q/quasten.shtml. About the origins of the liturgical movement in the United States, see Keith Pecklers, *The Unread Vision: The Liturgical Movement in the United States of America; 1926–1955* (Collegeville, MN: Liturgical Press, 1998).
[22] Vatican Secret Archives, Concilio Vaticano II, 1370, "Documenta sessionum aprilii 1961, X De aptatione liturgiae ad ingenium et traditiones populorum": *"Canones in forma contracta definite recogniti.* [. . .] 1) Ut perveniatur ad formam liturgiae, quae necessitatibus et indoli variorum populorum plane respondeat magis activa requiritur collaboratio Antistitum. Episcopi enim, qui in contactu immediato cum fidelibus proprii territorii munere apostolico funguntur, iudices maxime qualificati sunt tum de modo tum de mensura aptationis expetendae [. . .] 2) [. . .] valde desideratur explicita declaratio Concilii de munere Episcopi [. . .] 3) Quaestiones de aptatione in Conferentiis regionalibus Episcoporum ordinentur [. . .] 4) [. . .] nova forma semper organice ex forma iam existenti proveniat oportet. 5) [. . .] Conferentia regionalis Episcoporum indiget facultate permittendi, dirigendi atque custodiendi experimenta necessaria circa mutationem introducendam. [. . .] 7) Ut unitas fidei et cultus integra et manifesta servetur et congrua quoque ac bene ordinata varietas rituum externoum suum locum habeat, limites aptationis accurate determinentur. Qui limites statuantur ex libris liturgicis a Sancta Sede editis aut edendis, qui uti norma 'typica' habeantur, loco tamen relicto variationibus et aptationibus localibus sicut nunc fit in ritu matrimoniali. 8) Tamquam cardo tempestivae aptationis liturgicae sine dubio considerandum est problema linguae vernaculae, cui secundum indigentiam nostrorum temporum notabilior latior usus concedendus est praesertim in Missa ubique terrarum, sed maxime et urgentissime in Missionibus. Sine nitida solutione huius problematis, tota aptatio liturgica manca et inefficax manebit."

The urgency of an ecclesiological "recentering" of the Catholic Church in light of the liturgical debate became even more visible at the opening of the council because it was ecumenical. In the words of Pierre Duprey:

> This is just a first step in the opportunity of the liturgical reform. Other steps will follow; the rights of the bishops' conferences in regulating the liturgy will have to be built and elaborated on the theological level. That will be the task of the debate *De episcopatu* that many would like to be the next one following the liturgy debate.[23]

The attempt to nuance the change taking place in Catholic ecclesiology through an amendment that revised the expression "visible and invisible" (referring to the Church) into "visible yet endowed with invisible resources" was not successful in stopping the evolution of the concept of the Church,[24] that is, from an anti-Protestant, apologetic, and Bellarminian ecclesiology to a sacramental and ecumenical ecclesiology.

3.2. The Core Ecclesiology of *Sacrosanctum Concilium*

The debate on the floor of St. Peter's between 1962 and 1963 framed the liturgy on the background of a theology of the Church in which the elements were put together in an entirely different system than

---

[23] "Ce n'est d'ailleurs qu'un premier pas important à l'occasion de la réforme liturgique. D'autres suivront: ce fait, des pouvoirs des conférences épiscopales en matière liturgique devra être construit et élaboré sur le plan théologique et canonique: ce sera l'œuvre du *De épiscopatu* que beaucoup voudrait voir venir en discussion après la liturgie" (Letter of Pierre Duprey from Rome to the Monastery of St. Anne [Jerusalem], November 1, 1962, in Archive of the John XXIII Foundation for Religious Studies in Bologna). About the monastery of Sainte-Anne in Jerusalem, Pierre Duprey (1922–2007), and the contribution to Vatican II, see the obituary in *Orient Chrétien-Proche Dominique* 2–1 (2007): 57; Dominique Trimbur, "Sainte-Anne: lieu de mémoire et lieu de vie français à Jérusalem," in *Chrétiens et sociétés XVIe-XXe siècles* 7 (2000): 39–69; Mauro Velati, *Dialogo e rinnovamento. Verbali e testi del segretariato per l'unità dei cristiani nella preparazione del concilio Vaticano II (1960–1962)* (Bologna: Il Mulino, 2011).

[24] See Bugnini, *The Reform of the Liturgy*, 33; Lamberigts, "The Liturgy Debate," in *History of Vatican II*, vol. 2, 107–66.

that to which the pre–Vatican II Church was accustomed.[25] The text of SC 2 contains a first, profound statement on the Church, which undoubtedly puts the liturgical constitution in the corpus of the core ecclesiological texts of Vatican II:

> The Church is essentially both human and divine, visible but endowed with invisible realities, zealous in action and dedicated to contemplation, present in the world, but as a pilgrim, so constituted that in her the human is directed toward and subordinated to the divine, the visible to the invisible, action to contemplation, and this present world to that city yet to come, the object of our quest. (SC 2)

This passage was not casually worded: on November 17, 1962, the expression "visible and invisible" was changed to "visible but endowed with invisible realities."[26] The mention of the theandric—human and divine—dimension of the Church in SC 2 is ecclesiologically central and of great importance for the ecclesiological roots of the ecumenical impulse given by Vatican II. The Church is described here not in its juridical structure but in its sacramental character; that is why "many Fathers were astonished at this manner of speech about the Church, which differs from the view especially as developed by Bellarmine during the struggle of post-Tridentine theology with the Reformation."[27]

A second profound ecclesiological statement in the liturgical constitution deals with the issue of change and tradition. According to *Sacrosanctum Concilium*, the Church is both active in the world and dedicated to contemplation, lives in world history and transmits the mystery of Christ. Its human and visible dimension needs to understand the modern times; this is why the council decided that liturgy had to be "revised carefully in the light of sound tradition [. . .] to meet present-day circumstances and needs" (SC 4). The liturgical constitution embraces *aggiornamento* and "sound tradition," showing here

[25] See Cipriano Vagaggini, "Fundamental Ideas of the Constitution in *The Liturgy of Vatican II: A Symposium*, ed. William Baraúna, English ed. by J. Lang, 2 vols. (Chicago: Franciscan Herald Press, 1966), 1:96–129, esp. 99.

[26] Bugnini, *The Reform of the Liturgy*, 33; William Baraúna, "Chronicle of the Amendments of the Constitution," in Baraúna, *The Liturgy of Vatican II*, vol. 1, 73.

[27] Josef Andreas Jungmann, "Constitution on the Sacred Liturgy," in *Commentary on the Documents of Vatican II*, ed. Herbert Vorgrimler, vol. 1 (New York: Herder and Herder, 1967), 9.

all its Roncallian taste, and the awareness that the different versions of change—*aggiornamento*, tradition, *ressourcement*, reform—in Catholicism are closely connected to one another.[28] These different versions of change are implied also in SC 4, an "equal right and dignity" for all the liturgical rites of the Catholic Church. This statement has enormous ecclesiological implications: in the liturgical constitution Vatican II not only acknowledged the role of the rites different from the Roman but also stated that change in "sound tradition" is an operational principle that concerns the reform of the Roman Rite and the other rites in order "to meet present-day circumstances and needs" (SC 4).[29]

A third core element of the ecclesiology of *Sacrosanctum Concilium* deals with the sacramental view of the Church. The profound connection between Christology and ecclesiology was not less important than the acceptance of a visible-invisible dimension of the Church. Liturgy, like the history of salvation, is the work of Christ and thus expresses the human-divine dimensions of the Church: "For it was from the side of Christ as he slept the sleep of death upon the cross that there came forth 'the wondrous sacrament of the whole Church.'" (SC 5). The sacramental dimension of the Church, the Church as sacrament of Christ, expressed in *Sacrosanctum Concilium* witnesses the changes in Catholic ecclesiology in the three decades before Vatican II, especially thanks to the works of Yves Congar, Henri de Lubac, Hans Urs von Balthasar, and Otto Semmelroth.

This expression in SC 5—"there came forth 'the wondrous sacrament of the whole Church,'" which is a quotation from a prayer of the fifth century—became the central statement on the "Church as a sacrament" in the ecclesiological constitution *Lumen Gentium* 1: "Since the Church, in Christ, is in the nature of sacrament—a sign and instrument, that is, of communion with God and of unity among all men." In the corpus of Vatican II, we have three different formulations of the "Church as sacrament": sacrament of Christ, sacrament of unity,

---

[28] About John XXIII's theology, see Giuseppe Ruggieri, "Appunti per una teologia in papa Roncalli," in *Papa Giovanni*, ed. Giuseppe Alberigo (Bari: Laterza, 1987), 245–71. About the use of *aggiornamento*, development, and *ressourcement* as "euphemisms" for change, see O'Malley, *What Happened*, 298–301.

[29] About the ecclesiological shift implied in the plurality of liturgical rites, see Giuseppe Alberigo, "Dalla uniformità liturgica del concilio di Trento al pluralismo del Vaticano II," *Rivista Liturgica* 69, no. 5 (1982): 604–19.

universal sacrament of salvation for humankind and the world. But in *Sacrosanctum Concilium* the focus is originally christological.[30] This fact has deep implications for the understanding of the nature of the liturgical reform and its role in the process of inculturation. As Avery Dulles put it, "The Church therefore is in the first instance a sign. It must signify in a historically tangible form the redeeming grace of Christ. It signifies that grace as relevantly given to men of every age, race, kind, and condition. Hence the Church must incarnate itself in every human culture."[31]

The theological background of this view of the liturgy expressed in SC 1–5 is the history of salvation, which culminates with the *mysterium paschale*, a concept that entered the text during Vatican II, thanks to the French liturgist and bishop Henri Jenny.[32] *Mysterium paschale* is repeated many times in the text of the constitution and is a "heart word" not only for the liturgical constitution but also for Vatican II as such.[33]

The centrality of baptism and Eucharist in SC 6 is a witness to the powerful ecclesiology of the liturgical constitution. A mention of the "sacraments" in the first draft of the document was replaced by a more focused reference to the Eucharist.[34] That is why, different from *Lumen Gentium*, where in chapter 1 the definition of the Church is inclined to adopt a sociological tone, in the liturgical constitution the gathering of the faithful around the Eucharist is constitutive of the Church: "From that time onwards the Church has never failed to come together to celebrate the paschal mystery" (SC 6). The liturgical constitution revolves around the Eucharist: the communion in the Church is not sociologically defined but theologically as a product of the Eucharist.[35]

---

[30] See Salvador Pié-Ninot, *Ecclesiologia. La sacramentalità della comunità cristiana* (Queriniana: Brescia, 2008), 192–93.

[31] Dulles, *Models of the Church*, 60.

[32] See Henri Jenny, *The Paschal Mystery in the Christian Year*, trans. Allan Stehling and John Lundberg (Notre Dame, IN: Fides Publishers, 1962).

[33] Kaczynski, *Kommentar*, 61–63.

[34] For the change between the first draft and the final version of SC 6 and the recentering in the Eucharist ("sacrifice") in the sentence, "His purpose also was that they might accomplish the work of salvation which they had proclaimed, by means of *sacrifice and sacraments*, around which the entire liturgical life revolves" (emphasis mine), see Kaczynski, *Kommentar*, 64; and Bugnini, *The Reform of the Liturgy*, 33.

[35] See Dossetti, *Chiesa eucaristica*, 61–63.

SC 7 and its assertion of liturgy as the communication to the faithful of the *opus nostrae redemptionis* is "probably the most important statement in the Constitution and the key to a rethinking of the liturgy."[36] Even if SC 7 does not contain a definition of what the liturgy is,[37] it talks about "sacred action surpassing all others." This passage was one of the most disputed passages in the debate on the constitution, because many fathers compared this "definition by comparison" to the heroic virtues practiced by saintly men in the Church:[38]

> In [the liturgy] full public worship is performed by the Mystical Body of Jesus Christ, that is, by the Head and his members.
> From this it follows that every liturgical celebration, because it is an action of Christ the Priest and of his Body, which is the Church, is a sacred action surpassing all others. No other action of the Church can equal its efficacy by the same title and to the same degree. (SC 7)

The sanctification of the faithful begins with the reading of the Scripture and with the announcement of the Word; these are the basic elements of worship. The text of SC 7 took as its basis a passage in Pius XII's encyclical *Mediator Dei* and added a phrase about the presence of Christ in the reading of the Scripture but omitted the expression "and in the explanation of Scripture" because it was "a doctrinal development not sufficiently advanced for a conciliar document."[39] *Sacrosanctum Concilium* affirms clearly here that Christ, not the congregation, is the subject of the liturgy in the form of the sacrifice on the altar, in the person of the priest, and under the species of the Eucharist. The quotation from Augustine's *Tractatus in Ioannem* strengthens this idea and liberates the liturgical constitution from one of the major

---

[36] Reiner Kaczynski, "Toward the Reform of the Liturgy," in *History of Vatican II*, vol. 3: *The Mature Council, Second Period and Intercession, September 1963–September 1964* (Maryknoll, NY: Orbis; Leuven: Peeters, 2000), 223. See also Pietro Damiano Scardilli, *I nuclei ecclesiologici nella costituzione liturgica del Vaticano II* (Roma: Pontificia Università Gregoriana, 2007), 186–87.

[37] See Jungmann, "Constitution on the Sacred Liturgy," 3.

[38] The phrase "sacred action surpassing all others" was already in the German Catechism of 1955; see ibid., 14.

[39] Bugnini, *The Reform of the Liturgy*, 34. The phrase "and in the explanation of Scripture" had been proposed during the sessions of the Central Preparatory Commission by Bishop Denis Hurley (Durban, South Africa); Kaczynski, *Kommentar*, 66–67.

accusations, that is, of transforming the paschal mystery, which "is not the action of a man, but an action of God. [. . .] It is precisely this 'work of Jesus' which is the real content of the Liturgy."[40]

SC 7 was crucial also in abandoning the understanding of the liturgy as "public worship" (*cultus publicus*), as it was described in the Code of Canon Law of 1917 but also in paragraph 20 of the encyclical *Mediator Dei* (1947), and in giving liturgy a central place in the life of the Church. In SC 7 the liturgical constitution explains that liturgy: (a) is the fulfillment of the *sacerdotium* of Christ, (b) is the sanctification of Christians and the worshiping of God, and (c) has to be perceptible to the senses. In SC 7 the Church becomes, much more clearly than in *Lumen Gentium*, a communion of grace with Christ that is sacramentally manifested, implementing the passage from a Christocentric and "vertical" ecclesiology before Vatican II to the more trinitarian ecclesiology of Vatican II.[41]

A progression is visible between SC 7 (liturgy in the Church) and SC 8 (liturgy and eschatology). In SC 8 liturgy is defined as the continuation of the action of Christ until his return, and this is where the liturgical constitution becomes visibly unaffected by the accusations of "panliturgism," that is, of absorbing the whole life of the Church in its liturgical dimension. SC 9 is a clear statement against the accusation of "panliturgism" moved by the opponents of the liturgical movement well before Vatican II: "The sacred liturgy does not exhaust the entire activity of the Church. Before men can come to the liturgy they must be called to faith and to conversion" (SC 9). The ecclesiology of the liturgical constitution is based on the Eucharist, but it does not see the Eucharist as the only reality in the life of the Church. The Eucharist presupposes preliminaries and implies consequences. Three different aspects—Eucharist, community life, and kerygmatic moment—have become one in the liturgy: Christ's priestly, kingly, and prophetic offices are represented in the understanding of the Church offered by the liturgical constitution.

The centrality of the Eucharist and its foundational function for ecclesiology comes back at the end of chapter 1, which is about liturgical life in parishes and dioceses. The passages of *Sacrosanctum Con-*

---

[40] See Joseph Ratzinger, "The Theology of Liturgy," in *Looking Again at the Question of the Liturgy with Cardinal Ratzinger*, Proceedings of the July 2001 Fontgombault Liturgical Conference (Saint Michael's Abbey Press, 2003), 18–32, esp. 18–19.

[41] See Acerbi, *Due ecclesiologie*, 486–99.

cilium, stating that "the principal manifestation of the Church consists in the full, active participation of all God's holy people in the same liturgical celebrations, especially in the same eucharist, in one prayer, at one altar, at which the bishop presides, surrounded by his college of priests and by his ministers" (SC 41) and that the eucharistic celebrations in parishes "in some manner [. . .] represent the visible Church constituted throughout the world" (SC 42), were not less essential in affirming the eucharistic ecclesiology of the liturgical constitution.

It is clear that, although there is a unity of the *ecclesiologies* of Vatican II, there is a difference between the eucharistic ecclesiology of *Sacrosanctum Concilium* and the ecclesiology of *Lumen Gentium*: "In *Lumen Gentium* there is no systematic discussion of the ecclesiological role of the Eucharist."[42] In this respect, the eucharistic ecclesiology of *Sacrosanctum Concilium* was received more by the decree on ecumenism, *Unitatis Redintegratio*, than by the constitution *Lumen Gentium*.[43] This fact tells us the importance of the liturgical constitution—and of the liturgical reform of Vatican II—in the overall ecclesiological balance of the council. *Sacrosanctum Concilium* holds a position of priority in the hermeneutics of Vatican II, not because it was the first document that was approved, but because in all the other fundamental texts of the council there are textual and conceptual connections to the theological reorientation operated by the liturgical constitution. This theological reorientation was guided by the idea of *ressourcement*.

3.3. Liturgy and Ecclesiological *Ressourcement*

Much of the recent debate on the "reform of the liturgical reform" has focused on the loss of the sense of beauty and solemnity in post–Vatican II liturgies. In a sense, the polemics about Vatican II is a polemics on the supposed loss of the sense of aesthetics in a definitively globalized Catholicism.[44] The liturgical constitution addresses

[42] "Il ruolo ecclesiologico dell'eucaristia non trova in *Lumen Gentium* una trattazione organica" (ibid., 505).

[43] "Hence, through the celebration of the Eucharist of the Lord in each of these Churches, the Church of God is built up and grows in stature, and through concelebration, their communion with one another is made manifest" (*Unitatis Redintegratio* 15).

[44] See John F. Baldovin, *Reforming the Liturgy: A Response to the Critics* (Collegeville, MN: Liturgical Press, 2008), 19–26.

71

this problem in many passages of the text, most visibly when the constitution advocates for the "noble simplicity" (SC 34) of the celebrations. This is an ecclesiological option more than a purely aesthetical "option for the primitive" and for the minimalist.[45] It is one of the results of ecclesiological *ressourcement* manifested and fueled by the reform of the liturgy.

The ecclesiology of *ressourcement* proclaims that the origins of Christianity are, if not strictly normative, very significant in order to reshape the image and the understanding of the Church: it is a "back to the future" ecclesiology that we find in *Sacrosanctum Concilium*. Appreciating the *ressourcement* ecclesiology of the liturgical constitution requires an understanding of the different "political alignments" at Vatican II and the theological perspectives from which the document originated, in comparison to *Lumen Gentium*.

If we consider the political alignment in the *aula* of St. Peter's that voted for the reform of the liturgy, the ecclesiology of *Sacrosanctum Concilium* represents the "summit" and "fount" (SC 10) of the ecclesiology of Vatican II because its theological content was formed and shaped before the fight about the continuity with Vatican I began in the second session, in the fall of 1963.[46] On one side, *Sacrosanctum Concilium* did not suffer the wounds of the war waged by the conciliar minority against episcopal collegiality as it was worded in chapter 3 of *Lumen Gentium* and subsequently "reinterpreted" in the "Nota Explicativa Praevia" to *Lumen Gentium*.[47] On the other side, the rejection of the *schema De fontibus revelationis* on divine revelation in November 1962 had made clear that no document could be approved at Vatican II without a profound *ressourcement*—biblical, patristic, liturgical.[48]

---

[45] One of the many critical views of the liturgical reform can be found in Romanus Cessario, "The Sacraments of the Church," in *Vatican II: Renewal within Tradition*, ed. Matthew L. Lamb and Matthew Levering (Oxford and New York: Oxford University Press, 2008), 129–46.

[46] See Alberto Melloni, "The Beginning of the Second Period: The Great Debate on the Church," in *History of Vatican II*, vol. 3, 1–115.

[47] On the impact of the "Nota Explicativa Praevia" on the dynamics of Vatican II between 1964 and 1965, see Luis Antonio Tagle, "'The Black Week' of Vatican II (November 14–21, 1964)," in *History of Vatican II*, vol. 4: *Church as Communion: Third Period and Intercession; September 1964–September 1965* (Maryknoll, NY: Orbis; Leuven: Peeters, 2003), 388–452.

[48] See Giuseppe Ruggieri, "The First Doctrinal Clash," in *History of Vatican II*, vol. 2, 233–66; Gianotti, *I Padri della Chiesa al Concilio*, 412.

That is why in the liturgical constitution the ecclesiological core not only is tied to the Eucharist but also maintains a strong section on the *communio ecclesiarum*, one of the key concepts for the *ressourcement* of Catholic ecclesiology according to the model of the early Church. *Lumen Gentium* is silent on the practical application of episcopal collegiality whereas *Sacrosanctum Concilium* is not, and, as a matter of fact, it opened the door to the most important practical implementation of episcopal collegiality in modern Catholicism: national bishops' conferences.[49]

There are not only differences between the two ecclesiologies of *Sacrosanctum Concilium* and *Lumen Gentium* but also similarities. One of these similarities is the focus on *ressourcement* as a fundamental option for the renewal of theology. Both in the liturgical constitution and in the ecclesiological constitution we see *ressourcement* as a "listening to" the fathers of the Church, not a historical and philological assessment of their doctrine. In this sense, *Sacrosanctum Concilium* embodies the patristic perspective of Vatican II and its effort toward renewal in the spirit of a theological integration of Scripture and liturgy.[50] The liturgical constitution was crucial in opening the ecclesiological debate of Vatican II to the perspective of *ressourcement*.

The first *ressourcement* was ushered into the council by the liturgical constitution and it had to do with the participation of the faithful in the liturgy. It was no accident that during the debate (which left paragraphs 14–20 of the constitution relatively untouched)[51] many fathers underlined the role of liturgy in the early Church as the primary set for catechesis.[52] Accordingly, the quotation of the letter of Peter in SC 14 introduced the need for a conscious and active participation, just like in the early, pre-Constantine Church, in which the nature of the liturgy was matched and fulfilled by the mind of the participants and not by the force of social networks, nor by the embedding of liturgy in a

---

[49] See Acerbi, *Due ecclesiologie*, 535–53. See also Massimo Faggioli, "Prassi e norme relative alle conferenze episcopali tra concilio Vaticano II e post-concilio (1959–1998)," in *Synod and Synodality: Theology, History, Canon Law and Ecumenism in New Contact*, ed. Alberto Melloni and Silvia Scatena (Münster: LIT, 2005), 265–96.

[50] See Gianotti, *I Padri della Chiesa al concilio*, 417–19.

[51] See Jungmann, "Constitution on the Sacred Liturgy," 17.

[52] See the intervention of Archbishop Maurice Feltin (Paris) in *Acta Synodalia*, vol. 1, bk. 1, 368 (October 23, 1962).

political and cultural context, "the enchanted, porous world of our ancestors":[53]

> Mother Church earnestly desires that all the faithful should be led to that full, conscious, and active participation in liturgical celebrations which is demanded by the very nature of the liturgy, and to which the Christian people, "a chosen race, a royal priesthood, a holy nation, a redeemed people" (1 Pet 2:9, 4-5) have a right and obligation by reason of their baptism. (SC 14)

"Active participation"—called the "refrain" of the constitution[54]—recurs in eleven other places in the constitution. It is worth remembering that the idea of *actuosa participatio* was totally absent, in reference to the liturgy, in the Code of Canon Law of 1917. In Pius X's effort to renew liturgical music, with the *motu proprio Tra le sollecitudini* (1903), the expression *actuosa participatio* "seems to be mentioned in a casual way, without a strong doctrinal content."[55] It was only with Dom Lambert Beauduin that "active participation" became the slogan of the liturgical movement, thus planting one of the most important seeds of the future liturgical reform of Vatican II.[56]

With Vatican II, it became clear that active participation of the faithful is not an optional and accessory element of liturgy; it belongs to the very nature of liturgical action. Liturgical contemplation is a contemplation mediated through words, through the community, through something tangible; it is not pure interiority. This is the meaning of *per ritus et preces*—"through a good understanding of the rites and prayers" (SC 48). The liturgical celebration touches concretely the existential and bodily dimensions of men and women assembled in liturgical prayer, because this is how liturgy leads to a comprehension experience of the mystery of Christ.[57]

---

[53] Charles Taylor, *A Secular Age* (Cambridge, MA, and London: Harvard University Press, Belknap Press, 2007), 42.

[54] Jungmann, "Constitution on the Sacred Liturgy," 17.

[55] Paul De Clerck, "La participation active. Perspective historico-liturgiques, de Pie X à Vatican II," in *The Active Participation Revisited—La participation active. 100 ans après Pie X et 40 ans après Vatican II*, ed. Jozef Lamberts (Leuven: Peeters, 2005), 13–31, quotation at 15.

[56] See Lambert Beauduin, *La piété de l'Église. Principes et faits* (Louvain: Abbaye du Mont-César, 1914); *Liturgy the Life of the Church*, trans. Virgil Michel (Collegeville, MN: Liturgical Press, 1926).

[57] See Andrea Grillo and Matteo Ferrari, *La riforma liturgica e il Vaticano II. Quale futuro?* (Rimini: Pazzini, 2009), 60–61.

At Vatican II, the idea of active participation became something more than the "innocuous" version of the liturgical movement endorsed by many otherwise skeptical bishops in the decades before Vatican II,[58] when there was a tension between the two streams of the liturgical movement: one in favor of the vernacular language and other reforms and the other advocating active participation in the liturgy as it was in Latin. The solution to this tension came from the contribution of the non-European bishops at Vatican II.[59] At the council and in *Sacrosanctum Concilium* there is a connection between active participation and ecclesiology of the local Church.

SC 14 and the emphasis on active participation are the necessary foundation for the *ressourcement* of the theology of the Church and of the local Churches, as it is expressed in LG 26: "This Church of Christ is really present in all legitimately organized local groups of the faithful, which, in so far as they are united to their pastors, are also quite appropriately called Churches in the New Testament. [. . .] In them the faithful are gathered together through the preaching of the Gospel of Christ, and the mystery of the Lord's Supper is celebrated 'so that, by means of the flesh and blood of the Lord the whole brotherhood of the Body may be welded together.'" Another proof of the ecclesiological content of *Sacrosanctum Concilium* is paragraph 27, which gives priority to community liturgies over the "individual and quasi-private" celebrations.[60]

But the *ressourcement* here is evident in the statement that the membership in the Church is ecclesiologically defined through participation in the liturgy: "the liturgy is the first and necessary source for a life in the true spirit of Christ."[61] It is therefore true that "beginning with the Constitution on the Liturgy, Vatican II sought to retrieve the early centuries' vision of a Church as a particular or local community gathered for the Eucharist presided at by a bishop."[62] This is what drew opposition from the conciliar minority, still reluctant to abandon

[58] See Bernard Botte, *From Silence to Participation: An Insider's View of the Liturgical Renewal*, trans. John Sullivan (Washington, DC: Pastoral Press, 1988; original French: Paris: Desclée, 1973), 57–58.

[59] See Paul Pulikkan, *Indian Church at Vatican II: A Historico-Theological Study of the Indian Participation in the Second Vatican Council* (Trichur: Marymatha, 2001), 210–20; Lamberigts, "The Liturgy Debate," in *History of Vatican II*, vol. 2, 116–25.

[60] See Jungmann, "Constitution on the Sacred Liturgy," 21.

[61] Kaczynski, *Kommentar*, 80.

[62] Bernard P. Prusak, *The Church Unfinished: Ecclesiology through the Centuries* (Mahwah, NJ: Paulist Press, 2004), 274.

a Tridentine ecclesiology that identified the essence of the Church with its juridical element and, ultimately, with the authority of the pope. Cardinal Ernesto Ruffini (Palermo) explained this attitude in speaking of the refusal of Trent to concede "the chalice to the laity": "At the Council of Trent there were proposals to concede exceptions to some nations and kingdoms [to administer Holy Communion under both species], but the council decided not to consider those proposals and to defer the whole matter to the pope. And until now, for four centuries, if I am not mistaken, in the Roman Rite there has been no exception conceded by the popes."[63]

On the one hand, SC 14 stresses the primary identity of Christians as baptized. On the other hand, the ecclesiology of *Sacrosanctum Concilium* maintains a traditional and bishop-centered view of the Church, with a pivotal role for the bishop as the presider of the Eucharist in the local Church. Here we see the deep implications of *ressourcement* for liturgy and ecclesiology. If it is true that *Sacrosanctum Concilium* "refers to the 'hierarchic and communal nature of the liturgy' [but] it does not have in mind a return to pyramidal ecclesiology,"[64] it is also true in *Sacrosanctum Concilium* (and in the whole corpus of Vatican II, for that matter) that the episcopacy is given great liturgical and ecclesiological preeminence, and we do not yet find a "ressourced" understanding of the diversity of the ecclesial ministries. But in the words of Walter Kasper, "the council meant a powerful push for the development of ecclesiology. The systematization of its affirmations certainly could not be a task for the council itself."[65]

Along with the new, less juridical yet "transitional" ecclesiology of the encyclical *Mystici Corporis* (June 29, 1943), the liturgical *ressourcement* put on the agenda of Catholic ecclesiology the rediscovery of the episcopacy in a far more effective and politically less risky way than a

[63] *Acta Synodalia*, vol. 1, bk. 1, 600–601, speech given by Cardinal Ernesto Ruffini (Palermo) on October 29, 1962: "Cum autem in Concilio Tridentino proposita sit quaestio, an exceptio pro aliqua natione vel regno, ob peculiares rationes et sub certis conditionibus concedenda esset, Concilium noluit eam considerare, sed integrum negotium ad Summum Pontificem esse referendum decrevit. Iamvero usque ad hunc diem, per quattuor secula, nulla exceptio, ni fallor, in ritu romano a Pontificibus concessa est."

[64] Gaillardetz, *Ecclesiology for a Global Church*, 133.

[65] Walter Kasper, "Der Weg der eucharistischen Ekklesiologie in der katholischen Kirche," in *Die Liturgie der Kirche*, Walter Kasper Gesammelte Schriften 10 (Freiburg i.B.: Herder, 2010), 323.

constitutional "balance of power" between papacy and bishops—a kind of "rematch of Vatican I."[66] The ecclesiological *ressourcement* introduced by *Sacrosanctum Concilium* was just the first step in the long path toward the crafting of the ecclesiologies of Vatican II. From the cautious wording of paragraph 22 we can perceive the council's uncertain awareness of the ecclesiological implications of *Sacrosanctum Concilium*: "(1) Regulation of the sacred liturgy depends solely on the authority of the Church, that is, on the Apostolic See, and, as laws may determine, on the bishop. (2) In virtue of power conceded by law, the regulation of the liturgy within certain defined limits belongs also to various kinds of bishops' conferences, legitimately established, with competence in given territories" (SC 22).

Ressourcement here meant the end of four hundred years of centralization of liturgical law making in the Roman Catholic Church and a definitive overcoming of the Code of Canon Law of 1917 (canon 1257).[67] The pope was no longer the only legislator on liturgy in the Catholic Church, and the power to regulate liturgy was apportioned to bishops and bishops' conferences.[68] "In virtue of power conceded by the law" but on theological grounds—and not merely to pursue a micro-monarchical model for the dioceses—paragraph 41 puts the bishop at the center of the liturgical life of the local Church:

> The bishop is to be considered as the High Priest of his flock from whom the life in Christ of his faithful is in some way derived and upon whom it in some way depends.
>
> Therefore all should hold in the greatest esteem the liturgical life of the diocese centered around the bishop, especially in his cathedral church. They must be convinced that the principal manifestation of the

[66] See Hermann Josef Pottmeyer, *Towards a Papacy in Communion: Perspectives from Vatican Councils I and II* (New York: Crossroad, 1998); *Papstamt und Ökumene. Zum Petrusdienst und der Einheit aller Getauften*, ed. Peter Hünermann (Regensburg: Pustet, 1997); John R. Quinn, *The Reform of the Papacy: The Costly Call to Christian Unity* (New York: Crossroad, 2000); Massimo Faggioli, *Il vescovo e il concilio. Modello episcopale e aggiornamento al Vaticano II* (Bologna: Il Mulino, 2005), 27–36.

[67] See Jungmann, "Constitution on the Sacred Liturgy," 19; Dossetti, *Chiesa eucaristica*, 40.

[68] About the short-lived period of decentralization in the Church after Vatican II, see Heribert Schmitz, "Tendenzen nachkonziliarer Gesetzgebung. Sichtung und Wertung," *Archiv für katholisches Kirchenrecht* 146 (1977): 381–419; Martin Klöckener, "La reception de la éforme liturgique du concile Vatican II: une approche historique," *La Maison-Dieu* 268 (December 2011): 41–62.

Church consists in the full, active participation of all God's holy people in the same liturgical celebrations, especially in the same Eucharist, in one prayer, at one altar, at which the bishop presides, surrounded by his college of priests and by his ministers. (SC 41)[69]

In the debate of October 1962, in St. Peter's, Cardinals Ruffini and Browne reminded the council fathers that in Tridentine Catholicism the pope was the only legislator and that every decision in liturgical matters belonged to the pope.[70] In this respect, the liturgical debate of Vatican II was a watershed in Catholic ecclesiology. Long before the hard-reached balance between the ecclesiology of the universal and local Church could be set in *Lumen Gentium*'s watchful wording, the liturgical constitution put forward the role of the local bishop, underlining the episcopal character of liturgy and the unity of the local Church with its bishop and the clergy.

It is not an overstatement to say that the ecclesiological *ressourcement* of *Sacrosanctum Concilium* recovered the ecclesiology of the monarchic episcopate of Ignatius of Antioch, especially at paragraph 41, which footnote quotes Ignatius's letters *To the Smyrnians*, *To the Magnesians*, and *To the Philadelphians*. The ecclesiology of the local Church thus emerges, in the first constitution of Vatican II, not as a political, ideological, or institutional option to reverse the trend of the second millennium of Church history, but as the natural outcome of the new centrality of the Eucharist in Church life.[71] Ecclesiological *ressourcement* owes much more to the final outcomes of the liturgical renewal and its "conservative" aim (restoring the liturgical life in secularized Western society) than to the allegedly radical or liberal ecclesiologists active at Vatican II.

Although the ecclesiological *ressourcement* of *Sacrosanctum Concilium* exceeds the issue of the role of bishops in the Church, this issue evidently plays a key role in assessing the path of the Church of Vatican II. Often the assessment of the fate of the ecclesiology of the episcopate in the last fifty years has overlapped with the assessment of the reception

[69] On the genesis of SC 41 and the conciliar debate, see Scardilli, *I nuclei ecclesiologici*, 270–82.

[70] For the speeches of Ruffini and Browne (October 23, 1962), see *Acta Synodalia*, vol. 1, bk. 1, 364–67 and 376–77. About the debate, see Lamberigts, "The Liturgy Debate," in *History of Vatican II*, vol. 2, 120.

[71] See Jean-Marie R. Tillard, *L'Église locale. Ecclésiologie de communion et catholicité* (Paris: Cerf, 1995), esp. 251–66.

of *Lumen Gentium,* and the assessment of the fate of the ecclesiology of Vatican II has overlapped with the assessment of the collegiality in the post–Vatican II Church.[72] But the ecclesiological issue and the role of the episcopate specifically was no secondary step in the path of the liturgical reform as it was intended by the liturgical constitution of Vatican II. The restoration of the rights of the bishops in regulating the liturgical life in their Churches was a major step in the direction of an ecclesiological *ressourcement* operated through the liturgical reform of Vatican II.[73] The power of regulating the devotions proper to individual Churches (SC 13), the creation of episcopal commissions for the liturgy (SC 45–46), permission for concelebration (SC 57), and the catechumenate for adults (SC 64): these were just a few signs of the beginning of the new role for the bishops in the life of the Church, after centuries of a Catholicism where liturgical life, and not only that, was legislated ultimately by and through the pope.[74]

The episcopal and "local" character of liturgical life as presented in the liturgical constitution of Vatican II was received only partially by the ecclesiological constitution, paragraphs 23 and 28. *Lumen Gentium* 23 especially developed a historical-juridical, rather than liturgical, case for the role of bishops in their "particular Churches" and revealed, in its lack of liturgical basis, the burden of a "too much abstract and abrupt opposition between jurisdiction and *sollicitudo* [. . .] and between universal and particular Church."[75]

All this considered, the ecclesiological *ressourcement* of the first constitution of Vatican II needs to be measured carefully, especially if we take into account the pondering of *ecclesiologies* during the first two years of Vatican II (October 1962–December 1963). The developing of a tension between the "ecclesiology of the monarchy" (papal monarchy

---

[72] Especially in the first twenty years after the end of Vatican II; see Massimo Faggioli, *Vatican II: The Battle for Meaning* (Mahwah, NJ: Paulist Press, 2012).

[73] See Emmanuel Lanne, "Chiesa locale," in *Dizionario del concilio Vaticano II,* ed. Tommaso Federici (Roma, 1969), 797–826.

[74] See Dossetti, *Chiesa eucaristica,* 40.

[75] "Nicht nur an einer abstrakten und unvermittelten Entgegensetzung von Jurisdiktion und a-rechtlicher sollicitudo leiden, sondern ebenso an der abstrakten Polarität von Universalkirche und Particularkirche" (Peter Hünermann, "Theologischer Kommentar zur dogmatischen Konstitution über die Kirche Lumen Gentium," in *Herders Theologischer Kommentar zum Zweiten Vatikanischen Konzil,* ed. Hans Jochen Hilberath and Peter Hünermann, vol. 2 [Freiburg i.B.: Herder, 2004], 431).

and/or episcopal monarchy) and its opponents undermined a possible alternative ecclesiological approach to the Church. Excluded by the clash inside the "supreme" theological commission about the balance of power between pope and bishops, the sacramental/eucharistic ecclesiology survived in the liturgical constitution, rooted in a less juridical approach to the life of the Church and somehow sheltered by the fierce debate on bishops' collegiality that was taking place about *Lumen Gentium*.[76] In this sense, it is accurate to define the ecclesiology of the liturgical constitution as more "original" to Vatican II and less compromised by the need to redeem or correct the trajectories of the recent past of nineteenth- and early twentieth-century ecclesiology.[77]

The need for some institutional reform in order to give way to a more eucharistic Church was certainly not absent from the minds of the council fathers. Thanks to the liturgical debate, Vatican II began to discuss the role of the bishops' conferences from a much more general perspective, following the examples of strong national and international conferences of bishops (such as the German bishops' conference and CELAM for Latin America) and trying to connect this institution born in the nineteenth and twentieth centuries with the councils and synods of the first centuries.[78] But this new role of the bishops in the life of local Churches was supported by the final outcome of the liturgical debate, not by the quite active (later during Vatican II) bishops' lobbying in favor of an institutional *decentralization* in the global Catholic Church (that is, more autonomy from Rome for the bishops) and *centralization* in the local Church (abolition of the immovability for parish priests and more control of the religious orders active in the diocese).[79]

Compared to the central place occupied by the "new Catholic movements" in the Catholic Church of the twentieth century, the absence of a "revival of the episcopacy" in post–Vatican I and pre–Vatican II

<hr />

[76] See Alberto Melloni, "Ecclesiologie al Vaticano II (autunno 1962–estate 1963)," in *Les commissions conciliaires à Vatican II*, ed. Mathijs Lamberigts, Claude Soetens, and Jan Grootaers (Leuven: KUL, 1996), 91–179, esp. 136–38; Melloni, "The Beginning of the Second Period," in *History of Vatican II*, vol. 3, esp. 102–8.

[77] See also Acerbi, *Due ecclesiologie*, 485–553; Komonchak, "The Significance of Vatican II for Ecclesiology."

[78] See, for example, the intervention of Bishop Wilhelm Bekkers (s'Hertogenbosch, Holland) in *Acta Synodalia*, vol. 1, bk. 2, 313–14 (November 7, 1962).

[79] See Faggioli, *Il vescovo e il concilio*, 443–48.

Catholicism is striking.[80] This absence (which was followed by a crisis of authority of the bishops in the post–Vatican II Church) during the council made the push for an institutional reform in the Church difficult to articulate in its theological, cultural, and ideological subtexts. But the theological and cultural contribution of the liturgical revival between the late nineteenth century and the first half of the twentieth century made possible, though indirectly, the discovery of the episcopacy in a theologically more balanced form and in a way that was institutionally less hostile for the papacy and the Roman Curia. The liturgical movement and the patristic revival succeeded where the theology of the episcopate failed at Vatican II, proving difficult the attempt to balance the most vertical ecclesiology of Vatican I with the same juridical approach (but with much less firepower than the papacy).[81] In the post–Vatican II Church the new role of the bishops in the ecclesiology of Vatican II succeeded insofar as the liturgical ecclesiology of *Sacrosanctum Concilium* was received, and it failed through the fading of the council's self-awareness before papal primacy and its executive branch, the Roman Curia. The theological and ecclesial debate about the results and the fate of the liturgical reform should not conceal the relevance of the ecclesiological *ressourcement* and its sources for and in the liturgical renewal approved in 1963.

3.4. Ecclesiological Consequences of the New Liturgy

The very fact that the liturgy was to change is a firstfruit of Vatican II. Previously, a generation of Catholics had been educated to believe that in the Catholic Church "tradition" meant "immutability," but the decision of the liturgical reform was the most patent proof that the Church *changes*: "No more endless roll of *saecula saeculorum*. No more neat ahistorical belief that what one did on Sunday morning looked (with minor adjustments) like what the church had always done, from the time of the catacombs."[82] The reform of the liturgy was also

---

[80] See Massimo Faggioli, *Breve storia dei movimenti cattolici* (Roma: Carocci, 2008); Spanish translation: *Historia y evolución de los movimientos católicos. De León XIII a Benedicto XVI* (Madrid: PPC Editorial, 2011).

[81] A similar, "compensating" approach between Vatican I and Vatican II in Pottmeyer, *Towards a Papacy in Communion*.

[82] See Garry Wills, *Bare Ruined Choirs: Doubt, Prophecy, and Prophetic Religion* (Garden City, NY: Doubleday, 1972), 21.

founded on the fact that liturgy had always been changing during Church history. The identification, so popular in some quarters of early twenty-first-century Catholicism, of the "liturgy of Pius V" (the preconciliar rite) with the perfect and immutable form of the Roman Rite does not take into account the fact that Pius V himself reformed the liturgy after the Council of Trent.[83]

From the very beginning of the debate at the council, the fathers stressed the need to "adapt" the liturgy to the new catholicity of the Church. The cardinal of Tokyo, Tatsuo Doi, declared that it was time for a "major adaptation of the sacred liturgy to the culture and sensibility of the people of the Far East."[84] Cardinal Rugambwa (Rutabo, Tanzania) affirmed that the *schema* on the liturgy was important because "it offered non-Western cultures the chance to express themselves in prayer to God and in the catechesis to our people in manners that suit our culture."[85]

The debate on the reception of Vatican II and of its liturgical reform recently has been dominated more by the "narratives" than by a serious historical approach. Rejecting the liturgical reform is not a disapproval of the *idea* that the Church should change, but it is the refusal to admit the *fact* that the Church has always been a community of change within tradition. In the words of *Sacrosanctum Concilium*:

> In order that the Christian people may more certainly derive an abundance of graces from the sacred liturgy, holy Mother Church desires to undertake with great care a general restoration of the liturgy itself. For the liturgy is made up of unchangeable elements divinely instituted, and of elements subject to change. These latter not only may be changed but ought to be changed with the passage of time, if they have suffered from the intrusion of anything out of harmony with the inner nature of the liturgy or have become less suitable. (SC 21)

---

[83] See Josef A. Jungmann, *Missarum Sollemnia: The Mass of the Roman Rite*, 2 vols. (New York: Benziger Bros., 1951–55), 96–106; *Missarum sollemnia. Eine genetische erklärung der römischen Messe* (Wien: Herder, 1948). See also John Baldovin, "The Body of Christ in Celebration: On Eucharistic Liturgy, Theology, and Pastoral Practice," in *Source and Summit: Commemorating Josef A. Jungmann, S.J.*, ed. Joanne M. Pierce and Michael Downey (Collegeville, MN: Liturgical Press, 1999), 49–61.

[84] Cardinal Paul Tatsuo Doi (Tokyo) in *Acta Synodalia*, vol. 1, bk. 1, 323 (October 22, 1962).

[85] Cardinal Laurean Rugambwa (Rutabo, Tanzania) in *Acta Synodalia*, vol. 1, bk. 1, 333 (October 22, 1962).

The historicity of the liturgy and the emphasis, in the liturgical constitution, of the visible-invisible dimension of the Church signaled the end of the post-Tridentine ecclesiology of the *societas perfecta*, in which "tradition" and "immutability" were misused as synonyms. But the importance of the ecclesiological consequences of *Sacrosanctum Concilium* reaches far beyond the undeniable result of legitimizing "change within tradition." It opened up a path in the ecclesiological debate of Vatican II, showing a possible way to develop Catholic ecclesiology, alternate to the controversies about the juridical and sociological representations of the Church in Vatican II Catholicism. Focusing on the ecclesiology of the Vatican II liturgy offers contemporary Catholicism many resources for a fruitful escape from the clash of the interpretation of the council.[86]

On one side, we need to counter the usual accusations against the "liturgy of Vatican II" as having placed the community itself as the subject of the liturgy. In fact, the liturgical constitution sets up a reversal in the focus of the relationship between Church and liturgy, but in the sense that *Sacrosanctum Concilium* proposes an ecclesiology centered not on the Church itself but on the "mystery of Christ," the *Herzwort* of Vatican II.[87] On the other side, this sacramental ecclesiology proves to have a much more coherent and lasting equilibrium than the precarious balance between the juridical ecclesiology and the communion ecclesiology of *Lumen Gentium*, where the first chapter, centered on the *mysterium*, is followed by a sequence of chapters dealing with a more sociological and juridical concept of the Church, even though it is very different from the preconciliar, hierarchical way of describing the Church.[88]

Despite the fact that in *Sacrosanctum Concilium* we do not have a definition of the liturgy, we have a definition of the Church (SC 2) that points out an ecclesiology more harmonious than that found in *Lumen*

---

[86] See Faggioli, *Vatican II*, chap. 5.

[87] See Kaczynski, *Kommentar*, 63. See also Angelus A. Häussling, "Pascha-Mysterium. Kritisches zu einem Beitrag in der dritten Auflage des Lexicon für Theologie und Kirche," *Archiv für Liturgiewissenschaft* 41 (1999): 157–65.

[88] See Gérard Philips, *L'Église et son mystère au IIe Concile du Vatican. Histoire, text et commentaire de la constitution "Lumen Gentium,"* 2 vols. (Paris-Tournai: Desclée, 1967). For the latest commentary on *Lumen Gentium*, see Richard R. Gaillardetz, *The Church in the Making:* Lumen Gentium, Christus Dominus, Orientalium Ecclesiarum (New York: Paulist Press, 2006); Hünermann, "Theologischer Kommentar," 265–582, esp. 557–58.

Gentium: the liturgical constitution "postulates, in its affirmation about the subject of the Catholic liturgy and about the liturgical activity of the Church, a people-of-God ecclesiology."[89] Theology of liturgy, and implicitly ecclesiology, built up *Sacrosanctum Concilium* and thus outlined an image of Church that is not found in the ecclesiological constitution: the mystery of the Church is the mystery of the death and resurrection of Christ. In doing so, the liturgical constitution can afford to avoid the concerns for the institutional description of the Church and its canonical and sociological definitions. While *Sacrosanctum Concilium* expresses that Church and Eucharist are overlapping, an idea we cannot find in *Lumen Gentium*, we see in *Lumen Gentium*— after the first chapter on the Church as a mystery—a more sociological concept of Church, which can potentially be detached from the Eucharist, and it actually is detached when it comes to the definition of the ecclesiastical hierarchy, giving room for a more juridical perspective.[90]

Sacrosanctum Concilium anticipated the ecclesiological evolution of *Lumen Gentium* and escaped the alternative between "people-of-God ecclesiology" and "communio ecclesiology":[91] "By asserting that liturgy is a communal action, normally involving a congregation, and always an action of the Church as a whole, not a private or individual function, firmly grounds the liturgical renewal in the idea of the Church as the people of God."[92] It is therefore clear that the ecclesiology of *Sacrosanctum Concilium* does not contradict but ushers in and anticipates the communion ecclesiology of Vatican II as a pillar of the liturgical reform: the Church as a communion of life thanks to the grace, the expression, of the communion in the life of the Trinity; the power of the grace, received in faith and through the sacraments, especially the Eucharist, that unifies Christians as the people of God and Mystical Body of Christ; a people of God, walking toward the kingdom of God, but also active witnesses of Christ in the world,

---

[89] See Jean-Pierre Jossua, "La constitution Sacrosanctum Concilium dans l'ensemble de l'oeuvre conciliaire," in Jossua and Congar, *La liturgie après Vatican II*, 127–56, esp. 128–29.

[90] See Dossetti, *Chiesa eucaristica*, 62.

[91] About this shift in the ecclesiological debate, see Severino Dianich and Serena Noceti, *Trattato sulla chiesa* (Brescia: Queriniana, 2002), 217; Hermann Pottmeyer, "Dal Sinodo del 1985 al grande giubileo dell'anno 2000," in *Il Concilio Vaticano II. Recezione e attualità alla luce del Grande Giubileo*, ed. Rino Fisichella (Milano: San Paolo, 2001), 17–20.

[92] Rita Ferrone, *Liturgy:* Sacrosanctum Concilium (New York: Paulist Press, 2007), 33.

visible in its ecclesial institutions and led by the bishops in the local Churches and the pope.[93]

Even if the most complete assertion of the Church as "people of God" is in *Lumen Gentium* 13, the liturgical constitution introduced also the ecclesiology of the local Church that has been tamed in the ecclesiological constitution and neglected in the Church of post–Vatican II.[94] After a long silence by Catholic theology on the subject,[95] the liturgical constitution stresses the importance of the local Church through the biblical and patristic renewal, which points to the roots of early Christianity as a communion of local communities; through the rediscovery of the Eucharist as the very heart of the Church; through the empowerment of the local bishop as first celebrant within the local Church. The eucharistic focus of the ecclesiology of *Sacrosanctum Concilium* especially revived the role of the local presbyterium with the bishop, carrying a very important ecumenical contribution to the relationship with the Eastern traditions. According to St. Ignatius of Antioch, "*the Eucharist is an act of the presbyterium, not of the priest.* The ancients acknowledged only one altar symbol of Christ."[96]

[93] See Cipriano Vagaggini, "La ecclesiologia di comunione come fondamento teologico principale della riforma liturgica nei suoi punti maggiori," in *Liturgia, opera divina e umana. Studi sulla riforma liturgica offerti a S.E. Mons. Annibale Bugnini in occasione del suo 70° compleanno*, ed. Pierre Jounel, Reiner Kaczynski, and Gottardo Pasqualetti (Roma: C.L.V. Edizioni Liturgiche, 1982), 59–131.

[94] In 2001, then-Cardinal Ratzinger delivered a harsh assessment of the ecclesiological consequences of the liturgical constitution of Vatican II: "Il me semble que le passage de l'Eglise universelle à l'Eglise locale, et de l'Eglise locale à la communauté locale—comme nous a dit le professeur [Roberto] de Mattei—a été à l'heure actuelle un des plus gros problèmes. [. . .] Avec la fragmentation de la liturgie considérée come l'acte particulie des communautés locales, on perd l'Eglise, et avec l'Eglise la foi et le mystère" (Joseph Ratzinger [Benedikt XVI], "Bilan et perspectives," Actes des journées liturgiques de Fontgombault, 22–24 juillet 2001, in *Theologie der Liturgie. Die Sakramentale Begründung christlicher Existenz*, Joseph Ratzinger Gesammelte Schriften, Band 11 [Freiburg i.B.: Herder, 2008], 665–66).

[95] The first courageous attempt to reflect on the local Church in modern times had been by Adrien Gréa, *De l'Église et de sa divine constitution* (Paris: Société Générale de Librairie Catholique, 1885; second edition, Paris: Maison de la Bonne Presse, 1907). See Angel Antón, *El misterio de la Iglesia. Evolución historica de las ideas eclesiologicas*, 2 vols. (Madrid and Toledo: Editorial Católica, 1986), 2:458–63; Joseph A. Komonchak, "Chiesa locale e Chiesa cattolica. La problematica teologica contemporanea," in *Chiese locali e cattolicità*, ed. Hervé-Marie Legrand, Julio Manzanares, Antonio García y García (Bologna: EDB, 1994), 433–57.

[96] "Rappelle la phrase de St. Ignace: *l'eucharistie n'est pas l'acte du prêtre mais du présbyterium*. Les anciens ne connaissaient qu'un seul autel symbole du Christ"

The ecclesiology of the liturgical constitution seems to be able to overcome many of the controversies about the supposed contradiction between the "collegiality" of bishops at the universal level and the "synodal church" at the local level.[97] The synodal-local level has a clear priority in the eucharistic ecclesiology of *Sacrosanctum Concilium* where the "full, conscious, and active participation in liturgical celebrations" (SC 14) implies also a conscious and active participation in the life of the local Church, since the Church is "the sacrament of unity" (SC 26) and the Eucharist is the celebration of the whole Church, not just the clergy.[98] The focus of the liturgical constitution on baptism and Eucharist not only has an ecumenical projection but also aims indirectly at a declericalization of the Church. That is why the ecclesiology of *Sacrosanctum Concilium* proves its durability fifty years after the liturgy debate of Vatican II: because it fits the "expansion zone" of the Catholic Church in the path ahead.[99]

Questioning the liturgical reform of Vatican II means undoing also the ecclesiology of the liturgical reform and the ecclesiology of Vatican II. Benedict XVI's *motu proprio Summorum Pontificum* (July 7, 2007), which reintroduced the pre–Vatican II missal, entailed extraordinary consequences from an ecclesiological point of view:

> The rehabilitation of the Missal of 1962 accompanies the comeback of the preconciliar theology of episcopacy in liturgical matters, that is, a theology according to which the bishops are just executors of the right application of the norms as they are set by the Apostolic See. In the

---

(letter of Pierre Duprey from Rome to the Monastery in St. Anne [Jerusalem], November 1, 1962, in Archive of the John XXIII Foundation for Religious Studies in Bologna). See Jean Zizioulas, "L'église locale dans une perspective eucharistique," in Jean Zizioulas, *L'Etre ecclésial* (Genève: Labor et Fides, 1981), 181–94; Emmanuel Lanne, "L'église locale et l'église universelle. Actualité et portée du theme," *Irénikon* 43 (1970): 481–511.

[97] For this debate see Kilian McDonnell, "The Ratzinger/Kasper Debate: The Universal Church and Local Churches," *Theological Studies* 63 (June 2002): 222–50. See also Scardilli, *I nuclei ecclesiologici*, 235–319.

[98] For a stereotypical characterization of the concept of *actuosa participatio*, see Eamon Duffy, "Benedict XVI and the Liturgy," in *The Genius of the Roman Rite: Historical, Theological, and Pastoral Perspectives on Catholic Liturgy*, ed. Uwe Michael Lang (Chicago and Mundelein, IL: Hillebrand Books, 2010), 14–16.

[99] Such as seen, for example, by Dulles, *Models of the Church*, 188–90: modernization of structures, ecumenical interplay, internal pluralism, provisionality, and voluntariness.

motu proprio there is no mention of the episcopal conferences and of their authority.[100]

Far from being a technical or purely aesthetic makeup, the liturgical reform of Vatican II expressed and represented, from early in the history of the council, some elements of the theological "constitutional core" of Vatican II. Both the reception and the rejection of the liturgical reform embody in many cases the very reception and rejection of Vatican II, especially of its ecclesiological change.[101]

3.5. *Lex Orandi, Lex Credendi* and the Reception of the Liturgical Constitution

By approving the liturgical constitution in 1963, Vatican II set in motion a programmatic reform of Roman Catholic liturgy "unlike anything that had ever been attempted before."[102] Half a century later, one of the most overlooked principles for the understanding of the liturgical reform (and for understanding the impossibility of the undoing of the liturgical reform of Vatican II) is *lex orandi, lex credendi*. Its author, the fifth-century theologian Prosper of Aquitaine, is one of the witnesses of the ressourced character of Vatican II and of the reform in theology implicitly declared in the reform of the liturgy:

> The *lex credendi*—the "law of belief" about the nature of the Church, a law that Prosper of Aquitaine recognized as being so profoundly shaped by ritual experience—was now powerfully reshaped by a new *lex orandi*. The older, static, juridical identity of "church" described by Cardinal Bellarmine that had served Roman Catholicism so well (and ill) in the centuries after the Reformation was now reexperienced as, in some sense, untrue to experience.[103]

It is, however, hard to recognize a clear reception by the other final documents of Vatican II of this idea of the liturgy as *theologia prima*.

---

[100] Laurent Villemin, "L'autorité des conférences épiscopales en matière de liturgie. Interprétations et réinterprétations récentes," in *L'autorité et les autorités. L'herméneutique théologique de Vatican II*, ed. Gilles Routhier and Guy Jobin (Paris: Cerf, 2010), 151–65, quotation at 163.

[101] See Baldovin, *Reforming the Liturgy*, 134–40.

[102] O'Malley, *What Happened*, 139.

[103] See Mark S. Massa, *Catholics and American Culture: Fulton Sheen, Dorothy Day, and the Notre Dame Football Team* (New York: Herder and Herder, 1999), 170.

Lumen Gentium quotes the liturgical constitution for stressing the role of the clergy in the celebration[104] as does *Christus Dominus*, which quotes paragraphs 4 and 5 of the liturgical constitution in order to assert the role of the bishops' conferences.[105] Other council documents rely on *Sacrosanctum Concilium* for the movement created in the Church by the liturgical reform and its most practical aspects: the catechetical instruction (*Gravissimum Educationis* 4), the reform of the calendar (*Orientalium Ecclesiarum* 20), the ministry of priests and the priests' functions (*Presbyterorum Ordinis* 4–5), and liturgical education (*Ad Gentes* 16; *Optatam Totius* 8 and 16). Some insights come from the use of the liturgical constitution by the conciliar decree *Ad Gentes*, which recognizes the ties between the liturgical reform and the catechumenate,[106] and from the decree *Apostolicam Actuositatem*, which underlines the role of the liturgy in the spiritual life of lay faithful.[107]

Many elements of the liturgical constitution were received by other documents of the corpus of Vatican II. But the most important ecclesiological shifts operated by *Sacrosanctum Concilium*—from a juridical ecclesiology to one based on communion and a new understanding of the priesthood from a sacral model to a sacramental model—were not received by the documents of Vatican II debated and approved after

[104] In *Lumen Gentium* 50–51, but especially *Lumen Gentium* 28: "They exercise in a supreme degree their sacred functions; there, acting in the person of Christ and proclaiming his mystery, they unite the votive offerings of the faithful to the sacrifice of Christ their head, and in the sacrifice of the Mass they make present again and apply, until the coming of the Lord (cf. 1 Cor. 11:26), the unique sacrifice of the New Testament, that namely of Christ offering himself once for all a spotless victim to the Father."

[105] "It is therefore bishops who are the principal dispensers of the mysteries of God, and it is their function to control, promote and protect the entire liturgical life of the Church entrusted to them" (*Christus Dominus* 15).

[106] "Those who have received from God the gift of faith in Christ, through the Church, should be admitted with liturgical rites to the catechumenate which is not a mere exposition of dogmatic truths and norms of morality, but a period of formation in the whole Christian life, an apprenticeship of sufficient duration, during which the disciples will be joined to Christ their teacher. The catechumens should be properly initiated into the mystery of salvation and the practice of the evangelical virtues, and they should be introduced into the life of faith, liturgy and charity of the People of God by successive sacred rites" (*Ad Gentes* 14).

[107] "This life of intimate union with Christ in the Church is maintained by the spiritual helps common to all the faithful, chiefly by active participation in the sacred liturgy" (*Apostolicam Actuositatem* 4).

Sacrosanctum Concilium, that is, between fall 1963 and the end of the council in December 1965. Interestingly enough, the ecclesiological constitution, *Lumen Gentium*, and the debates that shaped the constitution in the second session (fall 1963) tapped the almost completed and ready-to-vote-on liturgical constitution, but with a narrow and exploitative approach. In fact, the theologians in charge of the drafting of the liturgical constitution used the ties between episcopal collegiality, the sacramentality of the episcopate, and episcopal consecration in order to demonstrate—and to secure the votes to be cast on October 30, 1963—the liturgical-theological roots of the episcopate as "the fullness of the sacrament of Orders" (*Lumen Gentium* 21 and 26).[108]

This underdevelopment of the ecclesiology of Vatican II meant also an underdevelopment of the ecclesiology of the local Church.[109] What remained of the liturgical constitution in the legacy of Vatican II was, however, the beginning of a new theological and juridical awareness of the need for a new balance of power between pope, local bishops, and bishops' conferences in the Catholic Church.[110] The history of the ecclesiology of the local Church is closely tied with the history of the liturgical movement; they will probably also share the same future path.[111] A rejection of the liturgical reform of Vatican II would mean a premature death of the ecclesiology of the local Church in Catholic theology and its ecclesial praxis.

In one of the most important and overlooked discontinuities of the liturgical constitution compared to Pius XII's encyclical *Mediator Dei*, Vatican II affirmed that the power to regulate liturgy is not in the hands of the pope or of the Holy See only.[112] Also, thanks to *Sacrosanctum*

---

[108] See Joseph Lécuyer, "Le sacrement de l'épiscopat," *Divinitas* 2 (1952): 201–31; Charles Moeller, "Il fermento delle idee nella elaborazione della Costituzione," in *La Chiesa del Vaticano II*, ed. Guilherme Barauna (Firenze: Vallecchi, 1965), 155–89, esp. 168–69.

[109] See Gilles Routhier, *Vatican II. Herméneutique et reception* (Montréal: Fides, 2006), 87–137; Hervé-Marie Legrand, "Les évêques, les Églises locales et l'Église entière. Évolutions institutionelles depuis Vatican II et chantiers actuels de recherche," *Revue de Sciences philosophiques et théologiques* 85 (2001): 461–509.

[110] See Dossetti, *Chiesa eucaristica*, 40.

[111] See Aimé G. Martimort, *De l'évêque* (Paris: Cerf, 1946). About Martimort, see Benoît-Marie Solaberrieta, *Aimé-Georges Martimort. Un promoteur du Mouvement liturgique en France (1943–1962)* (Paris: Cerf, 2011).

[112] See, for example, Pius XII's 1947 encyclical *Mediator Dei* 60: "The use of the Latin language, customary in a considerable portion of the Church, is a manifest

Concilium, at Vatican II the episcopal conferences established and reinforced their power, far beyond the diverse and sometimes improvised traditions of the individual national bishops' conferences.[113] The drafting of the liturgical constitution took for granted not only the existence of the national bishops' conferences but also their future development in the Church of Vatican II. Without the first experiences of the national bishops' conferences before Vatican II, we would not have *Sacrosanctum Concilium* (and Vatican II as it happened); without *Sacrosanctum Concilium* the national bishops' conferences would have remained in the embryonic stage they were in until 1963.

It can be said that the reception of the liturgical constitution worked both at the institutional and at the theological level. At the institutional level, the swift adoption of the new rite witnessed the preparation and the need of the Church for such a change, the most significant in the last four centuries in the history of Catholicism. At the theological level, the liturgical reform proved more than a renovation of the way of celebrating; it was the coming to life of a new understanding of the liturgy as a crucial moment in the self-understanding of the Church. *Sacrosanctum Concilium* is aware that "the life of the Church cannot be reduced to the sole Eucharistic moment" (SC 9–10)[114] and that liturgy has its role in the Church as a *theologia prima*, as *locus theologicus*, and as *culmen et fons*.[115] As a matter of fact, the liturgical constitution not only sponsored a new awareness within the Roman Catholic Church that *things change*[116] but revived the old axiom *lex orandi, lex credendi*: "the law of praying grounds the law of believing."

---

and beautiful sign of unity, as well as an effective antidote for any corruption of doctrinal truth. In spite of this, the use of the mother tongue in connection with several of the rites may be of much advantage to the people. But the Apostolic See alone is empowered to grant this permission. It is forbidden, therefore, to take any action whatever of this nature without having requested and obtained such consent, since the sacred liturgy, as we have said, is entirely subject to the discretion and approval of the Holy See."

[113] See Faggioli, "Prassi e norme relative alle conferenze episcopali."

[114] See Dossetti, *Chiesa eucaristica*, 67; for a reference to the Orthodox ecclesiology, see Nicholas Afanasiev, *The Church of the Holy Spirit*, trans. Vitaly Permiakov, ed. with an introduction by Michael Plekon, foreword by Rowan Williams (Notre Dame, IN: University of Notre Dame Press, 2007).

[115] See Andrea Grillo, *La nascita della liturgia nel XX secolo. Saggio sul rapporto tra movimento liturgico e (post-) modernità* (Assisi: Cittadella, 2003), 143.

[116] For an analysis of the US Church, see Mark S. Massa, *The American Catholic Revolution: How the Sixties Changed the Church Forever* (New York: Oxford Univer-

That is why the liturgical reform of Vatican II and the most recent calls for a "reform of the reform" touch the essence of Vatican II,[117] not to mention the theological and canonical issues raised by the coexistence of two different *leges orandi* tied to one *lex credendi*:[118] "If worship shapes belief, and experience forms doctrine, then the 'changes' mandated in worship by the Second Vatican Council represented something considerably more dramatic and profound than simply 'updating' the liturgy."[119] Changing worship sponsors a theological rethinking of ecclesiology, in a more profound and long-lasting way than the definition of the Church worded by *Lumen Gentium*: "A great number of criticisms against the liturgical reform and its application come from a misunderstanding or from a refusal of a renewed ecclesiology."[120]

The fact that liturgy is not only "summit" but also "source" implies a series of "operational principles" tied to the role and the form of liturgy—principles that can operate only along the lines of the deep

---

sity Press, 2010), 15–28. For other cases of reception of the liturgical reform, see Stephan Steger, "Die Liturgiereform im Bistum Würzburg nach dem Zweiten Vatikanum, Schlaglichter und Entwicklungslinien," *Liturgisches Jahrbuch* 57 (2007): 266–88; Wolfgang Steck, "Der Beginn der Liturgiereform in der Erzdiözese München und Freising. Eine chronologische Spurensuche," *Liturgisches Jahrbuch* 57 (2007): 135–51; Mathijs Lamberigts, "Entwicklungen nach dem II. Vatikanum in den Niederlanden. Die liturgische Entwicklung als Fallstudie," in *Das Zweite Vatikanische Konzil und die Zeichen der Zeit heute*, ed. Peter Hünermann (Freiburg i.B.: Herder, 2006), 283–312; Angel Unzueta, "L'action liturgique, expression de la Pentecôte" (about the liturgical reform in the Basque region of Spain) and Rémy Kurowski, "La messe dominicale comme creuset de la réception de la réforme liturgique en Pologne: Le cas de la diocèse de Gniezno," in *Réceptions de Vatican II: Le Concile au risque de l'histoire et des espaces humaines*, ed. Gilles Routhier (Leuven: Peeters, 2004), 91–129; Gilles Routhier, "Les avents de la constitution sur la liturgie au Canada francophone," *Questions Liturgique* 87 (2006): 233–63; Gilles Routhier, "Le mouvement liturgique au Québec: attentes et espérances de l'aggiornamento conciliaire," in *Vatican II au Canada: enracinement et réception*, ed. Gilles Routhier (Montréal: Les Editions Fides, 2001), 129–61.
[117] See Baldovin, *Reforming the Liturgy*.
[118] See Andrea Grillo, "Ende der Liturgiereform? Das Motuproprio 'Summorum Pontificum,'" *Stimmen der Zeit* 225, no. 11 (2007): 730–40; and *Oltre Pio V. La Riforma liturgica nel conflitto di interpretazioni* (Brescia: Queriniana, 2007).
[119] For an explanation of the "Durkheimian" understanding of the liturgical reform, see Massa, *Catholics and American Culture*, 148–71, quotation at 158.
[120] Laurent Villemin, "Principes ecclésiologiques de la réforme liturgique de Vatican II," *Lumière et Vie* 279 (Juillet–Septembre 2008): 71–79, quotation at 77.

implications of the liturgical reform of Vatican II. The new rite's language (comprehensible modern languages), symbols (inculturated traditions), scriptural passages (taken both from the Old Testament and the New Testament) contribute to shape a new *lex credendi*.[121]

If through the reintroduction of an already-abrogated liturgical rite, the *lex orandi* of Vatican II goes away, so goes the *lex credendi* and the basic form (*Gestalt*) of the faith[122] expressed by Vatican II from an ecclesiological standpoint in the liturgical constitution and then developed (or sometimes underdeveloped) not only by *Lumen Gentium* but also by *Dei Verbum* (ecclesiology and revelation), *Dignitatis Humanae* (ecclesiology and religious freedom), *Unitatis Redintegratio* (ecclesiology and ecumenism), and *Nostra Aetate* (ecclesiology and non-Christian religions).[123]

---

[121] On the relationship between *lex orandi* and *lex credendi* and the misuse of this axiom, see Paul De Clerck, " 'Lex orandi, lex credendi'. Un principe heuristique," *La Maison-Dieu* 222, no. 2 (2000): 61–78.

[122] See Peter Hünermann, *Dogmatische Prinzipienlehre. Glaube, Überlieferung, Theologie als Sprach- und Wahrheitsgeschehen* (Münster: Aschendorff, 2003).

[123] About the relations between the "issues" at Vatican II, see O'Malley, *What Happened*, 309–11.

Chapter 4

Liturgical Reform and *Rapprochement*

One of the main aims of the council announced by John XXIII was to summon the Church and celebrate its unity in a new relationship with the outer world:

> The forthcoming Council will meet therefore and at a moment in which the Church finds very alive the desire to fortify its faith, and to contemplate itself in its own awe-inspiring unity. In the same way, it feels the more urgent the duty to give greater efficiency to its sound vitality and to promote the sanctification of its members, the diffusion of revealed truth, the consolidation of its agencies.[1]

The same emphasis on "unity" was also a leitmotif in John XXIII's opening speech of the council, *Gaudet Mater Ecclesia* (October 11, 1962), in which the pope explained the threefold importance of "unity" for Vatican II:

> Indeed, if one considers well this same unity which Christ implored for His Church, it seems to shine, as it were, with a triple ray of beneficent supernal light: namely, the unity of Catholics among themselves, which must always be kept exemplary and most firm; the unity of prayers and ardent desires with which those Christians separated from this Apostolic See aspire to be united with us; and the unity in esteem and respect for the Catholic Church which animates those who follow non-Christian religions.[2]

---

[1] John XXIII, Apostolic Constitution *Humanae salutis*, with which the pope solemnly convoked the Second Vatican Ecumenical Council on December 25, 1961, in *Acta Apostolicae Sedis* 54 (1962): 5–13; English translation in *The Documents of Vatican II*, ed. Walter M. Abbott (New York: Herder and Herder, 1966), 703–9, quotation at 705–6.

[2] John XXIII, opening speech of Vatican II, *Gaudet Mater Ecclesia* (October 11, 1962), in *Acta Apostolicae Sedis* 54 (1962): 786–95; English translation in Abbott, *The Documents of Vatican II*, 710–19, quotation at 717. For the importance of the idea of

But Vatican II was meant to be a "celebration" in the most profound liturgical sense[3]—not a mere display of false unanimity, but a living experience of communion within the Church and with the world through the interaction of different cultural sensibilities, historical backgrounds, and theological orientations. The contribution of the liturgical reform to this aim of Vatican II has been dismissed for too long, being judged as a merely technical reform of the council that gave way to theological debates that took place in the years after the approval of *Sacrosanctum Concilium*.

The liturgical tradition of the Church has always contained the clear expression of the unity of the Church,[4] a unity that was liturgically visible until Vatican II under the Tridentine rule but that was already under a lot of pressure for changes that everybody—not only those in the milieu of the liturgical movement—saw coming. The liturgical movement and the theology of Vatican II reflected the impact of the "dialogical principle" on twentieth-century Western philosophy: Edmund Husserl, Martin Buber, Emmanuel Levinas, Hans-Georg Gadamer.[5] At the same time, the liturgical reform expressed the deep theological aspiration of the Church to shape itself in the form of Jesus "the universal brother of all human beings" ("le Frère universel de tous les humains," "mort pour tous les hommes sans exception"), in the words of Charles de Foucauld (1858–1916), a French Catholic religious and priest living among the Tuareg in the Sahara in Algeria. This theological insight was expressed not only by the two constitutions on the Church, *Lumen Gentium* and *Gaudium et Spes*, but also and first by the liturgical constitution, *Sacrosanctum Concilium*.

Vatican II continued the tradition of a unity expressed through liturgy, but it did so through an understanding of *rapprochement*—re-approaching, reaching out, and reconciliation—that expressed more clearly the attempt of Vatican II to make of the "Church a sacrament of

---

"unity" in Angelo Roncalli's biography and theology, see Alberto Melloni, *Papa Giovanni. Un cristiano e il suo concilio* (Torino: Einaudi, 2009), 149–64 and 195–225.

[3] See Giuseppe Alberigo, "Sinodo come liturgia?," *Cristianesimo nella storia* 28, no. 1 (2007): 1–40.

[4] See Henri de Lubac, *Catholicisme. Les aspects sociaux du dogme* (Paris: Cerf, 1938), 69–74.

[5] See Werner Stegmaier, "Heimsuchung. Das Dialogische in der Philosophie des 20. Jahrhunderts," in *Dialog als Selbstvollzug der Kirche?*, ed. Gebhard Fürst (Freiburg i.B.: Herder, 1997), 9–29.

reconciliation" for humankind.[6] The idea of *rapprochement*—a term used many times by Dom Lambert Beauduin, the pioneer of ecumenism and a liturgist[7]—is not part of the corpus of Vatican II in a material way, but it belongs fully to the aims of Vatican II. The liturgical reform of Vatican II plays a significant role in developing (during Vatican II) and performing (after Vatican II) this key feature of the council in a way that is not less important than other, better-known "*rapprochement* manifestos" of Vatican II, such as the decree *Unitatis Redintegratio*, the declaration *Nostra Aetate*, and the pastoral constitution *Gaudium et Spes*.[8]

The main *rapprochement* carried out by *Sacrosanctum Concilium* consists of a reconciled and unifying vision of the Church, of Christian life, of the existential condition of the faithful in the world, and of the coexistence between Church and world.[9] Far from being a purely aesthetical option, the theological starting point of the liturgical reform aimed at "resetting" the relationship between Christian liturgy, spiritual needs of the faithful, and Catholic theological reading of the modern world in its historical and social dimensions.[10] In a way, the

---

[6] See Peter Smulders, "La Chiesa sacramento della salvezza," and Jan L. Witte, "La Chiesa 'sacramentum unitatis' del cosmo e del genere umano," in *La Chiesa del Vaticano II. Studi e commenti intorno alla Costituzione dommatica Lumen gentium*, ed. Guilherme Barauna (Firenze: Vallecchi, 1965), 363–86 and 491–521. For the use of *sacramentum* in the ecclesiological debate at Vatican II, see Daniele Gianotti, *I Padri della Chiesa al concilio Vaticano II. La teologia patristica nella Lumen Gentium* (Bologna: EDB, 2010).

[7] See Raymond Loonbeek and Jacques Mortiau, *Un pionnier, Dom Lambert Beauduin (1873–1960). Liturgie et unité des chrétiens*, 2 vols. (Louvain-la-Neuve: Collège Erasme, 2001), 1:907–9. See also Jacques Mortiau and Raymond Loonbeek, *Dom Lambert Beauduin visionnaire et précurseur (1873–1960). Un moine au coeur libre* (Paris: Cerf, 2005); R.-Ferdinand Poswick and Lambert Vos, "Autour d'un centenaire (1909–2009). Les débuts du mouvement liturgique: Beauduin, Marmion, Festugière et . . . les autres," *Questions Liturgiques* 92, no. 1 (2011): 3–28.

[8] On the use of the word "dialogue," from the encyclical *Ecclesiam Suam* to the council texts, see O'Malley, *What Happened*, 204.

[9] See Dossetti, *Chiesa eucaristica*, 41.

[10] See Giovanni Turbanti, *Un concilio per il mondo moderno. La redazione della costituzione pastorale "Gaudium et spes" del Vaticano II* (Bologna: Il Mulino, 2000); Giuseppe Alberigo, "Das II. Vatikanum und der kulturelle Wandel in Europa," in *Das II Vatikanum. Christlicher Glaube im Horizont globaler Modernisierung*, ed. Peter Hünermann (Paderborn: F. Schöning, 1998), 139–57 (now republished: "Il concilio Vaticano II e le trasformazioni culturali in Europa," in Giuseppe Alberigo, *Transizione epocale. Studi sul Vaticano II* [Bologna: Il Mulino, 2009], 601–27).

rapprochement expressed by the liturgical constitution was the first, if partially unconscious, act of moving beyond the negative *Weltanschauung* marked in the Catholic intellectual world by the French Revolution and prolonged through the nineteenth and the first half of the twentieth centuries.[11]

The steps of the *rapprochement* embedded in the liturgical constitution proceed in multiple directions: with the outside world, within the Church, between the Catholic Church and other Christians, and with the Jews.[12]

4.1. *Pòlis* and Liturgy in the Church of Vatican II

In recent years a good number of studies in theology and Christian history have focused on the conciliar liturgical reform to discuss the meaning and to take stock of Vatican II. The observers of this debate know that the subtext is also "political," because the background of the liturgical reform was a complex idea of the relationship between liturgy, theology, ecclesiology, culture, and history.

In fact, the link between *lex orandi* and *lex credendi* is embodied also in the relationship between liturgy, prayer, and "worldview" in the various religious traditions. No need to remember the events of September 11, 2001, and the violence that occurred "in the name of God" to understand that there is a link between forms of personal prayer and the whole human community and to grasp the basic idea that private prayer is also "public theology."[13] For this we must take into account the "course" of the liturgy as a political "action of the people," public expression of prayer as a human act.

The liturgical constitution of Vatican II, which stated in the introduction that the Church is a "sign lifted up among the nations" (SC 2), was aware of this "public-political" character of the liturgy. Although the constitution does not mention the council's "political culture," it

[11] See Giovanni Miccoli, *Fra mito della cristianità e secolarizzazione. Studi sul rapporto chiesa-società nell'età contemporanea* (Casale Monferrato: Marietti, 1985).

[12] For the idea of *rapprochement* in post–Vatican II Catholicism, see Alberto Melloni, "Da *Nostra aetate* ad Assisi '86. Cornici e fatti di una ricezione creativa del concilio Vaticano II," *Convivium Assisense* 9, no. 1 (2007): 63–89.

[13] See *The 9/11 Handbook: Annotated Translation and Interpretation of the Attackers' Spiritual Manual*, ed. Hans G. Kippenberg and Tilman Seidensticker (London and Oakville: Equinox Pub., 2006).

does build a discourse on the Eucharist for the Church that lives on earth. The relationship between revelation, tradition, history, and ecumenism has a "political" meaning because it starts from an acceptance of the basic ideas of theological movements that are fed into Vatican II—the biblical, patristic, liturgical, and ecumenical movements—and accepts history as a "theological" source in framing liturgy as "source and summit" of the Church.[14]

The consciousness of the "political" content of Vatican II does justice to the liturgy of the apparent "exceptionalism" of the monotheistic religions of Christianity in terms of the relationship between religion and politics.[15] The link between politics as the "idea of the *pòlis*," on the one hand, and liturgy as an "action of the people," on the other, applies not only to the theologies of liberation or revolution and to political Islam but also to Catholicism, which is only apparently a neutral political form of religion. Vatican II had a "political culture," a view of the modern world that was expressed by many documents *ad extra* (the documents on ecumenism, on religious freedom, on non-Christian religions, and the pastoral constitution). But ultimately this political culture and its connection to the longing for *rapprochement* was expressed also by the documents *ad intra* (on the Church, on revelation), first and foremost by the constitution on the liturgy.

This is where Vatican II substantially clarifies the ideological use of the temptations of Catholicism as a "civil religion," that is, as a belief that (as has been explained by Robert Bellah) cements the civil and political cohesion of a people to some beliefs, values, and rituals—regardless of the religion professed by individuals and communities.[16] While the weakening of the social fabric of the Church in Europe has led some to see in "civil religion" the remedy for a conversion of Catholicism that for too long has served as a symbolic identification between nation and religion, the liturgical ecclesiology processed from the reform launched by Vatican II radically contradicts such a possibility. The idea of civil religion is far removed from the idea of the

---

[14] See Andrea Grillo, *La nascita della liturgia nel XX secolo. Saggio sul rapporto tra movimento liturgico e (post-) modernità* (Assisi: Cittadella, 2003), 123–52.

[15] For the definition of "politically indirect ecclesiology," see William T. Cavanaugh, *Migrations of the Holy: God, State, and the Political Meaning of the Church* (Grand Rapids, MI, and Cambridge, UK: Eerdmans, 2011), 123–40.

[16] See Robert Bellah, "Civil Religion in America," *Journal of the American Academy of Arts and Sciences* 96, no. 1 (1967): 1–21.

liturgy of the Church of Vatican II. The basic ideas of the conciliar liturgical reform are closely linked to the conception of the Church of Vatican II, which Georges Dejaifve has summarized in five characteristics: the distinction between Church and kingdom, the idea of communion, the sacramental aspect, catholicity, and political character.[17]

The liturgical reform of Vatican II is based on certain theological and cultural insights that are substantiated in the movement toward a reform of the Church in the ecumenical sense of *rapprochement*, made possible by a conversion to the sources of the Church and its theological and spiritual reflection of early theologians (*ressourcement*). John O'Malley's lesson on the "style of Vatican II" as "expressive value" is of great importance for understanding the relationship between liturgy and politics at the Vatican.[18]

The beginning of the liturgical constitution, in fact, marks the "pragmatic" of Vatican II, not through a theoretical description of the liturgy, but through a narrative of the relationship between God and his people that is distinctly catholic as "universal," and offers Christ and the Eucharist as the center of gravity in a clear *ressourcement* to the patristic idea of the Eucharist as *sacramentum unitatis*.[19]

Sacrosanctum Concilium aspires not to a purely aesthetic purification of the liturgy but to a refocusing on the Eucharist and the liturgy within the Church, with clear implications for the self-understanding of the community praying in space and time. This refocusing on the eucharistic liturgy has consequences for the way Christians look to the *pòlis* as a community in which to incarnate the Gospel, proclaim it, and live it well through prayer and liturgy. The liturgy reformed by the council expresses a clear vision of the Church attached to a worldview that proclaims a desire to foster unity: "The sacred Council has set out to impart an ever-increasing vigor to the Christian life of the faithful; to adapt more closely to the needs of our age those institutions which are subject to change; to foster whatever can promote union among all who believe in Christ; to strengthen whatever can help to call all mankind into the Church's fold" (SC 1).

It is no coincidence that the liturgical constitution was the first document to be debated and approved at the council after the Message to

[17] See Georges Dejaifve, "L'ecclesiologia del concilio Vaticano II," in *L'ecclesiologia dal Vaticano I al Vaticano II* (Brescia: La Scuola, 1973), 87–98.

[18] See O'Malley, *What Happened*, 305–7.

[19] See Gianotti, *I Padri della chiesa al concilio*, 399.

the World, which expressed the determination of the council to be of comfort to the anxieties that plague humanity in the present. The commitment to universal *rapprochement* envelopes the entire liturgical constitution, so that chapter 5 on the liturgical year encourages the narrative of reconciliation through a universal salvific will of God, not excluding any category of humanity.[20]

The idea of *rapprochement* also becomes visible in the constitution in paragraph 7: "The liturgy, then, is rightly seen as an exercise of the priestly office of Jesus Christ. It involves the presentation of man's sanctification under the guise of signs perceptible by the senses and its accomplishment in ways appropriate to each of these signs" (SC 7). The constitution changed not the doctrine on the Eucharist but the experience of it with a new focus on "the senses" as a gateway for participation in the liturgy as "sacred action surpassing all others" (SC 7). Making the senses part of the experience of the liturgy redirects the orientation of the Church and its emphasis in its public role. The liturgical life of the Church, therefore, has a "political" side that does not abstract from the *pòlis*:

> Liturgical services are not private functions but are celebrations of the Church which is "the sacrament of unity," namely, "the holy people united and arranged under their bishops."
>
> Therefore, liturgical services pertain to the whole Body of the Church. They manifest it, and have effects upon it. But they also touch individual members of the Church in different ways, depending on their orders, their role in the liturgical services, and their actual participation in them. (SC 26)

The preference for communal celebration (SC 27) de-emphasizes the purely hierarchical ecclesiology. It is clear, therefore, that the liturgical reform of theology and the renewed ecclesiology of the council expressed a "political" content in the broadest sense: "the politics of power and domination is to be transformed from the cross in a political *diakonia*. For God's sake the Christian cannot withdraw from politics; for the way of the cross does not slide over this-worldly reality but runs straight through it, with all that ensues from that."[21]

---

[20] See Dossetti, *Chiesa eucaristica*, 49.

[21] Herman Schmidt, "Lines of Political Action in Contemporary Liturgy," in *Politics and Liturgy*, ed. Herman Schmidt and David Power (New York: Herder and Herder, 1974), 13–33, quotation at 29.

The liturgical reform and the council are inextricably linked, because all the major theological ferments of Vatican II have left traces in the liturgical constitution: the rediscovery of the Word of God, ecclesiology, ecumenism, relations with the Jews, the Church and the modern world. The liturgical movement, together with the preconciliar renewal of pastoral theology, was able to bring to the council the need to develop new instruments that could show the bonds of earthly realities with the liturgical prayer. Just think of the retrieval of the prayer of the faithful: "To pray for real needs of the church and the world is to show that one is intimately concerned with political realities, that the word and the sacramental point to the salvation of the world in which we live."[22]

But if it is clear that a genuine inculturation of the liturgy is crucial for reconciliation among all Christians and between Christians and contemporary humanity, the relationship between liturgy and the *pòlis* is more problematic, not just for the liturgical reform, but for being considered in the *pòlis* as a concrete phenomenon that has deeply influenced both society and Christianity.

The transition from early Christianity to the Imperial Church, and from there to the National Churches after the Reformation and the Peace of Westphalia in 1648, seemed destined—at least back in the 1960s—to make way for a decidedly post-Constantinian World Church. The picture now seems more fragmented: if the council had anticipated the success of a democratic and participatory Church in the world to come,[23] now it seems the culture of antipolitics is unaware of the relationship between liturgy and *pòlis*.[24]

The forms of the liturgical celebration are not "indifferent" to the world in which the contemporary Church lives. As shown by recent reactions to the schism of Archbishop Marcel Lefebvre, who refused to recognize Vatican II, it is evident, even for observers apparently more distant from the World Church (non-Catholic churches, Jewish communities, political observers, and public intellectuals), that there is a direct link between forms of the liturgy, theological cultural reference,

---

[22] Joseph Gelineau, "Celebrating the Paschal Liberation," in Schmidt and Power, *Politics and Liturgy*, 107–19, quotation at 110.

[23] For the "insights" of Vatican II about democratization in the non-Western world, see Samuel P. Huntington, *The Third Wave: Democratization in the Late Twentieth Century* (Norman and London: University of Oklahoma Press, 1991).

[24] See Jean Daniélou, *L'oraison comme probléme politique* (Paris: Fayard, 1965), 23–30.

and worldview.[25] The theological content of the liturgical constitution (especially SC 5, 6, and 8) has intertextual connections with other council documents (*Dei Verbum*, *Nostra Aetate*) that are crucial for the overall theological balance of Vatican II.

The liturgical celebration gained, thanks to the council, a new centrality in the proclamation of the Gospel in the world. An undistorted reading of *Sacrosanctum Concilium* of Vatican II is not only a prerequisite for any discussion of liturgy and politics but also the first vaccine against any temptation to misuse religion as *instrumentum regni*—especially today, the dawn of the twenty-first century, when Roman Catholicism seems to be for some an ideological and geopolitical option rather than a witness to the Gospel call to unity among Christians and between Christians and humanity.

4.2. *Rapprochement* within the Church

Vatican II was a great event of *rapprochement* within the Church, a Church that had become bigger and more diverse between the Council of Trent and the twentieth century. The experience of the council made the bishops converge on the idea that the liturgical movement and the liturgical reform were responding to the signs of the time. As Cardinal Giacomo Lercaro (archbishop of Bologna) noted, the principle of liturgical adaptation "is in line with the missionary work inspired by Benedict XV, and today even more urgent in this moment in history, when different peoples pursue cultural and civil development."[26] Many bishops and groups of bishops experienced at Vatican II a Church that they did not know before, and that changed their minds, beginning with their ideas about the liturgical reform. Yves Congar recalled an exchange with the Dominican French liturgist Pierre-Marie Gy: "[Father Gy] tells me that the atmosphere of the council has an impact: entire episcopates (USA, for example, or South Africa) have changed a lot already in fifteen days."[27]

---

[25] See Massimo Faggioli, "Il Vaticano II come 'costituzione' e la 'recexione politica' del concilio," *Rassegna di Teologia* 50 (2009): 107–22.

[26] Cardinal Giacomo Lercaro (Bologna) in *Acta Synodalia*, vol. 1, bk. 1, 312 (October 22, 1962).

[27] Yves Congar, *Journal du concile*, 144 (entry of October 23, 1962): "[Le P. Gy] est plus que jamais dans son rôle de négociateur. Il me dit que l'atmosphere du concile

"The liturgy is the summit toward which the activity of the Church is directed; it is also the fount from which all her power flows" (SC 10). Liturgy as "the summit" is one of the "non-definitive definitions" of liturgy in *Sacrosanctum Concilium*, and at the same time it is a graphic description of the movement supposedly created by the new liturgy within the Church. The new drive toward this summit—the Eucharist celebrated in the liturgy of the Christian community—is meant to create "through Christ, the Mediator, [. . .] ever more perfect union[28] with God and each other, so that finally God may be all in all" (SC 48).

In the liturgical constitution, the idea of *rapprochement* in Christian life has both social and anthropological features. Liturgy is not meant to be the only occasion for spiritual life (SC 12), but liturgical prayer is also defined as "prayer with others" according to a "style."[29] In this sense, it is clear that liturgy is not primarily "public" or "private" but an act of the *community* whose center is the Eucharist and not a predetermined setting of social norms or a "civil religion." The liturgy of Vatican II is a liturgy for a "post-Durkheimian" Church.[30] The opposition to the liturgical reform is only another form of nostalgia for a Christendom for which the *Feindbild*, the idea of "enemy," was key in order to maintain internal order.[31]

Rapprochement in the Church through the Eucharist means getting rid of other mechanisms of social, cultural, and aesthetical cohesion.

---

agit: des épiscopats (USA par example ou Sud-Afrique) ont changé beaucoup déjà en quinze jours."

[28] To appreciate the riches of the English translation and its resonant character with the opening lines of the Constitution of the United States of America, see the Latin: "Una cum ipso offerentes, seipsos offerre discant, et de die in diem consummentur, Christo Mediatore, in unitatem cum Deo et inter se, ut sit tandem Deus omnia in omnibus."

[29] For the issue of the "style" of Catholicism, see John W. O'Malley, "The Style of Vatican II," *America* (February 24, 2003). For a theological perspective on dialogue as "style of Christianity" see Christoph Theobald, *Le Christianisme comme style. Une manière de faire de la théologie en post-modernité*, 2 vols. (Paris: Cerf, 2007).

[30] See Charles Taylor, *A Secular Age* (Cambridge, MA: Harvard University Press, Belknap Press, 2007), 505–35.

[31] See *I nemici della cristianità*, ed. Giuseppe Ruggieri (Bologna: Il Mulino, 1997); Jean Flori, *La guerre sainte: la formation de l'idee de croisade dans l'occident chretien* (Paris: Aubier, 2001); Paul Alphandéry and Alphonse Dupront, *La Chrétienté et l'Idée de Croisade* (Paris: Albin Michel, 1954); *"Gott mit uns". Nation, Religion und Gewalt im 19. und frühen 20. Jahrhundert*, ed. Gerd Krumeich and Hartmut Lehmann (Göttingen: Vandenhoeck & Ruprecht, 2000).

Bible and Eucharist are the filters for the liturgical *rapprochement* according to *Sacrosanctum Concilium*. The connection expressed in the liturgical constitution between the eucharistic dimension of the Church and the new centrality of the Bible in the liturgy and in the spiritual life of the faithful makes possible the statement that "liturgy by its very nature is far superior to" devotions (SC 13); the centrality of the Eucharist is not only superior to the spiritual and cultural particularism of devotions but also more effective in creating the union with God and in fostering the communion of its people. The desire that "the faithful should be led to that full, conscious, and active participation in liturgical celebrations which is demanded by the very nature of the liturgy" (SC 14) is consequent with the aspiration to a unity of a people celebrating as a whole—as an assembly and as individuals, according to an "active participation, both internal and external" (SC 19). If we eliminate from liturgy the concept of active participation, what remains is mostly adoration.

Rapprochement also works for the physical presence of the people gathered: "To promote active participation, the people should be encouraged to take part by means of acclamations, responses, psalms, antiphons, hymns, as well as by actions, gestures and bodily attitudes. And at the proper time a reverent silence should be observed" (SC 30). Thus, the new liturgy represents not an accommodation to modern times but the way to *rapprocher* the different dimensions of human life and to foster among the faithful the tangible effects of the communion celebrated through the Eucharist during the liturgy.

The drive to *rapprochement* through the liturgical reform also works internally, within the local Church, where the bishop is the center of liturgical unity of the Christian community: "The bishop is to be considered as the High Priest of his flock from whom the life in Christ of his faithful is in some way derived and dependent" (SC 41). The liturgical aspects of the role of the bishops express the emphasis of Vatican II on the local/particular Church—far beyond the direct statements of *Lumen Gentium* about the universal dimension of episcopal collegiality. The first *rapprochement* elaborated by Vatican II was aimed at the local Churches and operated by the bishops in their dioceses before and more concretely than the long and not yet finished debate about the possible forms of expressions of "collegial" unity between the bishops and the bishop of Rome. The constitution on the liturgy emphasizes the centrality of the local Church in its actual realization in the parish: the idea of *actuosa participatio* (SC 41) connects with the role of the Eucharist in the Church (SC 42), together with the representation of the local Church gathered around the bishop in *Lumen Gentium* 26, the role of the clergy in *Lumen Gentium* 28, and the idea of the local Church as *portio populi Dei* in the conciliar decree on the pastoral ministry of the bishops, *Christus Dominus* 11.[32]

Without neglecting the fundamental importance of the debate about collegiality, it is clear that *rapprochement* has had a very tangible effect in shaping the post–Vatican II Church. The *rapprochement* expressed in the liturgical reform is made visible by the dialogical structure of every celebration and the appeal—made in the liturgy—to the five senses of the human being, in a call to a unity between the diverse dimensions of the existential life, but also in a call to the community as a whole as the "bearer" of liturgy.[33]

Rapprochement requires and fosters "active participation," and this asks for accessible rites, not only from a linguistic point of view, but also through the senses. From here, the idea of recentering the local Christian community close to its bishops is clear. In an attitude of adaptation, according to which "the regulation of the liturgy within certain defined limits belongs also to various kinds of bishops' conferences, legitimately established, with competence in given territories" (SC 22.2), the liturgical constitution keeps in mind the need for diversity in unity: "As far as possible, notable differences between the rites used in adjacent regions should be avoided" (SC 23). In the liturgical constitution the emphasis on the bishop and the ecclesiology of the local Church does not represent the revenge of the old elite (the bishops) in the life of Catholicism after Vatican I (which empowered the pope with new authority in the Church), but the awareness that the personal dimension of community takes place in a local Church presided over by a bishop in communion with the bishop of Rome and with its presbyterium and the people of God. The new ecclesiological balance of the liturgical constitution does not aim at an institutional revolution but expresses the possibility of a more *rapproched* Church in the light of the liturgical Tradition (capital T) of the Catholic Church.[34]

[32] See Giampietro Ziviani, *Una Chiesa di popolo. La parrocchia nel Vaticano II* (Bologna: EDB, 2011), 11.

[33] See Kaczynski, *Kommentar*, 201–10.

[34] See Yves Congar, *Tradition and Traditions: An Historical and a Theological Essay* (New York: Macmillan, 1966).

According to *Sacrosanctum Concilium*, the centripetal force of the Church is no longer a Rome-centered governance (also for liturgical matters); it is, rather, the idea that the Church is the "sacrament of unity" (SC 26), in which liturgy "performs" communion and unity both in the Church and beyond the boundaries of the Church. According to this internal *rapprochement*, the liturgical constitution displays at the same time the need for a declericalization of the liturgy (if not yet of the Church) and the theological roots for the priority of the communitarian celebration of liturgy.[35] The liturgical constitution does not challenge the tradition that there are different roles and functions within the Church regarding the liturgy, but it does assume the idea of the common priesthood of the faithful. In the liturgical constitution the idea of *rapprochement* in the local Church is connected with the Eucharist as *sacramentum unitatis*: "The Sunday Eucharist is the ultimate test of the Christian community, because if a minimum level of personal adherence to God's mercy is enough to save a believer, the *repraesentatio ecclesiae* requires much more."[36]

One of the consequences of the liturgical reform in the direction of *rapprochement* is the essential feature of the rediscovery of the role of the liturgical assembly as an "integral player of the liturgical act."[37] The Church is no longer primarily an idea; it is a real gathering.[38] And yet, "the liturgy of Vatican II is the image of what the Church aspires to be: not of what the Church is, but of what the Church aspires to be."[39] In fact, one of the most important implications of the liturgical reform for *rapprochement* in the Church is the notion that "participation" must be extended to other fields in the life of the Church: *leitourgia*,

---

[35] See Kaczynski, *Kommentar*, 92.

[36] Ziviani, *Una Chiesa di popolo*, 152.

[37] In the words of Yves Congar, "sujet integral de l'action liturgique." See Yves Congar, "L'Ecclesia ou communauté chrétienne, sujet intégral de l'action liturgique," in *La liturgie après Vatican II. Bilans, etudes, prospective*, ed. Jean-Pierre Jossua and Yves Congar (Paris: Cerf, 1967), 242–82; English translation: "The Ecclesia or Christian Community as a Whole Celebrates the Liturgy," in Yves Congar, *At the Heart of Christian Worship: Liturgical Essays of Yves Congar*, trans. and ed. Paul Philibert (Collegeville, MN: Liturgical Press, 2010), 15–68.

[38] See Laurent Villemin, "Principes ecclésiologiques de la réforme liturgique de Vatican II," *Lumière et Vie* 279 (Juillet–Septembre 2008): 71–79, esp. 74.

[39] Arnaud Join-Lambert, "Richesses de Vatican II à (re)découvrir," in *Questions liturgiques—Studies in Liturgy* 91, nos. 1–2 (2010): 42–63, quotation at 63.

diakonia, martyria, Church governance, teaching.[40] Here we find the foundation for the preeminence given to the liturgy celebrated by the community over that celebrated by the individual: "It must be emphasized that rites which are meant to be celebrated in common, with the faithful present and actively participating, should as far as possible be celebrated in that way rather than by an individual and quasi-privately" (SC 27).

This *rapprochement* is founded on the very idea of a fundamental unity of the people of God, which has to be expressed and strengthened through the liturgy: "In the liturgy, apart from the distinctions arising from liturgical function or sacred orders and apart from the honors due to civil authorities in accordance with liturgical law, no special exception is to be made for any private persons or classes of persons whether in the ceremonies or by external display" (SC 32).

But the fundamental move of the liturgical constitution in the direction of *rapprochement* in the Church is in stressing the nature of the Church as an extension of the mission of Jesus Christ. Here we have the connection between ecclesiology and Christology in the constitution. Giving centrality back to the liturgy means restoring, in a theologically transparent way, the understanding of the relationship between Church and liturgy and giving way to the liturgy as a *rapprochement* to its real center, the liturgy being "the line of *continuation* between the time of the Church and the time of Christ."[41] Liturgy is the ultimate source of *rapprochement* in the Church because it stresses the nature of the celebration as the time and place for a *community*, not for a sum of individuals, that meets Christ in the Eucharist.

The liturgical reform of Vatican II made a clear option for putting to an end the class-based legacy of Christendom when liturgy mirrored not only the culture of dominant Catholicism but also social and status differences between the wealthy and the poor, thus legitimizing and justifying the different roles played in the Church by the wealthy and the poor (bishops' appointments, lifestyle of the clergy, separate pews and separate liturgical services for wealthy and poor) in and through

[40] See the intervention of Cardinal Joseph Ritter (St. Louis, Missouri) of October 23, 1962, who during the debate on the liturgical reform reminded the assembly of the need to update the ways and forms of ministry in the Church; in *Acta Synodalia*, vol. 1, bk. 1, 351–53.

[41] See Pietro Damiano Scardilli, *I nuclei ecclesiologici nella costituzione liturgica del Vaticano II* (Roma: Pontificia Università Gregoriana, 2007), 176.

the liturgy.[42] But along with these "communitarian" sensibilities, the liturgical constitution also stresses the importance of the unity of the local Church through liturgy, which is not seen as a closed-door performance for initiates to be staged in pseudo-sectarian settings.[43]

The *rapprochement* expressed by the liturgical constitution, far from being the attempt of a small elite of liturgists trying to force their ideas about the liturgy into the Catholic Church, showed the need to rediscover the original and nonderivative nature of the liturgical language. Its purity is functional to the need to re-source the Church with the center of the Christian message.

4.3. Liturgy and Ecumenical *Rapprochement*

The role of the liturgy and eucharistic ecclesiology in paving the ecumenical way were emphasized in the debate on the liturgical constitution: "One of the best gifts of the Conciliar liturgical renewal was its ecumenical consciousness that had not been so acutely present in the years that preceded it."[44] Far from being an indirect contribution to the formation of the liturgical constitution, the ecumenical movement provided the liturgical debate with powerful insights.

The Italian archbishop of Catanzaro (southern Italy) in his intervention of October 23, 1962, affirmed: "Given that this liturgical constitution will be promulgated by an ecumenical council, the constitution has to be a 'magna carta' for every expert in the field of liturgy [. . .] and that means underlining the link between faith and liturgy. [. . .] In our world today it is of the utmost importance to seek unity through liturgy."[45] In his intervention on November 18, 1963, in the name of some other bishops of the United States, Cardinal Joseph Ritter (archbishop of St. Louis, Missouri) stressed that the Eucharist is sign and

---

[42] For an example of the change between the "class system" of burial liturgies to the post–Vatican II era, see Luc Perrin, *Paris à l'heure de Vatican II* (Paris: Éditions de l'Atelier, 1997).

[43] For the critical issue of liturgical practices in some post–Vatican II Catholic movements, see Massimo Faggioli, *Breve storia dei movimenti cattolici* (Roma: Carocci, 2008); Spanish-language edition: *Historia y evolución de los movimientos católicos. De León XIII a Benedicto XVI* (Madrid: PPC Editorial, 2011).

[44] Keith F. Pecklers, *Worship: A Primer in Christian Ritual* (Collegeville, MN: Liturgical Press, 2003), 114.

[45] Archbishop Armando Fares (Catanzaro, Italy) in *Acta Synodalia*, vol. 1, bk. 1, 353 (October 23, 1962).

cause for the Church's unity and emphasized the role of the liturgical movement in the history of Catholic ecumenism: "The meaning of the liturgy and of its renewal in the life of the Church are of great ecumenical importance and this needs to be declared explicitly in this document [*de Oecumenismo*]."[46]

It is not off the mark to say that the liturgical constitution, with its truly ecumenical stress on baptism and Eucharist for the understanding of the Church, serves the ecumenical aims of Vatican II no less than the ecclesiological constitution.[47] The introduction to *Sacrosanctum Concilium* (SC 1) states the aims of Vatican II: renewal of the liturgy, adaptation of what can be changed, creation of unity among Christians and humankind.

It is easy to see that the ecumenical intention constitutes one of the main pillars of the ecclesiology of the liturgical reform and also that the solemn declaration of the introduction has a direct ecumenical purpose.[48] The appealing (especially for the Orthodox Churches) role of liturgy as summit of the activity of the Church impressed the non-Catholic observers as a powerful "conversion" from more recent and divisive theological traditions and "schools" of second-millennium and confessional Catholicism. The emphasis (dear to the Protestant Churches) on the unity of Scripture and Tradition constitutes two ecumenically crucial, yet overlooked, contributions of *Sacrosanctum Concilium* to the ecumenical *rapprochement* expressed by Vatican II. But the liturgical constitution expresses one of the basic ideas of Catholic ecumenism come to new life after the condemnation of ecumenism in

[46] See *Acta Synodalia*, vol. 2, bk. 5, 536–37. See also Claude Soetens, "The Ecumenical Commitment of the Catholic Church," in *History of Vatican II*, vol. 3: *The Mature Council, Second Period and Intercession, September 1963–September 1964* (Maryknoll, NY: Orbis; Leuven: Peeters, 2000), 270–71; and Congar, *Journal du Concile*, vol. 1, 541 (entry of November 18, 1963). Ritter would return to the Eucharist as source and true center of unity between the Churches in his intervention on November 25, 1963; see Nicholas A. Schneider, *Joseph Elmer Cardinal Ritter: His Life and Times* (St. Louis, MO: Liguori Publications, 2008).

[47] See Dossetti, *Chiesa eucaristica*, 44–61.

[48] For the overall ecumenical debate within the Catholic Church before the council and at Vatican II, see Étienne Fouilloux, *Les catholiques et l'unité chrétienne du 19. au 20. siècle. Itinéraires européens d'expression française* (Paris: Le Centurion, 1982); Mauro Velati, *Una difficile transizione: il cattolicesimo tra unionismo ed ecumenismo (1952–1964)* (Bologna: Il Mulino, 1996); Mario Velati, ed., *Dialogo e rinnovamento. Verbali e testi del segretariato per l'unità dei cristiani nella preparazione del concilio Vaticano II (1960–1962)* (Bologna: Il Mulino, 2011), 409–37.

Pius XI's encyclical *Mortalium Animos* (1928).[49] Following the spirit of the late Dom Lambert Beauduin, at Vatican II Catholicism began to understand the deep connections between liturgy and ecumenism, between liturgical movement and ecumenical movement. In the words of the French ecumenist Paul Couturier, "l'un est l'aboutissement de l'autre" ("one is the outcome of the other").[50]

Theological *ressourcement* on one side and a further development of the ecclesiology of Pius XII's *Mystici Corporis* on the other played a major role in making the liturgical constitution able to express the image of the Church in ecumenical terms:

> The Church is essentially both human and divine, visible but endowed with invisible realities, zealous in action and dedicated to contemplation, present in the world, but as a pilgrim, so constituted that in her the human is directed toward and subordinated to the divine, the visible to the invisible, action to contemplation, and this present world to that city yet to come, the object of our quest. (SC 2)

Many elements signal not only a shift in Catholic ecclesiology but also the direction of this shift in a clearly ecumenical context: the new centrality of the mystery of Christ in Catholic spirituality; the idea of the Church as *Ursakrament*; the definition of the Church as visible and invisible, human and divine.[51] This shift was intentional and not casual in the minds of the council fathers. The acceptance of the idea of a necessary mix of "sound tradition" and "legitimate progress" (SC 23) for the sake of the liturgical reform indicates overcoming the idea from the Counter-Reformation of the unchangeability of the Church and its liturgy. In SC 50 the same attitude toward a polemical-apologetical "confessionalization of liturgy" and the liturgical aesthetics that took place during the last four centuries of anti-Protestant polemics is clearly visible: "the rites are to be simplified, due care being taken to preserve their substance. Parts which with the passage of time came to be duplicated, or were added with little advantage, are to be omitted. Other parts which suffered loss through accidents of

---

[49] See James F. Puglisi, ed., *Liturgical Renewal as a Way to Christian Unity* (Collegeville, MN: Liturgical Press, 2005).

[50] See Loonbeek and Mortiau, *Un pionnier*, vol. 1, 576.

[51] See Kaczynski, *Kommentar*, 54.

history are to be restored to the vigor they had in the days of the holy Fathers, as may seem useful or necessary" (SC 50).

The awareness of historicity of the Church implies not only the duty of remembering but also the chance to heal the wounds suffered through "accidents of history." Crusader mind-set, religious wars, spiritualization of the interconfessional polemics, and "theology of the enemy" had penetrated Catholic liturgy, especially in the last five centuries of the second millennium, due to the opposition between Rome and, first, the Lutheran Reform and the clash with the Muslim Turks in southern and central Europe and, after, with secularization.[52] The simplification of the rites of the liturgy at Vatican II was supposed to get rid of the devotions burdened with the yoke of historical contrapositions and restore liturgy to its original spiritual flavor in a spirit of dialogue between sound tradition and modern culture.

Strange as it may seem, the ecumenical implications of *Sacrosanctum Concilium* are not the fruit of a late, post–Vatican II interpretation of the constitution. During the liturgy debate, many fathers expressed the ties between liturgical reform and the ecumenical intention of Vatican II. On October 30, 1962, Bishops Bernard Alfrink, Augustin Bea, and Jean-Julien Weber, for example, supported the proposal to restore Communion under both species because it could be beneficial for ecumenical dialogue. Cardinal Alfrink, the archbishop of Utrecht, said that "in this ecumenical moment, the introduction of Communion under the two species is not without importance."[53] Cardinal Bea added that already "Paul III in 1548 conceded the chalice in Germany to everybody willing to acknowledge the eucharistic presence in both species. [. . .] I do not need to add further to what Cardinal Alfrink said about the ecumenical importance of such a decision."[54] The retired archbishop of Strasbourg, Weber, affirmed that Communion under both species would demonstrate that the Catholic Church "does not reject this venerable tradition that has been maintained by the Eastern Churches."[55]

---

[52] See *Santi, culti, simboli nell'età della secolarizzazione (1815–1915)*, ed. Emma Fattorini (Torino: Rosenberg & Sellier, 1997); Marina Caffiero, *La politica della santità. Nascita di un culto nell'età dei Lumi* (Bari: Laterza, 1996); *Les usages politiques des fêtes aux XIX–XX siècles*, ed. Alain Corbin, Noëlle Gérôme, Danielle Tartakowsky (Paris: Publications de la Sorbonne, 1994).

[53] *Acta Synodalia*, vol. 1, bk. 2, 17.

[54] *Acta Synodalia*, vol. 1, bk. 2, 24.

[55] *Acta Synodalia*, vol. 1, bk. 2, 79.

The ecumenical dimension of the liturgy debate was not as secondary as it has been judged by some recent commentators on the liturgical reform of Vatican II. The participation of the ecumenical observers to the theological and liturgical dimension of Vatican II is a key feature for the understanding of the relationship between liturgical reform and *rapprochement*.[56] The Lutheran theologian André Birmelè affirmed about the ecumenical observers at the council: "Their presence contributed undeniably to the new ecumenical awareness of the Catholic Church at Vatican II and influenced the work of the council."[57] The liturgical reform was welcomed by ecumenical observers such as Karl Barth (1886–1968) and even by the Orthodox theologian Olivier Clément (1921–2009), who saw in the reform an example for the Orthodox liturgy, in which the faithful assume a mere "passive role."[58]

The liturgical reform was nothing less than the realization of the aspirations of the council for a renewed form of public Church prayer in line with the theological development of the Catholic understanding of the relationship in the *oikumene*. In the words of Cipriano Vagaggini, "The Constitution reflects the more profound tendencies which were then manifested in the Council. During the writing of the Constitution, a mixed group that represented the Secretariate for the Union of Christians and another group that represented the liturgical commission held several joint meetings."[59] Differently enough from recently

[56] See Douglas Horton, *Vatican Diary*, 4 vols. (Philadelphia, PA: United Church Press, 1964–66); Giuseppe Alberigo, "Ecclesiologia in divenire. A proposito di Concilio pastorale e di Osservatori a-cattolici al Vaticano II," in Alberigo, *Transizione epocale*, 325–50.

[57] André Birmelè, "Le Concile Vatican II vu par les observateurs des autres traditions chrétiennes," in *Volti di fine concilio: Studi di storia e teologia sulla conclusione del Vaticano II*, ed. Joseph Dorè and Alberto Melloni (Bologna: Il Mulino, 2000), 225–64, quotation at 230; also, Mauro Velati, "Gli osservatori del Consiglio Ecumenico delle Chiese al Vaticano II," in *L'evento e le decisioni. Studi sulle dinamiche del concilio Vaticano II*, ed. Maria Teresa Fattori and Alberto Melloni (Bologna: Il Mulino, 1997), 189–257.

[58] See Olivier Clément, "Vers un dialogue avec le catholicisme," *Contacts* 14 (1965): 16–37, esp. 37; and Karl Barth, "Thoughts on the Second Vatican Council," in *Ad Limina Apostolorum: An Appraisal of Vatican II*, trans. Keith R. Crim (Richmond, VA: John Knox Press, 1968), 70. George Lindbeck provides a more critical position in "Liturgy: Summit and Source," in *The Future of Roman Catholic Theology: Vatican II—Catalyst for Change* (Philadelphia, PA: Fortress Press, 1970), 51–75.

[59] Cipriano Vagaggini, "Fundamental Ideas of the Constitution," in *The Liturgy of Vatican II: A Symposium*, ed. William Baraúna, English ed. by Jovian Lang, 2 vols. (Chicago: Franciscan Herald Press, 1966), 95–129, quotation at 125.

published skeptical portrayals of the liturgical movement vis-à-vis Vatican II, the ecumenical aim was fully shared by the overwhelming majority of the council, and it was equally one of the major arguments in the drafting and discussions to which those appealed who wished to introduce a wider use of vernacular in the Roman liturgy and to restore Communion under both forms as well as concelebration:[60]

> Notable is the importance given in the Constitution to readings, to solemn proclamations and to preaching the word of God contained in the scriptures together with the celebration of the sacrifice and the sacraments. [. . .] In all these points, the ecumenical aim made no small contribution. Especially in giving more liturgical importance to the Bible, the Council thereby wished to remove every pretext for the accusation that would like to see in Catholic worship a lack of perfect proportion between the celebration of the sacramental rites and the proclamation of the Word of God.[61]

Vatican II meant the beginning of an effort at composing common translations, especially in the English-speaking world.[62] But the new role of the Bible in Catholic liturgy meant not only a new and ecumenical approach to the relationship between the faithful and Scriptures but also a new consciousness of the complexity of the relationship between the Church and the Jews.[63]

4.4. Liturgy and the New Relationship with the Jews

In the rediscovery of the Old Testament as part of Christian liturgy,[64] the liturgical constitution of Vatican II expressed the idea that the his-

---

[60] See Mathijs Lamberigts, "The Liturgy Debate," in *History of Vatican II*, vol. 3, 107–66; Jean-Marie Tillard, "La réforme liturgique et le rapprochement des églises," in *Liturgia, opera divina e umana. Studi sulla riforma liturgica offerti a S. E. Mons. Annibale Bugnini in occasione del suo 70° compleanno*, ed. Pierre Jounel, Reiner Kaczynski, and Gottardo Pasqualetti (Roma: CLV–Edizioni Liturgiche, 1982), 215–40.

[61] Vagaggini, "Fundamental Ideas of the Constitution," 95–129, quotation at 125.

[62] See James F. Puglisi, "Introduction," in *Liturgical Renewal as a Way to Christian Unity*, ed. James F. Puglisi (Collegeville, MN: Liturgical Press, 2005), vii–ix.

[63] See Riccardo Burigana, *La Bibbia nel concilio. La redazione della costituzione "Dei Verbum" del Vaticano II* (Bologna: Il Mulino, 1998); Ronald D. Witherup, *Scripture:* Dei Verbum (Mahwah, NJ: Paulist Press, 2006).

[64] See Josef A. Jungmann, *The Mass of the Roman Rite: Its Origins and Development*, trans. Francis A. Brunner, rev. Charles K. Riepe (Westminster, MD: Christian

tory of salvation is a prism whose "rays come from the Old Testament and especially from Christ and reach out toward the heavenly Jerusalem." [65]

Rapprochement with the Jews is also expressed in *Sacrosanctum Concilium* through the *rapprochement* of Catholic tradition with the Word of God. This implies a theological impossibility to rescind the ties between the liturgical constitution and the constitution on revelation, *Dei Verbum*, and says a lot about the dire consequences of a rejection of the liturgical reform of Vatican II for the Catholic Church in the twenty-first century. Scriptural proclamation in the liturgy has a hermeneutics of its own. The liturgical reform is to be understood in deep connection with *Dei Verbum* and the fundamental idea of a unity between the Hebraic Scriptures and the New Testament. [66]

The importance of *Sacrosanctum Concilium* for the *rapprochement* with the Jews lies in the fact that the liturgical reform of Vatican II made a step forward in comparison to the liturgical reforms of Pius XII, not just in terms of the "quantity" of reforms enforced, but in terms of intimate connections between the issue of "change" in the Church (liturgy included) and the unfolding of a deep theological debate on the relations between the Church and the Jews. That is why every step back, or deviation, or second thought about the liturgical reform of Vatican II puts at risk much more than merely the way of performing liturgical ceremonies and has consequences even more dire than the restoring of the prayer *pro Iudaeis*. [67]

The whole concept of the liturgical reform proposed by *Sacrosanctum Concilium* is founded on a new approach to the Bible and a close connection between the Bible, liturgical renewal, and *ressourcement*. [68] The ties between a more confident contact with the Bible in the liturgy and the push for a "full, conscious, and active participation in liturgical

---

Classics, 1959), 260–62; original German: *Missarum solemnia. Eine genetische erklärung der römischen Messe* (Wien: Herder, 1949).

[65] Vagaggini, "Fundamental Ideas of the Constitution," 95–129, quotation at 112.

[66] See Dossetti, *Chiesa eucaristica*, 95.

[67] In response to the Statement of the Discussion Group "Jews and Christians" of the Central Committee of German Catholics: The Disruption to Christian-Jewish Relations by the Re-establishment of the Tridentine Rite (February 29, 2008), the statement of the Vatican Secretariat of State (April 4, 2008) mentions *Nostra Aetate*, *Lumen Gentium*, and *Dei Verbum*, but strangely enough it does not mention *Sacrosanctum Concilium*.

[68] See Jean Daniélou, *The Bible and the Liturgy* (Notre Dame, IN: University of Notre Dame Press, 1956).

113

celebrations" (SC 14) also necessarily produce a new emphasis on the need to read the Scriptures through the lens of the historical-critical method. Thus, the liturgical reform implies reconsideration, in the liturgy and through the liturgy, of the relationship between the Church and the Jews.[69]

This *rapprochement*, which is grounded in the theological identity and the spiritual needs of Christians before any historical or political considerations, is inseparable from the stress put by *Sacrosanctum Concilium* on the role of the Bible in liturgy: "The treasures of the Bible are to be opened up more lavishly so that a richer fare may be provided for the faithful at the table of God's word. In this way a more representative part of the sacred scriptures will be read to the people in the course of a prescribed number of years" (SC 51).

This inseparability of liturgical reform, biblical renewal, and new relationship with the Jews is confirmed by the reasons given by *Sacrosanctum Concilium* for a more abundant reading from Scripture in the liturgy—the history of salvation and the connection between God's works in the history of salvation, the mystery of Christ, and the celebration of the liturgy:

> That the intimate connection between rite and words may be apparent in the liturgy:
>
> (1) In sacred celebrations a more ample, more varied, and more suitable reading from sacred scripture should be restored.
>
> (2) The most suitable place for a sermon ought to be indicated in the rubrics, for a sermon is part of the liturgical action whenever a rite involves one. The ministry of preaching is to be fulfilled most faithfully and carefully. The sermon, moreover, should draw its content mainly from scriptural and liturgical sources, for it is the proclamation of God's wonderful works in the history of slavation, which is the mystery of Christ ever made present and active in us, especially in the celebration of the liturgy. (SC 35.1–2)

Sacrosanctum Concilium and its clear affirmation of the unity between the New Testament and the Old Testament is inseparable from *Dei Verbum*, as the new relationship with the Jews brought about by

---

[69] See *The Catholic Church and the Jewish People: Recent Reflections from Rome*, ed. Philip A. Cunningham, Norbert J. Hofmann, and Joseph Sievers (New York: Fordham University Press, 2007); Nostra Aetate: *Origins, Promulgation, Impact on Jewish-Catholic Relations*, ed. Neville Lamdan and Alberto Melloni (Berlin: LIT, 2007).

114

Vatican II is inseparable from the liturgical reform of the council. The liturgical constitution and the liturgical reform of Vatican II represent a fulfillment of and a step beyond the pre–Vatican II liturgical movement: "Eminent figures in the Liturgical Movement, such as Prosper Gueranger or Louis Bouyer, [. . .] wrote prior to the Council and had some very harsh things to say about the Jews, presenting them as a reprobate people, lost and condemned."[70] It is an undisputable fact that Vatican II articulated a new vision of the relationship between Jews and Catholics. The liturgical reform is an integral part of this new vision.

4.5. *Rapprochement* as Style of the Church

The liturgical reform deserves to be seen as a major act of "conversion," of change of direction of the Church toward her very source of life, liturgy as "summit and fount." That is what Cardinal Giacomo Lercaro meant in his December 6, 1962, speech about the need for the Church "to be culturally 'poor,'"[71] meaning that the glorious traditions of Catholicism should not limit the universality of the Church's language, should not divide rather than unite, should not repel many more men and women than they attract and convince.

Before and besides the technical content of the liturgical reform, this drive for a *rapprochement in the Church* and for a *rapprochement* made possible *through the Church* is one of the most fundamental features of the epoch-making shift of Vatican II. It comes as no surprise that during the debate on revelation (November 1962) the style of the liturgical constitution was proposed as a model for the amendments of the next document to be debated by the council.[72]

John O'Malley's insights about "the style of Vatican II" prove to be of the utmost importance for understanding the *rapprochement* expressed by the liturgical constitution. The incipit of *Sacrosanctum Concilium* is highly representative of the new style of council documents, made of words that "imbue Vatican II with a literary unity unique among

---

[70] Rita Ferrone, "Anti-Jewish Elements in the Extraordinary Form," *Worship* 84, no. 6 (November 2010): 498–512, quotation at 505.

[71] See Giuseppe Ruggieri, "Beyond an Ecclesiology of Polemics," in *History of Vatican II*, vol. 2: *The Formation of the Council's Identity, First Period and Intercession, October 1962–September 1963* (Maryknoll, NY: Orbis; Leuven: Peeters, 1997), 345–47.

[72] Bishop Casimiro Morcillo (Zaragoza) in *Acta Synodalia*, vol. 1, bk. 3, 61 (November 14, 1962).

councils." Vatican II was a language-event, whose "style of discourse was the medium that conveyed the message. [. . .] The style is thus values-expressive."[73] The beginning of the liturgical constitution marks, indeed, the "pragmatic" of Vatican II, not through a theoretical description of the liturgy, but through a narrative of the relationship between God and God's people expressed to the faithful in a "linguistical pragmatic."[74]

From the very beginning of the liturgical constitution, Vatican II expresses in its language the desire for a *rapprochement*: "has set out," "adapt," "promote union," "strengthen whatever can help to call all mankind into the Church's fold" (SC 1), "express [. . .] and manifest to others the mystery of Christ" (SC 2). These are the first words of the liturgical constitution, which was the first document to be debated, voted on, and approved by Vatican II after the Message to the World that expressed the determination of the council to be heedful of the world: "We urgently turn our thoughts to all the anxieties by which human beings are afflicted today."[75] Chapter 5 on the liturgical year, for example, abandons the spirit of the *reconquista* typical of medieval Christendom and fosters *rapprochement* through a narrative of God's will for a truly universal salvation, which does not exclude any category or area of humankind from the gift and mercy given by God:[76]

> In the course of the year, moreover, she unfolds the whole mystery of Christ from the incarnation and nativity to the ascension, to Pentecost and the expectation of the blessed hope of the coming of the Lord.
>
> Thus recalling the mysteries of redemption, she opens up to the faithful the riches of her Lord's powers and merits, so that these are in some way made present for all time; the faithful lay hold of them and are filled with saving grace. (SC 102)

---

[73] O'Malley, *What Happened*, 305–7.

[74] See Peter Hünermann, "Zur theologischen Arbeit am Beginn des dritten Millenniums," in *Das Zweite Vatikanische Konzil und die Zeichen der Zeit heute*, ed. Peter Hünermann (Freiburg i.B.: Herder, 2006), 569–93, esp. 580–81.

[75] The Message to the World was approved by the council on October 20, 1962; see *History of Vatican II*, vol. 2, 50; Turbanti, *Un concilio per il mondo moderno*, 119–35; O'Malley, *What Happened*, 99. About the contribution of Chenu to the Message to the World, see Marie-Dominique Chenu, *Notes quotidiennes au Concile: Journal de Vatican II, 1962–1963*, ed. Alberto Melloni (Paris: Cerf, 1995), 59–60.

[76] See Dossetti, *Chiesa eucaristica*, 49.

The liturgical reform of Vatican II thus deploys a deep theological and ecclesiological content. One element of this content of Vatican II is *rapprochement* as a movement toward reconciliation and retrieval of the elements that are in common between different Christian Churches and the Jews. This content was expressed by Vatican II first liturgically and then, in other council documents, with a more clear understanding of the "political" message of theological *rapprochement*: "The politics of power and dominion is to be transformed by the cross into a political *diakonia*. For God's sake the Christian cannot withdraw from politics; for the way of the cross does not slide over this-worldly reality but runs straight through it, with all that ensues from that."[77]

Full of "political" content is the affirmation of SC 26:

> Liturgical services are not private functions but are celebrations of the Church which is the "sacrament of unity," namely, "the holy people united and arranged under their bishops."
>
> Therefore, liturgical services pertain to the whole Body of the Church. They manifest it and have effects upon it. But they also touch individual members of the Church in different ways, depending on their orders, their role in the liturgical services, and their actual participation in them. (SC 26)

The political culture of Vatican II and its ecclesiology—both "local" and "universal" at the same time—reveals in SC 26 the source of its committment: the Eucharist.

The connections between world Church, ecclesiological *ressourcement*, and lessons learned from history formed the political culture of Vatican II. Part of it comes from the liturgical constitution and its complements from other council documents. It is time to rediscover that "the intertextual character of the sixteen documents is therefore the first step in uncovering the paradigm and therefore an essential step in constructing a hermeneutic for interpreting the council." It will thus be possible to appreciate the "political" contribution of the liturgical constitution to the message of Vatican II, through the reform of the "summit and fount" of the life of the Church: "In a world increasingly wracked with discord, hatred, war, and threats of war, the result was a

[77] Schmidt, "Lines of Political Action in Contemporary Liturgy," 13–33, quotation at 29.

message that was counter-cultural while at the same time responsive to the deepest human yearnings. Peace on earth. Good will to men."[78]

The style of the document and the new centrality of liturgy for the Church of Vatican II expresses *rapprochement* in the option, emphasized in the debate by the Melkite Greek bishop of Akka, Maximos V Hakim (November 18, 1962), of the "liturgical way" as a way to open the theological tradition of the Church to an intellectual tradition far broader and deeper than the neoscholastic school: "The ecumenical character of the council invites us not to close the Word of God in particular categories and not to eliminate another *intellectus fidei*."[79]

The pre–Vatican II liturgical movement and the pastoral renewal managed to deliver at Vatican II the need to put forward new texts able to show the connections of the liturgical prayer with the realities of this world: "The restoration of the prayer of the people is the most noteworthy element of this trend. To pray for the actual needs of the Church and the world is to show that one is intimately concerned with political realities, that the word and the sacrament point to the salvation of the world in which we live."[80] That is why a real inculturation of liturgy is crucial to the *rapprochement* called for by the liturgical reform.[81]

[78] O'Malley, *What Happened*, 310–11.

[79] Bishop Maximos V Hakim (Melkite Greek, Akka) in *Acta Synodalia*, vol. 1, bk. 3, 153 (November 17, 1962).

[80] Joseph Gelineau, "Celebrating the Paschal Liberation," 110.

[81] For the "political" content of the liturgy, see "Liturgy: A Spirituality of Human Liberation," in James L. Empereur and Christopher G. Kiesling, *The Liturgy That Does Justice* (Collegeville, MN: Liturgical Press, 1990), 15–38. For the shortcomings of *Sacrosanctum Concilium* with regard to liturgy, justice, and peace, see Paul De Clerck, "La liturgie comme lieu théologique," in *Liturgie lieu théologique*, ed. Paul De Clerck (Paris: Beauchesne, 1999), 125–42.

Chapter 5

Reforming the Liturgy—Reforming the Church

5.1. Liturgy at Vatican II:
Ressourcement–Development–Reform

The liturgical reform was not a surprise of the council, even if the consensus at the council around the fundamental issues of the reform was surprising: Mass, sacraments, calendar, liturgical language and formation, active participation, liturgical music, and liturgical art.[1] The liturgical movement had prepared the Church for Vatican II well before Vatican II was announced in 1959. The consensus about the need for liturgical reform was as bipartisan as it ever was as a debate at the council, but at the beginning of the council the attitude toward the liturgical reform seemed split into two tendencies, as the Dutch theologian Edward Schillebeeckx defined them:

> 1) *Renovatio liturgica* is unnecessary. Status quo.
>
> 2) A *universal* renewal is impossible because needs differ from country to country. (e.g. the disadvantages of the vernacular in a bilingual country). Thus: solution: grant primary competence to the episcopal conferences.[2]

The movement toward a reform of the liturgy implied a change in the Church: "The directives and principles set down in the Constitution amount to a general mobilization of the entire Church."[3] This

---

[1] See Johannes Wagner, *Mein Weg zur Liturgiereform, 1936–1986. Erinnerungen* (Freiburg i.B.: Herder, 1993), 45–77.
[2] Note of October 22, 1962, in *The Council Notes of Edward Schillebeeckx 1962–1963*, ed. Karim Schelkens (Leuven: Peeters, 2011), 8.
[3] Bugnini, *The Reform of the Liturgy*, 48.

general mobilization was founded on some basic principles.[4] First of all, the liturgy, in order to facilitate access to the riches of the mystery of Christ to the faithful and to strengthen their bond of union with the altar, is not *unchangeable*. Therefore, the constitution speaks boldly of a fundamental reform (*instauratio*) of the liturgy. Second, the relationship between the center and the periphery of the Catholic Church shifted, as the liturgical reform renounced the idea of a liturgy that is strictly uniform for all countries. Inculturation is a basic feature in the history of Christianity, and liturgy had made no exceptions. It was time to acknowledge what many bishops in missionary Churches took for granted. Third, if the faithful are expected to participate in the liturgy in a conscious way, it follows that the language enveloping the sacred texts must be made transparent, and the language had to be actualized in harmony with the different situations of a multifaceted reality. Fourth, the liturgical reform is a pastoral reform, fundamentally different from Pius V's reform:

> The last great reform of the liturgy, which was undertaken four hundred years ago, was not primarily of a pastoral character. It was apologetically and historically oriented. [. . .] The liturgical reform of the II Vatican Council also reaches back to old, indeed even older traditions— those in which the liturgy was still to be a living expression of the whole community. In this sense it even repeats the watchword with which Pius V at the time officially introduced the new missal: "the reform is to be carried out according to the norm of the old Fathers" (art. 50). Now, however, the orientation of the reform is wholly pastoral. This return to the past is to be carried out as "advantage or necessity may require." This reform takes a giant step toward the Christian people, in short, it is a pastoral reform.[5]

Vatican II was made through and by *ressourcement* (looking at the past sources of Christian theology), *aggiornamento* (updating for the present), and *development* (preparation for the future).[6] The liturgical constitution and the liturgical reform issued at Vatican II were the first and the major bearers of *ressourcement*, *aggiornamento*, and develop-

---

[4] See Josef Andreas Jungmann, "A Great Gift from God to the Church," in *The Liturgy of Vatican II: A Symposium*, ed. William Baraúna, English ed. by Jovian Lang, 2 vols. (Chicago: Franciscan Herald Press, 1966), 65–70.

[5] Ibid., 69.

[6] See O'Malley, *What Happened*, 37–43.

ment, and that made the liturgical reform the first and most important reform of Vatican II. John O'Malley affirms that "Vatican II falls under the rubric of a reform council,"[7] and the idea of "reform" is indeed intimately connected with the whole history of the liturgical debate at Vatican II; that is why the stakes are so high when it comes to a discussion about a "reform of the reform" of the liturgy of Vatican II.[8]

Strange as it may sound, Vatican II advocated for a strongly "traditional" concept of liturgy, against some "modernist" attempts to freeze the Roman Rite in its most recent forms as shaped by the interconnections between Western European culture and Tridentine Catholic piety. Vatican II decided to reshape liturgy also in order to reshape Bellarmine's ecclesiology and the "modernity" of Tridentine Catholicism.[9] *Sacrosanctum Concilium* is based on the principle of reform as a hermeneutical act of reassumption of the sources of the great tradition of the Church. In this sense, *ressourcement*, reform, and development are closely connected, and proof for that is the short-lived character of some other post–Vatican II institutional reforms that were based on a purely functionalistic and accomodationist mind-set.[10]

Any attempt to undermine the liturgical reform of Vatican II reveals a clearly reductionist view of Vatican II and its epoch-making changes. Liturgy and reform—personal reform as well as institutional reform— are at the very roots of Christian liturgy. More than fifty years ago Gerhart B. Ladner had pointed out the strong relationship between "purity and liturgy in the Christian world, where the liturgy culminates in a unique union between man and God." Vatican II recaptured that spirit of the early liturgies, where, "compared to other ancient mystery religions, the Christian conception of purity and purification is the least ritualistic and the Christian concept of penance is an example."[11]

---

[7] Ibid., 300.

[8] See John Baldovin, *Reforming the Liturgy: A Response to the Critics* (Collegeville, MN: Liturgical Press, 2008).

[9] See *Il concilio di Trento e il moderno*, ed. Paolo Prodi and Wolfgang Reinhard (Bologna: Il Mulino, 1996).

[10] For example, the Synod of Bishops. See Thomas J. Reese, *Inside the Vatican: The Politics and Organization of the Catholic Church* (Cambridge, MA: Harvard University Press, 1996); Antonino Indelicato, *Il sinodo dei vescovi. La collegialità sospesa (1965–1985)* (Bologna: Il Mulino, 2008).

[11] Gerhart B. Ladner, *The Idea of Reform: Its Impact on Christian Thought and Action in the Age of the Fathers* (Cambridge, MA: Harvard University Press, 1959), 296.

Already in 1950 Yves Congar had outlined the ties between liturgical renewal and "true" reform of the Church:

> It is to bring the neo-pagan world baptized in the living substance of liturgical prayer, perhaps [. . .] to find, in line with the tradition and from it, forms of worship that are more accessible. In any event, to get something that is less formal, less tight, less "past" and more *done for* and *done together*: anything that is truly a community prayer.[12]

Strangely enough for the debate unfolding within the walls of post–Vatican II Catholicism, supposedly conflicting between a "progressive" Thomistic theological mind-set and a "conservative" Augustinian worldview,[13] Congar argued that the power of Augustinianism in the Catholic tradition is not in conflict with the need of reform: "All reformism easily will find inspiration in Augustinianism, as the reformist spirit lives on an affirmation of the end beyond all means, the meaning of things beyond their external form."[14]

The link between liturgical reform and reform of the Church, and the need of the former for the latter, is rooted in the fact that the liturgy of Vatican II embodies the spirit for a true "reform within the Church," "reform of the Church," "reform without schism."[15] The history of the liturgical reform of Vatican II shows clearly that the council fathers opted for a "development" and not for a "perfectibility" of liturgy—

---

[12] "Il s'agit de faire entrer les néo-païens baptisés de notre monde dans la substance vivante de la prière liturgique; peut-être aussi [. . .] de retrouver, dans la ligne de la tradition et à partir d'elle, des formes cultuelles qui soient plus accessibles. En toute hypothèse, d'obtenir quelque chose qui soit moins formaliste, moins hermétique, moins 'se passant devant' et davantage *fait pour* et *fait avec*: quelque chose qui soit vraiment la prière d'une communauté" (Yves Congar, *Vraie et fausse réforme dans l'Église* [Paris: Cerf, 1950], 185. See also the English translation: *True and False Reform in the Church*, trans. Paul Philibert [Collegeville, MN: Liturgical Press, 2010]).

[13] See Joseph Komonchak, "Augustine, Aquinas, or the Gospel *sine glossa*? Divisions over *Gaudium et Spes*," in *Unfinished Journey: The Church 40 Years after Vatican II*, ed. John Wilkins (London: Continuum, 2004), 102–18.

[14] "Tout reformisme trouvera facilement son inspiration dans l'augustinisme, puisque l'esprit réformiste vit d'une affirmation de la fin au delà de tous les moyens, du sens des choses au delà de leur forme extérieure" (Congar, *Vraie et fausse réforme*, 225).

[15] See ibid., 333–35.

perfectibility being the driving principle of every schismatic tendency. One of the witnesses of the liturgical movement acutely noted:

> The role of the Council fathers was not to approve a completely finished reform that would be presented to them with all the details, but to establish the general principles and orientations for a reform. The practical application of these principles could be done only after the council. We had to avoid getting lost in the concrete details. Rather, we had to search for the main principles for today's reform of the liturgy in the study of tradition and in pastoral experience.[16]

The open-ended mind-set of the liturgical reform is the very proof of the "ressourced," nonmodernist attitude of Vatican II. But primary evidence of this basic feature of the liturgical reform is the fact that Vatican II was first of all "a sacred gathering"[17] that had, as every liturgical gathering, a synodal feature, open to the "spirit of reform"— personal and spiritual conversion as well as readiness to institutional reform.[18]

In the very beginning of its gathering, in the fall of 1962, Vatican II somehow anticipated and showed its own *mind*, with common prayer on the floor of St. Peter's, regarding the liturgical reform, experiencing its theology well before drafting and amending it. This is why Vatican II has to be considered much more than a legislative assembly[19] and has to be rediscovered liturgically:

> The council does not meet based on the ontological priority to deliberate or to legislate, but, obedient to the call of the Master, meets with Him to pray and glorify the Father for the sacrifice, to sum up in Christ a bit more time and space. [. . .] The liturgy, understood in its proper meaning, is an essential and nuclear part of the council. The council is a liturgical act, joined by both the Sacrament and the Sacrifice.[20]

[16] Bernard Botte, *From Silence to Participation: An Insider's View of Liturgical Renewal* (Washington, DC: Pastoral Press, 1988), 119.

[17] See O'Malley, *What Happened*, 32.

[18] See Peter De Mey, "Church Renewal and Reform in the Documents of Vatican II: History, Theology, Terminology," *The Jurist* 1–2 (2011): 369–99.

[19] See Giuseppe Alberigo, "Sinodo come liturgia?," *Cristianesimo nella Storia* 28, no. 1 (2007): 1–40.

[20] "El Concilio no se reune exclusivamente ni siquiera con prioridad ontologica para deliberar o para legislar, sino que obediente a la llamada del Maestro se reune con El para orar y glorificae al Padre, para realizar el Sacrificio, para recapitular en

If it is true that the Eucharist makes the Church,[21] a liturgical reform that reshapes the form of celebration of the Eucharist represents and anticipates a major reform of the Church:

> The eucharistic assembly, the Church gathered for the celebration of the Eucharist, that is, for the celebration of the paschal mystery, that eucharistic Church is really the Church *simpliciter*, the Church in its purest, most complete act, the Church that summarizes all other elements, all other purposes, all other functions and activities in that liturgical act, and that act takes its innermost being, and is also the model most typical and characteristic of its structure.[22]

But for now only in some circles has it been fully understood that liturgy forms a nuclear part of Vatican II because Vatican II itself was also a liturgical act. Therefore, Vatican II liturgy presupposes a theologically "serious" (that need not be "academic") hermeneutic of the council rooted in the *sensus fidelium*. The issue of "reform" in *Sacrosanctum Concilium* emerges not as a primarily ecclesiological issue but as an anthropological issue, in light of the rediscovery of the primacy of the ritual and symbolic experience in *Sacrosanctum Concilium* (mystery) as well as in *Dei Verbum* (Word), in *Lumen Gentium* (communion), and in *Gaudium et Spes* (dialogue). The anthropology of the liturgical movement was focused on recovering the connection between the internal and external dimension of the faithful—in Thomas Aquinas's terms, *ratio et manus* ("reason and hand"). The anthropology of *Sacrosanctum Concilium* is based on listening to the Word, the ecclesial communion, the opening to the world, and the celebration of the Eucharist.[23]

The recentering around the Eucharist and the liturgy has a significant impact on the future life of the Church, especially in the debate

---

Cristo un trozo màs de tiempo y de espacio [. . .] la liturgia, entendida en su recta acepcion, forma la parte esencial y nuclear del Concilio. El Concilio es un acto liturgico, unido por tanto al Sacramento y al Sacrificio" (Raimon Panikkar, "El concilio come 'misterio,'" *Criterio* [1963]: 167–68).

[21] See Paul McPartlan, *The Eucharist Makes the Church: Henri de Lubac and John Zizioulas in Dialogue* (Edinburgh: T & T Clark, 1993).

[22] Dossetti, *Chiesa eucaristica*, 70.

[23] See Andrea Grillo, "Maschile e/o femminile. Un confronto 'prospettico' tra concilio di Trento e concilio Vaticano II," in *Anatemi di ieri, sfide di oggi. Contrappunti di genere nella rilettura del concilio di Trento*, ed. Antonio Autiero and Marinella Perroni (Bologna: EDB, 2011), 199–212.

between "universal" and "local" ecclesiology and in reshaping the life of the local Churches.[24] The discourse on ministries in the Church is particularly important. *Sacrosanctum Concilium* 29 affirms that "Servers, readers, commentators, and members of the choir also exercise a genuine liturgical function." The reorientation of ecclesiology in light of the liturgical reform must help reorient the discourse on ministry in the Church: "These ministers do not compete with one another in the liturgy but cooperate. [. . .] A careful reading of the conciliar documents reveals that the council avoided the preconciliar emphasis on matters of power and jurisdiction where ministry was concerned."[25] This is where the liturgical reform shows its potential for "reform" in the Church according to the new understanding of the relationship between liturgy and ecclesiology.[26] Despite the overall character of the theological and historical debate about the relationship between the "letter" and the "spirit" of Vatican II, the case of the liturgical reform leaves no room for a strictly "originalist" interpretation of the texts of the council.

5.2. Reform of the Liturgy—Reform from the Liturgy

The recentering of the liturgy around the Eucharist announced by Vatican II set the whole Church in motion toward a movement of reform, but two issues need to be considered to understand the complexity of the connection between liturgy and Church reform.

On the one hand, the dynamics of the reception of Vatican II do not allow for a simple top-down "application" of the council decrees (as it happened for the council of Trent),[27] and the history of post–Vatican II Catholicism shows the shortcomings of such an interpretation of the relationship between the council and the real life of the Church, which has become a global Church.[28]

---

[24] See Gilles Routhier, "La synodalitè de l'église locale," *Studia canonica* 26 (1992): 111–61.

[25] Richard R. Gaillardetz, *Ecclesiology for a Global Church: A People Called and Sent* (Maryknoll, NY: Orbis, 2008), 135–36.

[26] See Henri Chirat, *L'assemblee chrétienne à l'âge apostolique* (Paris: Cerf, 1949).

[27] See Paolo Prodi, *Il paradigma tridentino. Un'epoca della storia della chiesa* (Brescia: Morcelliana, 2010); Vittorio Peri, "Trento: un concilio tutto occidentale," in Vittorio Peri, *Da Oriente a Occidente. Le Chiese cristiane dall'Impero romano all'Europa moderna* (Padova: Antenore, 2002), 397–459.

[28] About this debate see Massimo Faggioli, *Vatican II: The Battle for Meaning* (Mahwah, NJ: Paulist Press, 2012).

On the other hand, we see here a possible tension between the *hic et nunc* of the liturgical act and the long-term "theological project" expressed by the liturgical reform of Vatican II. But this issue is not unique to the liturgy of Vatican II. In the history of liturgy the "eternal" features of Christian worship have always coexisted with the development of theological contents, especially after the council of Trent and in the Baroque period.[29]

There is surely a tension and a nonidentity between the "here and now" of the Eucharist on the one side and the reform of the Church as a "plan" on the other side. But *Sacrosanctum Concilium* not only stated clearly the necessity of the liturgical reform for a more pastoral Church but also made clear the priority of liturgy as a basic element for the reform and the connection between reform of the liturgy and the spiritual-institutional needs of contemporary Catholicism. Recanting the liturgical reform is thus a not-so-subtle way to express not just a set of aesthetic preferences but also a mind-set of personal and institutional unwillingness to walk the path of Church reform.

Despite the differences of the relationships of the two popes of Vatican II with the assembly, both John XXIII and Paul VI had clearly in mind the connection between the liturgical reform and the reform of the Church. On the one side, John XXIII, resisting the pressures coming from some cardinals during the preparatory phase of Vatican II, stressed the importance of beginning every general congregation in St. Peter's with the celebration of the Mass, well aware of the liturgical character of the gathering of the council and of the *aggiornamento*. Most probably, both the very "traditional" Tridentine piety of Angelo Giuseppe Roncalli and his contacts with the Eastern theological and liturgical tradition played a role in the steadiness of his position about the liturgical celebrations during Vatican II.[30] On the other hand, John XXIII was cautious about the change of the liturgical language,

---

[29] See Josef Jungmann, *The Mass of the Roman Rite: Its Origins and Development*, trans. Francis A. Brunner, rev. Charles K. Riepe (Westminster, MD: Christian Classics, 1959), 106–19. More recently, see Andreas Odenthal, *Liturgie vom Frühen Mittelalter zum Zeitalter der Konfessionalisierung: Studien zur Geschichte des Gottesdienstes* (Tübingen: Mohr Siebeck, 2011).

[30] See *Giornale dell'Anima: soliloqui, note e diari spirituali*, ed. Alberto Melloni (Bologna: Istituto per le scienze religiose, 2003); Francesca Della Salda, *Obbedienza e pace. Il vescovo A.G. Roncalli tra Sofia e Roma 1925–1934* (Genova: Marietti, 1989); Angelo Giuseppe Roncalli (John XXIII), *Tener da conto. Le agendine di Bulgaria, 1925–1934*, ed. Massimo Faggioli (Bologna: Fondazione per le scienze religiose, 2008).

as we can read in his private diary during the second week of debate at Vatican II:

> The question of Latin certainly divides those who have never left home or Italy from those of other nations, especially in missionary lands, or who, although Italians, are living and sacrificing themselves in distant parts. On this matter of Latin in the liturgy, it will be necessary to proceed with slow steps and by degrees.[31]

But Roncalli also had a deep sense of the importance of change in the Catholic tradition. An admirer of the reformers of the Church after the council of Trent, John XXIII felt no nostalgia for that era.[32] The very opening celebration of Vatican II showed the need for liturgical renewal and the openness of John XXIII to that renewal, as Edward Schillebeeckx noted:

> No communion, no concelebration. No communal singing, just the Capella Sistina. No "Pax"!! Just a bow from the Pope towards the observers! The altar was invisible to almost everyone. Yet something new: during the Mass, the Pope forbade all the bows and genuflections commonly due to his person to avoid diverting attention from the altar. [. . .] No celebrations, just byzantinism! Need for liturgical renewal demonstrated by such an Opening![33]

On the other side, we cannot overlook the centrality of the process of the liturgical reform during the pontificate of Paul VI. Authoritatively defined "the reformist pope" *par excellence*,[34] but also the pope who reaffirmed the authority of the Roman pontiff and a very personal exercise of his office as a "mystic of the papacy," Paul VI never

---

[31] Angelo Giuseppe Roncalli (John XXIII), *Pater amabilis. Le agende del Pontefice 1958–1963*, ed. Mauro Velati (Bologna: Fondazione per le scienze religiose, 2008), 446, note of October 24, 1962.

[32] See the ten volumes of the *Edizione nazionale dei diari di Angelo Giuseppe Roncalli–Giovanni XXIII*, published by the Istituto per le scienze religiose, Fondazione per le scienze religiose Giovanni XXIII in Bologna between 2004 and 2008; Alberto Melloni, *Papa Giovanni. Un cristiano e il suo concilio* (Torino: Einaudi, 2009); and the seminal work by Angelina and Giuseppe Alberigo, *Giovanni XXIII. Profezia nella fedeltà* (Brescia: Queriniana, 1978).

[33] Note of October 11, 1962, in *The Council Notes of Edward Schillebeeckx*, 3.

[34] See Andrea Riccardi, *Il potere del papa da Pio XII a Giovanni Paolo II* (Roma-Bari: Laterza, 1993), 315.

considered the issues of the liturgical reform, of the reform of the Church, and the "romanocentrism" of his ecclesiology to be in conflict.[35] If it is true that in Paul VI the appreciation of the historicity of the Catholic tradition was not as deep as it was in John XXIII, nevertheless, Paul VI saw the liturgical reform as an authoritative way for the Church to express herself at Vatican II.

The council was the meeting point between the theological work of the theologians of the liturgical movement and the leadership of the bishops, particularly the bishops of Rome, in advancing the liturgical movement. The council fathers and popes embraced the long history of the liturgical movement and worked out the liturgical reform. This embrace was so strong that it survived the reshuffling of the liturgical commission, in favor of a much stronger presence of Roman Curia members, that took place in October 1962. The theological "lift" of the liturgical reform could not be stopped, not even by doubling the Roman members and getting rid of Annibale Bugnini as secretary of the commission.[36]

In his famous speech of September 29, 1963, the newly elected pope, Paul VI, said, "The time has come, it seems to us, when the truth about the Church of Christ must be explored, expressed and orderly, perhaps not with the solemn statements that are called dogmatic definitions, but with those statements with which the Church with more explicit and authoritative magisterium says what it thinks about herself."[37] There is no doubt that the pope was thinking not only about the eccle-

---

[35] See Jean-Pierre Torrell, "Paul VI et l'ecclésiologie de 'Lumen gentium,'" in *Paolo VI e i problemi ecclesiologici al Concilio* (Brescia: Istituto Paolo VI, 1989), 144–86.

[36] See Bugnini, *The Reform of the Liturgy*; see also Maria Paiano, "Les travaux de la commission liturgique conciliaire," in *Les commissions conciliaires à Vatican II*, ed. Mathijs Lamberigts, Claude Soetens, and Jan Grootaers (Leuven: Bibliotheek van de Faculteit Godgeleerdheid, 1996), 7; Henri de Lubac, *Carnets du Concile*, ed. Loïc Figoureux (Paris: Cerf, 2007), 104–5. During the mid-1970s the liturgical reform experienced the first strong oppositions coming from the Roman Curia: on January 4, 1976, the Vatican announced Annibale Bugnini's appointment as pronuncio to Iran. Bugnini was a liturgical scholar and not a diplomat, but during his diplomatic mission to Iran he wrote *La Chiesa in Iran* (Roma: Edizioni Vincenziane, 1981), and, more important, wrote the well-known *La riforma liturgica (1948–1975)* (Roma: CLV-Edizioni liturgiche, 1983; English translation by Matthew J. O'Connell, *The Reform of the Liturgy 1948–1975* [Collegeville, MN: Liturgical Press, 1990]).

[37] "È venuta l'ora, a noi sembra, in cui la verità circa la Chiesa di Cristo deve essere esplorata, ordinata ed espressa, non forse con quelle solenni enunciazioni che si chiamano definizioni dogmatiche, ma con quelle dichiarazioni con le quali la

siological constitution but also about the liturgical constitution that was to be approved in the second conciliar period.

Here, Paul VI was expressing a crucial concept of the idea of the connection between Church and reform at Vatican II: there is no point in repeating the dogmas of the Church without lived experience of Catholicity. Paul VI affirms the need to find a language as close as possible to the Christian experience, not in order to contradict the language of the abstract dogmatic canon of discernment, but in order to deepen the truth. "Language" here is more than the vernacular or Latin. That is why "a reading of Vatican II's Constitution on the Sacred Liturgy shows that the question of liturgical language is not treated anywhere *ex professo.*"[38]

Nevertheless, it was clear that the *incipient* character of the reform of the liturgical language was foreshadowing the character of the reform of the Church after Vatican II. The journal *Worship* prepared for the reception and the translation into action of the liturgical constitution through a long and detailed commentary by Frederick R. McManus.[39] The generally enthusiastic tone of the commentary was otherwise careful in offering a balanced and open-ended interpretation of the text of the constitution, for example, about the use of the vernacular language—an issue that received longer and more detailed comments than any other part of the constitution (twelve pages for SC 36 and twelve pages for SC 54). The interpretation of the passage on liturgical language was clearly directed toward a differentiated application of the documents, depending on the local demands of the liturgical movements:

Chiesa con più esplicito ed autorevole magistero dichiara ciò che essa pensa di sé" (*Acta Synodalia*, vol. 2, bk. 1, 183–200, quotation at 190).

[38] Botte, *From Silence to Participation*, 121. Already in 1957, in his *Il senso teologico della liturgia*, Cipriano Vagaggini had acknowledged that the issue of the language was the most difficult (*Il senso teologico della liturgia. Saggio di liturgia teologica generale* [Roma: Edizioni Paoline, 1957], 733). Along with the introduction of the vernacular, the most disputed question in the debate over the liturgy concerned allowing Communion under both species; see Joseph A. Komonchak, "The Council of Trent at the Second Vatican Council," in *From Trent to Vatican II: Historical and Theological Investigations*, ed. Raymond F. Bulman and Frederick J. Parrella (New York: Oxford University Press, 2006), 65.

[39] See Frederick R. McManus, "The Constitution on Liturgy: Commentary; Part One," *Worship* 38, no. 6 (1964): 314–74; "Part Two," *Worship* 38, no. 8 (1964): 450–98; "Part Three," *Worship* 38, no. 9 (1964): 515–65.

The purpose of this article [36] may be described as the widespread introduction of the vernacular languages, but in such a way as to respect the liberty of those areas where thus far there has not been any broad movement toward the use of the mother tongues. The article appears as a compromise between those who would retain the Latin language in the Roman rite and the other rites of the Western Church, and those who would on principle use the vernacular languages exclusively.[40]

The liturgical reform was an act of reform consciously balancing a decentralized aspect and a centralized one. The decentralized aspect gave more power to the national bishops' conferences about inculturation, translation of the liturgical texts, and adoption of the vernacular language in the liturgy. But the "Catholic reformism" of the liturgical reform was also centralized in character. The liturgical reform was enacted by the Holy See.[41] Thinking that the post–Vatican II liturgical reform "twisted the arm" of Paul VI is not only a grave misunderstanding of his pontificate but also a misinterpretation of the liturgical constitution and its fifty-year-long reception.[42] It was no accident that on November 17, 1962, the council voted overwhelmingly (2,175 yes to 21 no) to eliminate the following from the text of the constitution: "The present Constitution wishes to make no dogmatic definitions." On November 28, 1962, L'Osservatore Romano commented that this elimination was made "perhaps because the Fathers wished greater freedom to reform the liturgy. Instead of merely making a few rubrical changes they wished to touch even some liturgical elements which are not of divine institution."[43]

The liturgical reform of Vatican II acted as a centralized reform trying to defend unity in the diversity of cultures. The council fathers wanted to emphasize "the unity of liturgy in order to emphasize the

[40] McManus, "The Constitution on Liturgy: Commentary; Part One," 350–51.
[41] For the speeches of Paul VI about the liturgical reform, see Bugnini, The Reform of Liturgy, 278–301.
[42] See Piero Marini, A Challenging Reform: Realizing the Vision of the Liturgical Renewal, 1963–1975, ed. Mark R. Francis, John R. Page, and Keith F. Pecklers (Collegeville, MN: Liturgical Press, 2007). See also Paul De Clerck, "La Constitution Sacrosanctum Concilium. Réflexions sur sa réception dans le long terme," Questions Liturgiques 91 (2010): 142–55.
[43] See William Baraúna, "Chronicle of the Amendments of the Constitution," in Baraúna, The Liturgy of Vatican II, vol. 1, 73.

unity of the Paschal Mystery and the unity of the Church: in this sense it is a centralized reform."[44] In other words, it is a profound distortion of the liturgical reform to associate it with a particular "ideological" agenda of Vatican II, because the liturgical reform intended to give back to the Eucharist its powerful voice among the people of God.[45] The liturgical reform assumes the idea of a Church *semper reformanda*, where the Eucharist, not a particular ecclesiological interpretation, is the driving force of the communion. *Sacrosanctum Concilium* affirms God's truly universal will of salvation, which excludes no category or region of humankind, because through the Eucharist the Church can reach the Christ who entered with body and spirit into the dimensions of time and space.[46] *Sacrosanctum Concilium* reforms the liturgy through a rediscovery of the priesthood of Christ in liturgy by means of "tangible signs"—*signa sensibilia*.

The word "participation" recurs sixteen times in the liturgical constitution. The reform of the Church begins here with the maturation of the participation of the faithful in liturgy and the maturation of a fully ecclesial faith, made possible through the liturgical reform. The new statute of the participation in the Eucharist reveals that the liturgical reform is not primarily about a reform of the rites; it is first and foremost about the capacity to reform the space of Eucharist in the life of the Church. The rediscovery of the mystagogical dimension of the "new liturgy" is a potential for reform, because liturgical reform implies not a reform applied to the rites of liturgy but a reform that liturgy promotes through its rites.[47]

That is why the liturgical reform is a driving force for Church reform, much more than any "ecclesiological engineering" often proposed— but in truth never tested—in the first fifty years of post–Vatican II Catholicism.[48] Conversely, the undermining of the liturgical reform of

[44] See Laurent Villemin, "Principes ecclésiologiques de la réforme liturgique de Vatican II," *Lumière et Vie* 279 (Juillet–Septembre 2008): 71–79, quotation at 78.

[45] About ideologies and liturgical reform, see Marcel Metzger, "La réforme liturgique du Concile Vatican II et les idéologies qui résistent," *Revue des Sciences Religieuses* 85, no. 1 (2011): 101–10.

[46] See Dossetti, *Chiesa eucaristica*, 49–51.

[47] See Andrea Grillo, *La nascita della liturgia nel XX secolo. Saggio sul rapporto tra movimento liturgico e (post-) modernità* (Assisi: Cittadella, 2003), 147.

[48] But a study of institutional reform in the post–Vatican II Catholic Church is still much needed, in the wake of Patrick Granfield's *Ecclesial Cybernetics: A Study of Democracy in the Church* (New York: Macmillan, 1973).

Vatican II has a profound impact on the capability of the institution to be more open to the Eucharist and exposes the Church to the reaction of "modernistic" attempts of reform that are very far from the spirit of reform advocated by Vatican II.

5.3. Tradition, Language, and Style in the Liturgical Reform

The recent debate on the liturgical reform has often stressed the "abuses" that took place during the reception and implementation of *Sacrosanctum Concilium*. Much more important for the life of the Church and its intellectual and spiritual history is the extraordinary impact of the liturgical reform on the understanding of the Church and its relationship with a living tradition.

For some bishops at Vatican II it was clear that the liturgical reform had to be framed in the context of the need of the Church to speak to the modern world, as it was emphasized by Cardinal Paul-Émile Léger (archbishop of Montréal): "The need to adapt the liturgy does not come only from the mission countries, but also from the regions of the Western world where, in the last century, a new civilization was born." [49] For the vast majority of the bishops, the guiding principle of the liturgical reform had to be the pastoral need of the Church, not a particular attachment to an idiosyncratic view of the history of liturgy. The cardinal archbishop of Westminster, William Godfrey, explained, not without some "prophetic" insights, the real rationale of the liturgical reform against any kind of historical argument:

> In the debate about the reform of the liturgy the historical argument does not have to be the most important one. If somebody said "These ceremonies were introduced only in the twelfth century," I accept that as an assertion of an historical fact, not as an argument. What we have to consider is the pastoral issue: is it not our goal, here and now, to assess the usefulness and appropriateness of any element for our faithful? Maybe in a future council they will say about our decisions: "This was introduced only in 1962." Would that be a good argument against our resolutions? [50]

---

[49] Cardinal Paul-Émile Léger (archbishop of Montréal), speech of October 23, 1962, in *Acta Synodalia*, vol. 1, bk. 1, 372.

[50] Cardinal William Godfrey (archbishop of Westminster), speech of October 23, 1962, in *Acta Synodalia*, vol. 1, bk. 1, 374.

In his speech of October 24, 1962, Cardinal Eugène Tisserant, dean of the Sacred College of Cardinals and a famous expert in Eastern rites, defended the idea of liturgical translations in languages other than Latin, providing the council fathers with abundant historical examples: Slavonic, Croatian, Slovene, Syriac, etc.[51] The assumption of the legitimacy of liturgical translations of the Roman Rite came not only from Eastern Catholic bishops but also from Roman Rite bishops acquainted with the history of the liturgy.

The attitude of the American bishops during the first and second sessions of the council on the liturgical debate was in favor of the liturgical reform and in general often leaned toward a *via media* regarding the issue of the continuity/discontinuity with the previous liturgical tradition. Positions within an episcopate as large as the United States were diverse. Cardinals Francis Spellman (New York) and James Francis McIntyre (Los Angeles) and Archbishop Paul Hallinan (Atlanta) were clearly on different sides of the debate—Spellman, McIntyre, and Alfredo Ottaviani being among the most vocal opponents of changes to the Order of the Mass and to the Canon. The young Arab Melkite bishop Neophytos Edelby noted:

> We see in the debate two streams: a conservative stream, represented especially by Italian and North American bishops, and a reformist stream, but moderate, represented by the rest of the European bishops and by the missionary bishops. This second stream is likely to prevail.[52]

Already in the preparatory phase of Vatican II, many bishops from the United States had proposed the introduction of the vernacular in the liturgy.[53] But their inclination toward a global reform of the liturgy grew during Vatican II. When, on November 19, 1962, Archbishop Hallinan recruited a significant number of bishops from the United States, it became clear that the majority of the bishops were in favor of the liturgical reform and of the *schema* debated on the floor of

[51] Cardinal Eugène Tisserant, speech of October 24, 1962, in *Acta Synodalia*, vol. 1, bk. 1, 399–400. See also Étienne Fouilloux, *Eugène Cardinal Tisserant (1884–1972). Une biographie* (Paris: Desclée de Brouwer, 2011), 629.

[52] Neophytos Edelby, *Il Vaticano II nel diario di un vescovo arabo*, ed. Riccardo Cannelli (San Paolo: Cinisello Balsamo, 1996), 74 (entry of October 22, 1962).

[53] See, for example, Cardinal Richard Cushing (Boston), in *Acta et Documenta Concilio oecumenico apparando. Series prima (antepraeparatoria)* (Typis Polyglottis Vaticanis, 1960–1961) I,II/6, 283.

St. Peter's.[54] It also became clear that the North American bishops were not "Latin-minded" and that Hallinan represented a wide basis of a Catholic Church waiting and already preparing for this reform.[55]

In general, the very history of the debate on the liturgy at Vatican II shows the disconnect, before Vatican II, between the sentimental attachment to the glorious tradition of the Roman Church and its role in the life of the faithful, the bishops included. Cardinal McIntyre went as far as to affirm that "the challenge to the Latin language in the sacred liturgy is an indirect but real attack against the stability of the sacred dogmas."[56] But the delivery of that speech could not stop theologians like Schillebeeckx from remarking on the inconsistency between the advocacy for Latin and the fluency of the speaker:

> Spellman and McIntyre proclaim that Latin is the *only* liturgical language, but pronounce it in such an Americanised fashion that no one understands them: the worse one's spoken Latin the more one is inclined to favour it. It is a *"status symbol"* of priest-"intellectuals" as opposed to the "idiots."[57]

As a matter of fact, the issue of the Latin and the vernacular language came as no surprise in the debate at Vatican II.[58] Already in December

[54] Hallinan wrote a short text in which he stressed that the bishops of the United States wished to vote on chapter 1 of the *schema* during the first session, and 132 bishops signed the petition; see Mathijs Lamberigts, "The Liturgy Debate," in *History of Vatican II*, vol. 2: *The Formation of the Council's Identity, First Period and Intercession, October 1962–September 1963* (Maryknoll, NY: Orbis; Leuven: Peeters, 1997), 107–66, esp. 153. About Hallinan, see Thomas J. Shelley, *Paul J. Hallinan: First Archbishop of Atlanta* (Wilmington, DE: M. Glazier, 1989).

[55] See Paul J. Hallinan, "An American View," *Worship* 37, no. 8 (1963): 547–50.

[56] Cardinal James McIntyre (archbishop of Los Angeles), speech of October 23, 1962, in *Acta Synodalia*, vol. 1, bk. 1, 370.

[57] Note of October 26, 1962, in *The Council Notes of Edward Schillebeeckx*, 13.

[58] In the archives of letters sent to the liturgical commission in the summer of 1963, there is a letter from the young (born 1917) bishop of Boise (Idaho, USA), Sylvester Treinen: "As one of the Junior Bishops who will be attending the Second Session of the Second Vatican Council in September, I hesitate to make a petition or offer any suggestions. However, perhaps on the other hand it would be unwise for me to remain silent on something which I feel is important. With all due reverence then to Your Eminence [Cicognani, segretario di Stato] and acknowledging my own youth, I would like to say that I would be much in favor of having the Council Fathers be given a chance to vote on a proposition that would allow the priests to have an option of reciting the Divine Office in the vernacular language. I would

1960, during the preparation of the council, the subcommission *de lingua latina* of the liturgical preparatory commission had decided to deal with the issue of the vernacular language, saying that "it is time that Vatican II does what Trent did not do on the basis of the will to condemn the heretics" and affirming that the issue of the liturgical language was a matter of reform—and not a matter of "exceptions" or "indults." In the meeting of the subcommission of February 12, 1961, McManus quoted the *votum* of the Catholic University of America *in favor* of the vernacular:

> Patrum deliberationi proponimus: (a) regulam quae in usu Ecclesiarum Orientalium recepta et pro eis a Sede Apostolica agnita est, ut scil. actiones liturgicae ad incrementum pietatis populi in lingua vernacula celebrentur, ad Ecclesiam Latinam extendendam, versione tamen unaquaque ab auctoritate competenti ecclesiastica approbata.[59]

like to see the priests able to make this choice merely for the sake of their own personal devotion if they felt that this would add to their devotions. Perhaps it is not possible at this date, but I also feel that it would add much to the progress of the sessions of the Council if there were some kind of an instantaneous translation of the speeches into the four or five major languages. I am able to understand the Fathers, when they speak in Latin, if they speak distinctly and slowly. However, it is quite a strain to do this for several hours at a time. I have spoken with many other bishops who feel this same way. With sentiments of deep esteem and with best wishes, I remain very sincerely yours in Christ, Sylvester Treinen" (ASV, Vatican Secret Archives, Concilio Vaticano II, 1384, "Commissio conciliaris—Acta sessionum," letter of August 9, 1963).

[59] "We intend to submit for deliberation of the Fathers: (a) to extend to the Latin Church, in a version approved by the competent ecclesiastical authority, that rule, which has been in use and granted to the Eastern Catholic Churches by the Apostolic See, that allows the Eastern Catholic Churches to celebrate liturgy in the vernacular languages in order to foster the devotion of the faithful." ASV, Vatican Secret Archives, Concilio Vaticano II, 1360. See also the minutes of the meeting of the subcommission "de lingua latina" (Milan, December 10, 1960); present members included Joseph Malula, Lukas Brinkhoff, Frederick McManus, and Pietro Borella (who was taking these notes): "Domini Brinkhoff et McManus, vero, affirmant jam venit plenitudo temporum, et hora est, ut Concilium Vaticanum II hoc faciat, quod Tridentinum non fecit; nec fecit, ratione principii, ut damnaret errorem hereticorum ita expressum: 'linguam tantum vulgari missam celebrari debere'. [. . .] Nec placuit Consultoribus propositio haec: ut, extra linguam latinam, concederetur, singulis in casibus, ad judicium Metropolitarum, de consensu S. Sedis, major usu linguae vulgaris; ita ut mutatio linguae non fiat statim, per revolutionem, sed per gradus, per evolutionem. Juxta Consultores lex deberet esse pro Ecclesia universa et universa liturgia."

During the debate in St. Peter's in October 1962 it was clear that the issue of the liturgical language had evolved: the liturgical reform had become inextricably linked with the biblical movement. That is why the Roman Curia Cardinal Antonio Bacci said that it made no sense to translate the liturgy into the vernacular languages, given the low intellectual level of many of the faithful and the perils lurking in the biblical texts: "For the adolescents especially, reading the Bible might carry doubts and disturbing thoughts," coming, for example, from the story of Susanna or the Song of Songs. Furthermore, in some countries with a history of national or ethnic tensions (Northern Italy, Switzerland, Canada), Cardinal Bacci went further, "We have reason to fear that nationalism and disputes might spill over the altar and touch the eucharistic sacrifice."[60] In the following intervention immediately after Bacci, Cardinal Albert Meyer of Chicago reminded the council fathers that "to be sure, many faithful expect something in this liturgical matter from the Council," first of all in terms of use of the vernacular language.[61]

Cardinal Meyer interpreted the expectations of the vast majority of the council fathers. From a historical point of view, the liturgical reform of Vatican II marks a milestone in the pilgrimage of the Church through history. Cardinal Joseph Ritter of St. Louis reminded the fathers that Trent declared that "the Church always had the power, given changing circumstances, times and places, in administering the sacraments, of making dispositions and changes it judged expedient for the well-being of recipients, or for the reverence due to the sacraments themselves, provided their substance remained intact."[62]

Trent was in the minds of the council fathers, "not only as a set of teachings and laws but also as an event, an example of how the Church could vigorously and comprehensively address serious challenges, if necessary by innovations."[63] Differently from the Council of Trent,

[60] Cardinal Antonio Bacci (Roman Curia), speech of October 24, 1962, in *Acta Synodalia*, vol. 1, bk. 1, 409–10. In 1967 Cardinal Bacci wrote the preface to a pamphlet furiously denouncing the liturgical reform; Tito Casini, *La tunica stracciata. Lettera di un cattolico sulla riforma liturgica*, con prefazione del cardinale Antonio Bacci (Roma: SATES, 1967).

[61] Cardinal Albert Meyer (archbishop of Chicago), speech of October 24, 1962, in *Acta Synodalia*, vol. 1, bk. 1, 411.

[62] Cardinal Joseph Ritter (archbishop of St. Louis), speech of October 23, 1962, in *Acta Synodalia*, vol. 1, bk. 1, 351–53. About the relationship between Trent and Vatican II in the liturgical constitution, see Komonchak, "The Council of Trent at the Second Vatican Council," 61–80, esp. 63–66.

[63] Komonchak, "The Council of Trent at the Second Vatican Council," 76.

which did not reform the liturgy and did not debate the role of liturgy but simply "called to order" the abuses in sixteenth-century liturgical life of Catholicism,[64] Vatican II reformed liturgy on the solid basis of an international liturgical movement, a profound stream of theological *ressourcement*, and ecumenical hope. On the other side, the liturgical reform of Vatican II relied not only on the theological support of the preconciliar movements but also on the pastoral experiences (in some cases thanks to exceptions granted by the Holy See) going on in many dioceses all over the world in the 1940s and 1950s, as the bishop of Innsbruck (Austria), Paul Rausch, reminded the council fathers gathered in St. Peter's.[65]

Ressourcement's call to the great theological tradition of the Church was matched at Vatican II by the profound need for a new language in the liturgy and in the Church, concurrent with the shaping of a new style of Catholicism. If it is true that at Vatican II "the style of discourse was the medium that conveyed the message," the language being "values-expressive,"[66] we have no better example of this shift in vocabulary than the language of the liturgical reform. On October 22, 1962, the archbishop of Milan himself, Cardinal Giovanni Battista Montini (who was elected pope a few months later, on June 21, 1963), declared that "liturgy was instituted for the people, and not the people for liturgy."[67] Cardinal Raul Silva Henriquez (Santiago, Chile) added that "the liturgy should have appropriate room for the living language

[64] See Hubert Jedin, "Il Concilio di Trento e la riforma dei libri liturgici," in *Chiesa della fede—Chiesa della storia* (Brescia: Morcelliana, 1972), 392–425; Giuseppe Alberigo, "La riforma conciliare nel cammino storico del movimento liturgico e nella vita della chiesa," in *Transizione epocale. Studi sul Vaticano II* (Bologna: Il Mulino, 2009), 520.

[65] See Paul Rusch (auxiliary bishop of Innsbruck), speech of October 30, 1962, in *Acta Synodalia*, vol. 1, bk. 2, 35. Pius XII in 1943 had granted the German-speaking dioceses the permission to celebrate a "dialogue mass" with readings in vernacular language; see Theodor Maas-Ewerd, *Die Krise der liturgischen Bewegung in Deutschland und Österreich. Studien zu den Auseinandersetzungen um die "liturgische Frage" in den Jahren 1939 bis 1944* (Regensburg: Pustet, 1981); Rudolf Pacik, *"Last des Tages" oder "geistliche Nahrung"? Das Stundengebet im Werk Josef Andreas Jungmanns und in den offiziellen Reformen von Pius XII. bis zum II. Vaticanum* (Regensburg: Pustet, 1997).

[66] O'Malley, *What Happened*, 306–7.

[67] Cardinal Giovanni Battista Montini (Milano) in *Acta Synodalia*, vol. 1, bk. 1, 315 (October 22, 1962): "Liturgia nempe pro hominibus est instituta, non homines pro liturgia."

of the praying community. The sacramental signs are not to conceal the mysteries of faith but to reveal them."[68]

The converging theological paths of the liturgical reform and the new approach to divine revelation through the Bible expressed in *Dei Verbum* constitute the beginning of a new theological epistemology. Vatican II proved its courage in the foresightful effort to match the unspeakable fascination of the liturgy with the need—very much traditional if not absolutely "original," going back to the first Christian communities—for an understanding of the Word of God in the liturgy. From a cultural point of view, it is beyond dispute that the theological work done after Vatican II on the translation of liturgical language into the vernacular has enriched the vernacular without diminishing the "sacred character" of the Latin. After fifty years of liturgical inculturation, to withdraw the liturgy from the spoken language would mean to withdraw a fundamental dimension of human existence from the real-world linguistic realm.[69]

The connection between liturgical reform, ecclesiological *ressourcement*, patristic renewal, catechetical movement, and biblical renewal[70] multiplied the individual driving force of every element of the style of Vatican II and put the Church of Vatican II in the position to better respond to the "disenchantment" typical of the secular age. According to Charles Taylor, "A new poetic language can serve to find a way back to the God of Abraham."[71] Vatican II made it possible to open the Church to liturgy as the gateway to communion, tapping and re-creating a tradition that is conveyed by a style and a language typical of Vatican II. This is what the French liturgist Pierre-Marie Gy called "ressourcement en tradition."[72] In the wording of *Sacrosanctum Concilium*, "For

[68] Cardinal Raul Silva Henriquez (Santiago de Chile) in *Acta Synodalia*, vol. 1, bk. 1, 324 (October 22, 1962).

[69] For a historical example of the connection between language and the missionary element of the Church in the post-Tridentine era, see Sandra Mazzolini, "La lingua dell'altro come mezzo di propagazione della fede," in Autiero and Perroni, *Anatemi di ieri, sfide di oggi*, 187–98.

[70] See Achille M. Triacca, "Attuazione della Sacrosanctum Concilium," and Corrado Maggioni, "Rinnovamento liturgico," in *Il Concilio Vaticano II: recezione e attualità alla luce del giubileo*, ed. Rino Fisichella (Cinisello Balsamo: San Paolo, 2000), 232–55 and 256–75.

[71] See Charles Taylor, *A Secular Age* (Cambridge, MA: Harvard University Press, Belknap Press, 2007), 757.

[72] See Pierre-Marie Gy, "La liturgie de l'Église. La tradition vivante et Vatican II," *Revue de l'Institut Catholique de Paris* 50 (1994): 29–37. See also Patrick Prétot, "The

the liturgy is made up of unchangeable elements divinely instituted, and of elements subject to change. These latter not only may be changed but ought to be changed with the passage of time, if they have suffered from the intrusion of anything out of harmony with the inner nature of the liturgy or have become less suitable" (SC 21).

The "ressourced reform" of the Church adopted by Vatican II was possible in the space between Scripture and liturgy, integrating patristically different elements that up to Vatican II had remained separated: Scripture, tradition, and liturgy; Word and sacrament; Christology and pneumatology; hierarchy and faithful; episcopacy and primacy; universal and local Church. Vatican II turned Catholic theology back to liturgy and made of liturgy "the axis of its understanding of the Church. [. . .] The council positioned itself in a place in which *mysterium* becomes historically visible without simply becoming a sociological phenomenon."[73]

5.4. Liturgy at a Crossroads

One of the often-asked questions about the liturgical reform of Vatican II concerns the real "need" of the council to address the Latin Mass. This question presupposes a few assumptions seldom questioned. Among these, there are the assumption that the liturgical experience of the faithful before Vatican II was a golden age where liturgy corresponded to the needs of Catholics worldwide and the certitude (more psychological than historical) that the Latin Mass of Pius V was in a way the ultimate and not-to-be-changed form of Catholic liturgy. The former assumption discards easily the issue of the "catholicity" of the Catholic liturgy in a Church that after Trent had been defined not only by the separation from the churches of the Reformation but also by its new "global" character. The impression that the celebration of the Mass in the *aula* of St. Peter's in rites other than the Roman Rite made on the council fathers was a powerful one:

Sacraments as 'Celebrations of the Church': Liturgy's Impact on Sacramental Theology," in *Sacraments: Revelation of the Humanity of God; Engaging the Fundamental Theology of Louis-Marie Chauvet*, ed. Philippe Bordeyne and Bruce T. Morrill (Collegeville, MN: Liturgical Press, 2008), 25–41.

[73] Daniele Gianotti, *I Padri della Chiesa al concilio Vaticano II. La teologia patristica nella Lumen Gentium* (Bologna: EDB, 2010), 417.

Today the liturgy is celebrated in the Byzantine Rite by Bishop Nabaa. [. . .] This has made a great impression, now that the council debates concelebration, Communion under both species, and the use of the vernacular in the liturgy. Cardinal Gracias of Bombay said this morning: "We have been so touched by the concelebration in the Greek language, by his popular character, and by the use of the vernacular language that we all wish to be Eastern Catholics."[74]

The accusations against the liturgical reform of Vatican II question the legitimacy of "reforming the liturgy" during a council and during the postconciliar period. All that is often said with great ignorance of the history of the Tridentine period and of the liturgical changes after Trent. The Tridentine era has become the symbol of a crystallized, immobile, and perfect kind of Catholicism, as if it happened overnight, the day after the completion of the Council of Trent in 1563. In fact, the culture of Tridentinism (and of the liturgy of the post-Trent period) was a culture of "reform," of "Catholic reform." It is thus clear that the idea of "reforming the liturgy" was, in the minds of the council fathers at Vatican II, nothing less than reinterpreting the culture of Catholic reform that they had learned is part of Catholicism.

The Council of Trent did not become, as a culture and model for the Catholic Church, a universally accepted "paradigm" immediately; it took at least one century for Trent to become what we now suspect (or hope) that Trent was for the Catholic Church in the modern period.[75]

For some council fathers the attempt to renew the liturgy was a coup against the paradigm of Trent, as Schillebeeckx noted: "An 83-year old gentleman, bishop of Agrigento [Italy] spoke of the *crimen* that the Council Fathers present would inflict on future generations by introducing the vernacular, which is the beginning of Protestantism!"[76] But for the 98 percent of the bishops at Vatican II the liturgical reform was the best way to be creatively faithful to the "culture of reform" embodied (in its own way and according to the sensibility of its time) by the paradigm of Tridentine Catholicism.

---

[74] Edelby, *Il Vaticano II nel diario di un vescovo arabo*, 77–78 (entry of October 24, 1962).

[75] See Prodi, *Il paradigma tridentino*; Jean Bernhard, Charles Lefebvre, and Francis Rapp, *L'Epoque de la réforme et du concile de Trente*, vol. XIV of *Histoire du droit et des institutions de l'Église en occident* (Paris: Cujas, 1990).

[76] Entry of October 27, 1962, in *The Council Notes of Edward Schillebeeck*, 13. It was Bishop Giovanni Battista Peruzzo; see his intervention in *Acta Synodalia*, vol. 1, bk. 1, 594–95.

Already the first session of Vatican II saw an impressive growth of conciliar consciousness around the issue of liturgy, without any planning or maneuvering before the beginning of the council. Giuseppe Alberigo in his memoirs of the council describes those days:

> The rise [of] a completely unexpected and spontaneous majority, a very large number of votes that tended to converge on the major topics of the Council. It was a gradual but rapid process, without any planning or management; the Council fathers were simply becoming aware of their role and of the vast and unforeseen horizons of the Council itself. Their favorable response did not concern the proposed text on the liturgical reform alone; it also expressed the conviction that the time of fear, the era of the Church as a secure fortress, was over.[77]

The liturgical reform ushered in the *aula* of St. Peter's the feeling that reform was possible in the Church, but the ideas about the direction of this reform were not unanimous. In the conciliar debate about the liturgical reform three different positions may be distinguished:

> The first was a small group, systematically opposed to any significant reform, that included individuals who had been or continued to be active members of the Congregation of the Holy Office, the Congregation for Rites or the Congregation for Seminaries, as well as a part of the English-speaking episcopate, such as Spellman, McIntyre, and Godfrey. A second and quite numerous group was in favor of moderate adaptation to the times. A third group, consisting primarily of bishops from the Third World, included perhaps the most radical of the council fathers and called for a more thorough and fundamental adaptation of the rites to local situations and mentalities. This latter group enjoyed extraordinary support from the professional liturgists.[78]

The second and the third groups joined forces at Vatican II, vastly outnumbered the group that was systematically opposed to any significant reform, and launched a liturgical reform that was passed to the hands of the national bishops' conferences. It is thus not an overstatement to say that the type of reception of the liturgical reform mirrors the type of reception of Vatican II—not just because the liturgical reform is the most visible and direct reform in the life of the

---

[77] Giuseppe Alberigo, *A Brief History of Vatican II*, trans. Matthew Sherry (Maryknoll, NY: Orbis, 2006), 25–26.

[78] Lamberigts, "The Liturgy Debate," in *History of Vatican II*, vol. 2, 148.

faithful and Christian communities in the last four centuries. The liturgical reform opened by *Sacrosanctum Concilium* made liturgy the most powerful "container" of the profound values and attitudes of Vatican II and showed the possibility of the tensions active in the relations between Catholicism and modern times: faith and history, *ressourcement* and updating, visible communion and ecumenism, liturgical spirituality and "signs of the times." In the words of John Paul II:

> Such an overall reform of the Liturgy was in harmony with the general hope of the whole Church. In fact, the liturgical spirit had become more and more widespread together with the desire for an "active participation in the most holy mysteries and in the public and solemn prayer of the Church," and a wish to hear the word of God in more abundant measure. Together with the biblical renewal, the ecumenical movement, the missionary impetus and ecclesiological research, the reform of the Liturgy was to contribute to the overall renewal of the Church.[79]

For many, the vernacular Mass is the essence of the liturgical reform of Vatican II. The liturgical reform is, however, more than the vernacular and much more than the caricature created by its critics. The liturgical reform of Vatican II is a container that can hold the message of *reform as renewal* of tradition, of *change through* ressourcement; this message is impossible to convey by a liturgical mentality that rejects the very idea of the possibility and necessity of the "dirty little secret" of contemporary Catholicism—that is, things change in the Catholic Church too.[80]

Of course, from a historical point of view, the nature of this change is far from being entirely clear yet. The process of reception of a council is measured in generations, not in years, and this is exceptionally true for Vatican II, the first "global council" in the history of the Church.[81] The case of the liturgical reform is particularly important be-

---

[79] John Paul II, apostolic letter *Vicesimus quintus annus* (1988), 4.

[80] For the impact of the liturgical reform in US Catholicism, see Mark S. Massa, *The American Catholic Revolution: How the Sixties Changed the Church Forever* (New York: Oxford University Press, 2010), 15–28; Joseph P. Chinnici, "The Catholic Community at Prayer 1926–1976," in *Habits of Devotion. Catholic Religious Practice in Twentieth-Century America*, ed. James M. O'Toole (Ithaca, NY, and London: Cornell University Press, 2004), 9–87.

[81] See Gilles Routhier, *La réception d'un concile* (Paris: Cerf, 1993), and *Réceptions de Vatican II: le concile au risque de l'histoire et des espaces humains*, ed. Gilles Routhier

cause it represents the first "stress test" in the history of the reception of Vatican II: "The liturgical movement since Vatican II has become a battlefield, perhaps because it is the most visual representation of a paradigm shift that has gone too far for some and not far enough for others."[82]

The history of post–Vatican II Catholicism—well before Benedict XVI's *motu proprio Summorum Pontificum* of July 7, 2007—shows the centrality of the liturgical issue. The liturgical renewal of the first half of the twentieth century had many features typical of a "movement," and it is not an accident that for some of the "new Catholic movements" liturgy has been and still is the defining issue for their birth, existence, and relationship with the communion of the Catholic Church.[83] The liturgical reform carried with itself a new life for lay ministers in the Church, a new discovery of the liturgical assembly, concelebration as a sign of unity in the priesthood, the new role for the Word of God in the eucharistic celebration. All this tells us that the liturgical reform is the most important reform that was implemented by the Holy See of Paul VI immediately after Vatican II.

There are legitimate questions regarding the trajectories and the results of the liturgical reform.[84] But if a debate has to take place, it is about the "weight" of liturgy in contemporary Catholicism and the future of its spirituality and theological mind-set,[85] not about its legitimacy. A few questions clearly rise on the horizon, if we link the

---

(Leuven and Dudley, MA: Katholieke Universiteit Leuven, Peeters, 2004).

[82] See Christopher M. Bellitto, *Renewing Christianity: A History of Church Reform from Day One to Vatican II* (New York: Paulist Press, 2001), 209.

[83] See, for example, *Presence, Power, Praise: Documents on the Charismatic Renewal*, ed. Kilian McDonnell, 3 vols. (Collegeville, MN: Liturgical Press, 1980); Bernard Sven Anuth, *Der Neokatechumenale Weg: Geschichte, Erscheinungsbild, Rechtscharakter* (Würzburg: Echter, 2006); Massimo Faggioli, *Breve storia dei movimenti cattolici* (Roma: Carocci, 2008; Spanish translation: *Historia y evolución de los movimientos católicos. De León XIII a Benedicto XVI* [Madrid: PPC, 2011]).

[84] See Joseph Ratzinger (Benedict XVI), *The Spirit of the Liturgy* (San Francisco: Ignatius Press, 2000); and *Theologie der Liturgie: Die sakramentale Begründung christlicher Exisenz*, Gesammelte Schriften, Band 11 (Freiburg i.B.: Herder, 2008).

[85] Still valid are the issues about the "balance" of the new liturgy pointed out by Cipriano Vagaggini, "La ecclesiologia di comunione come fondamento teologico principale della riforma liturgica nei suoi punti maggiori," in *Liturgia, opera divina e umana. Studi sulla riforma liturgica offerti a S.E. Mons. Annibale Bugnini in occasione del suo 70° compleanno*, ed. Pierre Jounel, Reiner Kaczynski, and Gottardo Pasqualetti (Roma: C.L.V. Edizioni Liturgiche, 1982), 59–131, esp. 130–31.

history of the first decades of liturgical reform, its role in the Church, and the shape Catholicism will take in the future. Will future Catholicism be a *hardware Catholicism*, more focused on the devotional labels shaped in a traditionalist and neo-ultramontane fashion, where the hierarchical worldview is coming back via the calls for a "reform of the reform" of the liturgy? Or will it be a more *liturgical Catholicism*, capable of complementing its tradition with the new wave of evangelicalism that cannot leave the Catholic Church untouched?[86] The liturgical reform of Vatican II prepared a ground for a world Church, able to take the tradition from its European past but unwilling to be a prisoner of its history. In this respect, the reform of the language of the liturgy, the principle of adaptation and inculturation of the rites, and the decentralization of decision making in the matter of liturgy represented a huge step in the direction of a reform of the institutions of the Church.[87] Since *Sacrosanctum Concilium* is not a law or a regulation but clearly a "framework law" in the hands—for the first time in its history—of the national bishops' conferences, it set a path for a Church reform that implied not only a theological reform but also a reform of Church governance.

It has been correctly pointed out that creating distance from *Sacrosanctum Concilium* by "conceding" the indult to celebrate the preconciliar rite (the 1984 and 1988 indults) and by legitimizing the coexistence of two different ritual forms (ordinary and extraordinary; see *Summorum Pontificum* of 2007) is not far from renouncing Vatican II as such, stopping every pastoral effort aimed at receiving the liturgical reform and Vatican II through the liturgy.[88] Besides the fact that the unity of the Church expresses itself in the liturgy, *a fortiori* after Vatican II, the basic ideas of the liturgical reform are so connected with the core values of the council that renouncing the liturgical reform is a manifesto for the renunciation of Vatican II.

---

[86] It has been correctly pointed out that the liturgical constitution did not take into account the issue of legitimacy of "charismatic" celebrations; see ibid., 75.

[87] See Julio Manzanares, *Liturgia y descentralización en el Concilio Vaticano II. Las conferencias episcopales, eje de la reforma litúrgica conciliar* (Roma: Pontificia Università Gregoriana Editrice, 1970).

[88] See Maggioni, "Rinnovamento liturgico," 258. See also Andrea Grillo, "Ende der Liturgiereform? Das Motuproprio 'Summorum pontificum,'" *Stimmen der Zeit* 225 (2007): 730–40.

Chapter 6

The Liturgy of Vatican II and
Fifty Years of the Conciliar Reception

6.1. The Anniversaries of Vatican II and the Liturgical Issue

Celebrating anniversaries is a special kind of "public liturgy" in the contemporary world. They are often used to remember facts and events that are relevant only for a specific kind of person and are totally irrelevant or even annoying for all the others. This phenomenon of modern life strikes a note of caution, if we consider that the years 2012–15 mark the fiftieth anniversary of the Second Vatican Council (1962–65). Nevertheless, anniversaries have been, in the last decades, important occasions for the Church to remember and reevaluate the council. The twentieth anniversary saw the celebration of a decisive moment in the history of the reception of the council with the Extraordinary Synod of Bishops celebrated in Rome in 1985.[1] The fortieth anniversary of the conclusion of the council left significant traces in the Church in 2005—a year that was marked by the agony of John Paul II, the conclave that swiftly elected Cardinal Joseph Ratzinger, and the beginning of the pontificate of Pope Benedict XVI. The Great Jubilee of 2000 was much less significant for the debate about the reception of Vatican II. Except for the dispute between Cardinals Joseph Ratzinger and Walter Kasper on the relationship between ecclesiology of the local Church and of the universal Church, its legacy was largely celebratory.[2]

But there are also other anniversaries tied to the event of Vatican II. The fortieth anniversary of *Sacrosanctum Concilium* in 2003 saw the

---

[1] See Massimo Faggioli, *Vatican II: The Battle for Meaning* (Mahwah, NJ: Paulist Press, 2012).

[2] See Kilian McDonnell, "The Ratzinger/Kasper Debate: The Universal Church and Local Churches," *Theological Studies* (June 2002): 222–50.

first symptoms of the reappearance of a kind of public nostalgia for the Tridentine liturgy and the signs of the current "uprising" against the liturgical reform of Vatican II.[3] Not long after the beginning of the debate on the liturgical reform of Vatican II, the election of Benedict XVI in 2005 brought about a visible change in the approach to the liturgical debate in the Church, also for the direct statements, decisions, and liturgical style of the new pontiff.[4] Following the election of Pope Benedict, the Church was given a chance to reappreciate the importance of the liturgical reform also in its connections with the whole being of the Church in the modern world.

The chances to appreciate things that are mistakenly forgotten or taken for granted sometimes take the appearance of "incidents." When these incidents are public and shown to the public through the media, the cost of appreciating things that we should not have forgotten is much higher. In early 2009, the fiftieth anniversary of the announcement of the council (January 25, 1959) could have passed as an innocuous anniversary among so many others that crowd the calendar. Unexpectedly, the fiftieth anniversary instead took on the tones of an international incident and a call to reflection for the whole Catholic Church and showed a freedom of speech at all levels: bishops and episcopal conferences, the cardinals of the Curia, theological faculties, the Catholic press, Catholic and non-Catholic political leaders, Catholic and non-Catholic opinion makers. The decision by Benedict XVI on January 21, 2009, to lift the excommunication imposed by John Paul II in 1988 on the four bishops ordained by Msgr. Marcel Lefebvre went right back to the center of the discussion about the relationship between contemporary Catholicism and Vatican II. The council that this small schismatic sect created in the 1970s has always been accused

[3] See Joseph Ratzinger, " 'Der Geist der Liturgie' oder: Die Treue zum Konzil. Antwort an Pater Gy," *Liturgisches Jahrbuch* 52 (2002): 111–15; Joseph Ratzinger, "40 Jahre Konstitution über die Heilige Liturgie. Rückblick und Vorblick," *Liturgisches Jahrbuch* 53, no. 4 (2003), 209–21; Andrea Grillo, "40 anni prima e 40 anni dopo Sacrosanctum Concilium. Una 'considerazione inattuale' sulla attualità del movimento liturgico," *Ecclesia Orans* 21 (2004): 269–300; Reinhold Malcherek, "Liturgie als personaler Begegnung. Liturgietheologische Reflexionen im Licht von Sacrosanctum Concilium und theologischer Entwürfe im Umfeld des II. Vatikanischen Konzils," *Ecclesia Orans* 21 (2004): 365–87; Piero Marini, "Sacrosanctum Concilium 40 anni dopo. Tra consegne e impegni permanenti," *Rivista Liturgica* 91, no. 5 (2004): 771–80.

[4] See *Benedict XVI and the Sacred Liturgy*, ed. Neil J. Roy and Janet E. Rutherford (Dublin: Four Courts Press, 2010).

of heresy and of being the cause of all evil for the Church.[5] This decision of Benedict XVI moved the Catholic Church—along with other Christian churches, Jewish communities, and the public—to reflect on Vatican II far more than they could have done in any formal study or conference speech. The debate confirmed, if proof were needed, that "something happened" at Vatican II.[6]

Felix culpa, one is tempted to say. But the reactions to the lifting of the excommunication of the Lefebvrists were not exhausted in "damage control," which has become a special kind of communication in the "liturgies" of the social and political communication of the global era. The case has been much more of an international diplomatic incident, or a miscommunication, or mismanagement from the operatives of the political-administrative machine also known as the Roman Curia. The publication on the internet of the statements of Richard Williamson, one of the four bishops consecrated without papal permission by Marcel Lefebvre in 1988, denying the historical fact of the Holocaust, with outrageous statements that could be a surprise only to those who completely ignore the roots of the political and cultural phenomenon Lefebvre, was the trigger for a public reaction that has reached unheard tones, especially in Europe and in the Americas.[7]

The position concerning the decision of Benedict XVI led the Holy See to numerous and repeated explanations, not only by representatives of national bishops' conferences and individual bishops, but also by world and political leaders and parliamentary groups of Catholics, until they finally recognized the object of contention: Vatican II or, rather, the inability declared several times by Lefebvre and his followers to recognize Vatican II and in particular some elements of the whole theological balance of Vatican II, especially the document *Nostra Aetate* on relations with other religions and the *deploratio* of anti-Semitism expressed therein.[8] The attempts coming from Rome to

---

[5] See Peter Hünermann, "Excommunicatio—Communicatio Versuch einer Schichtenanalyse," *Herder Korrespondenz* 63, no. 3 (2009); Giovanni Miccoli, *La Chiesa dell'anticoncilio. I tradizionalisti alla riconquista di Roma* (Roma-Bari 2011), 8–57.

[6] See David G. Schultenover, ed., *Vatican II: Did Anything Happen?* (New York and London: Continuum, 2007); O'Malley, *What Happened.*

[7] See Peter Hünermann, ed., *Exkommunikation oder Kommunikation? Der Weg der Kirche nach dem II. Vatikanum und die Pius-Brüder* (Freiburg i.B.: Herder, 2009).

[8] About Lefebvrism and the tradition of Catholic anti-Judaism fully visible in its theology during Vatican II, see Nicla Buonasorte, *Tra Roma e Lefebvre: il tradizionalismo*

"buy off" the Lefebvrists with concessions in liturgical matters—for example, greater freedom to use the Tridentine liturgy in its preconciliar form—proved ineffective, since for the Lefebvrists the liturgy of Vatican II is the theological container of the paradigm shift that happened at the council.[9]

All the reactions against the lifting of the excommunications notwithstanding, Benedict XVI's attempts to absorb the Lefebvrist schism, created by the refusal of a small group to accept Vatican II, has made clear that, beyond the insignificant number of the schism created by Archbishop Marcel Lefebvre, the council represents for the Church of the twenty-first century an element of internal debate, and not only a "compass" for the Church—as John Paul II said in his testament.[10] This says something to scholars and observers of the Catholic Church's role on the world stage. But of course, it also speaks to historians of the hermeneutics of Vatican II, the greatest religious event of the twentieth century.[11]

Among the many possible reasons for interest in this "political-theological" case, three stand out. The first reason is that, in the eyes of contemporary Catholicism, of international politics, and of global public opinion, Vatican II undoubtedly has a role as a "guarantee," as "condition of citizenship" of the Catholic Church in the modern world. The second element is the fact that this "guarantee" has been identified, especially from the perspective of international politics and public opinion worldwide, with the final rejection of anti-Semitism as an element of premodern and antidemocratic social and political culture, and with some specific elements of the theology of Vatican II, in particular those that constitute the "break" from the traditional preconciliar framework: freedom of conscience and religious freedom,

---

cattolico italiano e il Concilio Vaticano II (Roma: Studium, 2003); Giovanni Miccoli, "Two Sensitive Issues: Religious Freedom and the Jews," in History of Vatican II, ed. Giuseppe Alberigo, English ed. Joseph A. Komonchak, trans. Matthew J. O'Connell, vol. 4: Church as Communion: Third Period and Intersession September 1964–September 1965 (Maryknoll, NY: Orbis; Leuven: Peeters, 2003), 95–193; Miccoli, La Chiesa dell'anticoncilio.

[9] See John Paul II, motu proprio Ecclesia Dei (July 2, 1988); Benedict XVI, motu proprio Summorum Pontificum (July 7, 2007).

[10] John Paul II, apostolic letter Novo millennio ineunte (January 6, 2001), n. 57.

[11] Among others, see Samuel P. Huntington, The Third Wave: Democratization in the Late Twentieth Century (Norman and London: University of Oklahoma Press, 1991).

ecumenism, dialogue with Judaism, dialogue with other religions, collegiality, and shared responsibility in the government of the church.

The third, and most relevant element concerning this book, is that these elements central to "public reception" of the council are essential to the content of the "liturgy of Vatican II" and that they are the ones that the Lefebvrist schism always declined to accept as the result of the "heresy" of Vatican II.[12]

6.2. The Liturgy of Vatican II and the Postconciliar Church

"Vatican II falls under the rubric of a reform council,"[13] and the liturgical reform launched by *Sacrosanctum Concilium* was the first of these reforms. The liturgy of Vatican II expressed "the style of Vatican II," a style that is "values-expressive."[14] The fundamental ideas of the liturgical constitution belong to the core theological content of Vatican II: pastoral bearing, connection between liturgy and ecclesiology, Church as a sacrament, and history of salvation. In the rediscovery of the Old Testament as part of Christian liturgy,[15] the liturgical constitution of Vatican II expressed the idea that the history of salvation is a prism whose "rays come from the Old Testament and especially from Christ, and reach out toward the heavenly Jerusalem."[16] This is only one example of the theological content of the liturgical constitution (especially SC 5, 6, and 8) whose intertextual connections with other council documents (*Dei Verbum*, *Nostra Aetate*) are crucial for the overall theological balance of Vatican II. Losing the connection between the liturgical reform and the rest of the theology of Vatican II means leaving the other documents of the council without their primary and ultimate framework of solemn expression in the Church, the liturgy.

[12] See Nicolas Senèze, *La crise intégriste: vingt ans après le schisme de Mgr Lefebvre* (Paris: Bayard, 2008).

[13] O'Malley, *What Happened*, 300.

[14] Ibid., 307.

[15] See Josef A. Jungmann, *The Mass of the Roman Rite: Its Origins and Development*, trans. Francis A. Brunner, rev. Charles K. Riepe (Westminster, MD: Christian Classics, 1959), 260–62.

[16] Cipriano Vagaggini, "Fundamental Ideas of the Constitution," in *The Liturgy of Vatican II: A Symposium*, ed. William Baraúna, English ed. by Jovian Lang, 2 vols. (Chicago: Franciscan Herald Press, 1966), 1:95–129, quotation at 112.

This connection between liturgical reform and the theology of Vatican II has been stronger during the history of the postconciliar Church than it is now, fifty years after the beginning of the council. The philosopher and friend of Paul VI, Jean Guitton, asked the pope why he did not concede "the Missal of 1962" to Lefebvre and his followers. The pope replied:

> Never. This Mass so called of Saint Pius V, the one we see in Écône, becomes the symbol of the condemnation of the council. I will not accept, under any circumstances, the condemnation of the council through a symbol. Should this exception to the liturgy of Vatican II have its way, the entire council would be shaken. And, as a consequence, the apostolic authority of the council would be shaken.[17]

In 1988, taking note of the excommunication *latae sententiae* against the Lefebvrist bishops, John Paul II's *motu proprio Ecclesia Dei* made the Lefebvrist schism an opportunity to reflect on the meaning of Vatican II. On that occasion, Pope John Paul II said:

> The outcome of the movement promoted by Archbishop Lefebvre can and must be, for all the Catholic faithful, a motive for sincere reflection concerning their own fidelity to the Church's tradition, authentically interpreted by the ecclesiastical magisterium, ordinary and extraordinary, especially in the ecumenical councils from Nicaea to Vatican II. From this reflection all should draw a renewed and efficacious conviction of the necessity of strengthening still more their fidelity by rejecting erroneous interpretations and arbitrary and unauthorized applications in matters of doctrine, liturgy, and discipline.[18]

This assessment of the Lefebvrists' fidelity to the magisterium of the Church was accompanied, a few months later in 1988, by an important statement of John Paul II about the liturgical reform. After a paragraph on the "difficulties" and before a section on the "erroneous applications" of the liturgical reform, John Paul II said:

---

[17] Jean Guitton, *Paul VI Secret* (Paris: Desclée De Brouwer, 1979), 158–59; see Paul Bovens, "Chronique inachevée des publications autour de la Lettre apostolique en forme de Motu proprio 'Summorum Pontificum' de Benoît XVI," *Ephemerides Theologicae Lovanienses* 84 (2008): 529–36.

[18] John Paul II, *motu proprio Ecclesia Dei* (July 2, 1988), n. 5. See also Miccoli, *La Chiesa dell'anticoncilio*, 162–212.

This should not lead anyone to forget that the vast majority of the pastors and the Christian people have accepted the liturgical reform in a spirit of obedience and indeed joyful fervour. For this we should give thanks to God for that movement of the Holy Spirit in the Church which the liturgical renewal represents; for the fact that the table of the word of God is now abundantly furnished for all; for the immense effort undertaken throughout the world to provide the Christian people with translations of the Bible, the Missal and other liturgical books; for the increased participation of the faithful by prayer and song, gesture and silence, in the Eucharist and the other sacraments; for the ministries exercised by lay people and the responsibilities that they have assumed in virtue of the common priesthood into which they have been initiated through Baptism and Confirmation; for the radiant vitality of so many Christian communities, a vitality drawn from the wellspring of the Liturgy.

These are all reasons for holding fast to the teaching of the Constitution *Sacrosanctum Concilium* and to the reforms which it has made possible. "the liturgical renewal is the most visible fruit of the whole work of the Council". For many people the message of the Second Vatican Council has been experienced principally through the liturgical reform.[19]

In a way, John Paul II was the first pope in charge of the ecclesial interpretation of Vatican II, of its "global" reception in various areas of the world, and of its "theological core" in terms of the relationship of the Catholic Church *ad extra*. John Paul II here connected the legacy of the global pontificate and his deep grasp of Vatican II as a lived experience for the Catholic Church. John Paul II showed a deep understanding of the Lefebvrist issue in connection with the need to defend Vatican II. For John Paul II, just as for the vast majority of the bishops of the early post–Vatican II Church, the liturgical issue was part of this debate on the reception/rejection of the council.

Until recently, it was clear that the rejection of the liturgical reform was only a maneuver to reject Vatican II as a whole, especially its "discontinuities" with the theological *traditions* (plural) of the past, as opposed to the great *Tradition* (singular) of the Church.[20] But in the last few years and for some time now in the Catholic Church it has become possible to advocate a rejection of the liturgical reform without directly

[19] John Paul II, apostolic letter *Vicesimus quintus annus* (December 4, 1988), n. 12.
[20] See Yves Congar, *La tradition et les traditions* (Paris: Fayard, 1960).

advocating a rejection of the council. The incident with the Lefebvrists in January 2009, however, has made this attempt more difficult. Discussions concerning the lifted excommunication of the four bishops of the Society of Saint Pius X, founded by Msgr. Lefebvre in 1970, showed clearly that the anti-Semitic statements of one of these bishops not only represented a political and diplomatic issue but also presented a theological issue. The positions of the schism of Lefebvre on Vatican II and, in particular, its core elements of novelty and discontinuity within the recent tradition of the Church were directly connected with the liturgical reform, in which the new orientation of Catholic theology was expressed in the documents enacting the liturgical reform and then in the liturgy itself.[21] In a way, the Lefebvrists' rejection of the liturgy of Vatican II was the ultimate proof that the liturgical reform of Vatican II also carries the value of *lex orandi, lex credendi*.[22]

The *lex credendi* of Vatican II is expressed in the *lex orandi* of the liturgical reform enacted by the council and implemented by the bishops in the decades after Vatican II. The theological core of Vatican II rejected by the Lefebvrists evidently has to do with the recognition of religious freedom and freedom of conscience, the commitment to ecumenical and interreligious dialogue, and the commitment to a new understanding of faith anchored in the Word of God. Through the liturgy of Vatican II, this core includes the position of Scripture in the Church and the existence and role of episcopal conferences and episcopal collegiality, rejected by Lefebvre as "discontinuity" with the Western European tradition (in truth, more imperial than biblical) of the monarchical model of Church government.

The theological statements of Vatican II constitute the new face of the Catholic Church, and they are necessary to reconcile the Church with its theological understanding of revelation (*ad intra*) and to reconcile the Church's role in the world, on a public level and international level, with the political and cultural consequences of the changes at the theological level (*ad extra*). For historians of the Vatican and interpreters of Vatican II this provides the debate with an interesting element of the latest episode of the "Lefebvre case": it touches

[21] See Simon Schrott, "The Need for Discontinuity: Considerations on a Hermeneutic of Liturgical Reform according to Sacrosanctum Concilium," *Studia Liturgica* 41 (2011): 56–67.

[22] See also Paul De Clerck, " 'Lex orandi, lex credendi'. Un principe heuristique," *La Maison-Dieu* 222, no. 2 (2000): 61–78.

Vatican II at a "constitutional core," which exists independently of the formal hierarchy of the texts (constitutions, decrees, declarations), because it has to do more with the lived history and theological hermeneutics of the Vatican II Church in the world than with the "technical" exegesis of the texts. As the Lutheran observer Edmund Schlink explained after Vatican II:

> In attempting to arrange the many conciliar decisions in systematic order based on their content, it must be borne in mind that it was no accident that the proposals on the sacred liturgy were discussed and adopted first of all. It is true that even in its first draft this document was in a more advanced stage than the other schemata. Yet the structure of themes suggested that this matter be considered first.[23]

Sacrosanctum Concilium is at the crossroads of the whole corpus of Vatican II: between God's revelation and personal conscience, between ecclesiology of the local Church and Church as "sacrament" and people of God.[24] That is why the rejection of the liturgical reform is not driven by the rejection of the "abuses" of the postconciliar years; it seems more and more the forefront of an overall rejection of the theology of Vatican II.[25]

6.3. The Liturgical Reform and the Reception/Rejection of the Council

The death of John Paul II—the last father of Vatican II to be elected bishop of Rome and pope—and the election of Benedict XVI in 2005 have undoubtedly provided the cultural landscape of contemporary Catholicism and the debate on the hermeneutics of Vatican II with two important elements. Since his election in April 2005, Benedict XVI has reignited the debate about the role of Vatican II, long accepted in large areas of the Church only in a "nominalistic" way, tying it to a

---

[23] Edmund Schlink, *After the Council*, trans. Herbert J. A. Bouman (Philadelphia, PA: Fortress Press, 1968), 41; original German: *Nach dem Konzil* (Munich and Hamburg: Siebenstern, 1966).

[24] See Christoph Theobald, *La réception du concile Vatican II. I. Accéder à la source* (Paris: Cerf, 2009), esp. 431.

[25] See Daniele Menozzi, "Opposition to the Council," in *The Reception of Vatican II*, ed. Giuseppe Alberigo, Jean-Pierre Jossua, and Joseph A. Komonchak (Washington, DC: The Catholic University of America Press, 1987), 325–48.

153

discussion on the legacy of the council for the Church and contemporary culture.[26]

But every attempt to frame the current debate over the council without, on the one side, an analysis of the "political" (broadly speaking) orientation of the interpreters of Vatican II and, on the other side, without an awareness of the political, cultural, and theological consequences, in the long term, of the minimization of Vatican II is unsuccessful. The current doctrinal policy of the Holy See led by Benedict XVI seems to have left behind the Wojtylian leading role in world politics, but it seems also to have left behind the awareness of the "global impact of the council," not least the global impact of the liturgical reform of Vatican II. The case of lifting the excommunication of the Lefebvrist bishops is proof of that. The concession of the Mass in the "extraordinary rite," in the hope of drawing the Lefebvrists back into communion with Rome, demonstrated the "disposability" of the liturgical reform of Vatican II in the eyes of the current leadership of the Church. So far, the Lefebvrists have not accepted the offer, being that the *lex orandi* is only the first step in their fight against the *lex credendi* of Vatican II.[27]

The reorientation of Catholic theology and ecclesiology toward *ressourcement* and *rapprochement* is at stake here. In the late 1950s, the choice to leave behind the "Constantine age" was a turning point in the life of Angelo Giuseppe Roncalli (Pope John XXIII), and it was brought to maturity in the years of the council. This reorientation showed all its implications during Vatican II, in which the identity of the universal, really "Catholic" Church was the necessary precondition for the culture of dialogue and the dialogue between cultures. It was a choice made by starting from the theological center of the Catholic Church, the liturgy, and followed by a more comprehensive theological-political reorientation of theology for a world Church. In the postconciliar period, the recent teaching on the "purification of memory" enhances the discontinuity of the gestures and symbols, as

[26] See Massimo Faggioli, "Concilio Vaticano II: bollettino bibliografico (2000–2002)," *Cristianesimo nella Storia* 24, no. 2 (2003): 335–60; "Concilio Vaticano II: bollettino bibliografico (2002–2005)," *Cristianesimo nella Storia* 26, no. 3 (2005): 743–67; "Council Vatican II: Bibliographical Overview 2005–2007," *Cristianesimo nella Storia* 29, no. 2 (2008): 567–610; "Council Vatican II: Bibliographical overview 2007–2010," *Cristianesimo nella Storia* 32, no. 2 (2011): 755–91.
[27] See Andrea Grillo, "Un bilancio del motu proprio 'Summorum pontificum'. Quattro paradossi e una intenzione dimenticata," *Concilium* 45, no. 2 (2009): 125–32.

well as the words, of the Church of Paul VI and John Paul II, in terms of perception of the whole and the relevance of religion to world peace. But in the Church at the beginning of the twenty-first century, the fascination with neoconservative ideology seems to be aimed at putting an end to the international course given to postconciliar Catholicism by Paul VI and John Paul II—a transformation of the culture and theology of the Catholic Church, with deep "political" ramifications.[28]

The liturgical reform, the firstfruit and the ultimate theological-pastoral expression of Vatican II, could become the first victim, in an astounding example of theological relativism, of the efforts to minimize the *aggiornamento* of Vatican II. It is not only an accident that these attempts to "reverse" Vatican II became apparent in the twists of a political-diplomatic flap like the one of 2009 with the Lefebvrists. The theology of Vatican II raised high expectations in the world, and the liturgical reform is the most visible way for the Church to declare its public identity. But from a theological-political point of view, some interpretations of Vatican II do not seem to understand the cost of a withdrawal of the Catholic Church from the international scene of dialogue between Churches and religions, after the last decades in which the Roman papacy has created expectations in its global audience (even in the most ill-disposed counterparts). The current vision of the role of the Church in the world has direct consequences for the way to read the council; the current views of many revisionists of the liturgical reform of Vatican II have direct consequences for future relations between the Church and the world. The incident regarding the Lefebvrists in January 2009 provided the Church with clear evidence of that.

The debate on the liturgy is part of this, because the liturgical reform is part of the "discontinuities" of Vatican II compared with the previous period (the relationship between Church and democracy, episcopal collegiality and synodality in the Church; religious freedom; ecumenism; interreligious dialogue). Rejecting the "discontinuities" in the interpretation of Vatican II has not only theological but also cultural effects, at the risk of ignoring the existence of a "constitutional core" within the Vatican, that is, a nucleus that "political" actors (here taken in a broad sense: political leaders, parliaments, public opinion,

---

[28] For an overview, see Ian Linden, *Global Catholicism: Diversity and Change since Vatican II* (New York: Columbia University Press, 2009), 91–236.

religious and cultural communities) who interact with the Church feel that the change has become permanent and irrevocable, and expressed by its liturgy. These actors give a contribution—albeit indirectly and perhaps unconsciously—to the debate on the Vatican because they are more sensitive to that "constitutional core" of the council that is rejected by the Lefebvrist schism.[29] Rejecting their views as "political interference" with the internal affairs of the Church does not solve the genuine theological issue of the relationship between the public culture of Catholicism and its *lex orandi*.

The role of Vatican II in the public sphere of the Catholic Church is undeniable, if we consider that *Nostra Aetate* (Declaration on the Church's Relations with Non-Christian Religions), *Dignitatis Humanae* (Declaration on Religious Liberty), and *Gaudium et Spes* (Pastoral Constitution on the Church in the Modern World) address in a special way the issue of the Church in modernity. On the other hand, it is impossible to deny that the three "issues under-the-issues"—identified recently by John O'Malley, namely, the change in the Church, relations between center and periphery of the Church, the council as a linguistic event and "style" of Catholicism—are closely interconnected, and the denial of one of them immediately entails sterilization for the other two issues.[30]

It is clear that the liturgical reform has to do with these three issues, which make of Vatican II an age of transition to a culturally new form of Catholicism whose more solemn (and more successful) expression worldwide is the liturgical reform begun by *Sacrosanctum Concilium*. Among the elements of the "transition age" of Vatican II, there is definitely a change in the categories of thinking, which implies—to take just two examples—a modern critical approach to exegetical interpretation of the Scriptures and a relationship between the pope, bishops, and laity characterized, from the point of view of institutions, by freedom and responsibility. From this epochal transition follows a form of faith that must be articulated in the form of "church-world" in order to be communicable and witnessed in the world.[31] The liturgy of Vatican II is an expression of all that. Rejecting the theological core of the liturgical reform is nothing less than rejecting the theology of

[29] See Massimo Faggioli, "Il Vaticano II come 'costituzione' e la 'recezione politica' del concilio," *Rassegna di Teologia* 50 (2009): 107–22.

[30] See O'Malley, *What Happened*, 309–11.

[31] See Giuseppe Alberigo, "Transizione epocale," in Giuseppe Alberigo, *Transizione epocale. Studi sul Concilio Vaticano II* (Bologna: Il Mulino, 2009), 765–859.

Vatican II and the chance to communicate the Gospel in an understandable way in our time and age.

It is evident that the epochal changes of Vatican II do not have an impact that is exclusively internal to the Church. In fact, they also have a direct effect on the contemporary political and cultural opinion on the substance of the Church in the modern world. All these elements belong to the cultural discontinuity of Vatican II, the same as what is rejected by the culture of the schism of Lefebvre, and correspond to the "constitutional" core Vatican.

If the year 2006 and the "incident of Regensburg" meant rediscovering relations with Islam after *Nostra Aetate*, the period from 2007 to 2009 was a milestone in the realization of the value of the council for the relationship between the Church and Judaism, also thanks to the debate on the liturgy. But beyond the reactions against anti-Semitism (which not coincidentally is inherent in much of the anti-council culture), in a broader perspective it is evident that the fiftieth anniversary of the beginning of the council and the reactions against the lifting of excommunications of the Lefebvrist bishops are "moments of reception" of Vatican II. We are now, at the beginning of the twenty-first century, in a crucial moment of ecclesial reception but also political and cultural reception of the council. The history of the reception of Vatican II has made clear the unsustainability of the view that advocates an absolute "continuity" of the council with past tradition, also because this view tends to dispose summarily of the council's theology associating Vatican II with "the Sixties" and with secularization in the Western world.

Rejecting the liturgical reform of the council has been, since the early 1970s with the Lefebvrist schism, the most direct and effective way to charge Vatican II of being a mistake or, worse, a heresy. In this sense, the liturgical reform of Vatican II (and its enablers, especially between 1964 and the mid-1970s) received a daunting task, since *Sacrosanctum Concilium*, the symbol of the Church of Vatican II, is a guarantee of its commitment to reform, to *aggiornamento*, to interreligious dialogue with Judaism, to ecumenism and peace among peoples and cultures, and to the Church's commitment to social justice. Liturgy is not only about aesthetics: "Social justice needs liturgy and liturgy needs social justice. Or we could say that advocates for justice need liturgists, and liturgists need advocates for justice."[32]

---

[32] Keith F. Pecklers, *Worship: A Primer in Christian Ritual* (Collegeville, MN: Liturgical Press, 2003), 190.

The revisionist interpretations of the greatest religious event of the twentieth century are powered by a neoconservative ideological view that sees the pre–Vatican II Church as the only way out for a Western civilization in crisis, a sort of preservative for a traditionalist Catholic identity tempted by the sirens of "neo-maurrasisme."[33] If it is true that the council did not become "the Constitution" of the Church, or the revolution against the tradition, but it was and is a dynamic reality,[34] it is also legitimate to observe that Vatican II and its liturgy have emerged clearly as the absolute elements for the reception of Catholicism in the political and social culture of the contemporary world—the Western culture, but also and especially, at a time of an attempted new Europeanization of Catholicism, non-Western and non-European cultures.

The liturgy of Vatican II is not only the first and foremost medium of Vatican II but also an integral part of the theological message of Vatican II. Its core content is essential for the core content of Vatican II. The liturgy of Vatican II is constitutionally necessary for the theological survival of Vatican II. Undoing the liturgical reform of Vatican II leads to the dismantling of the Church of Vatican II. This is why it is necessary to understand the deep connections between the liturgical reform and theology of Vatican II in its entirety.

The attempt to preserve and revitalize the council through the concept of Vatican II as a "constitution" is recent,[35] but the idea of a core internal detail is not new to the interpreters of the council.[36] In particular, the idea of Vatican II as a "constitutional text for the faith" is useful for understanding the centrality of the liturgical reform for the

[33] About the monarchist, nationalist, antiparliamentarist, and counter-revolutionary Charles Maurras (1868–1952), see Philippe Chenaux, *Entre Maurras et Maritain: une generation intellectuelle catholique (1920–1930)* (Paris: Cerf, 1999), and Jacques Prévotat, *Les catholiques et l'Action Française: histoire d'une condamnation, 1899–1939* (Paris: Fayard, 2001).

[34] See Alberto Melloni, "Sacrosanctum Concilium 1963–2003. Lo spessore storico della riforma liturgica e la ricezione del Vaticano II," *Rivista liturgica* 90, no. 6 (2003): 915–30.

[35] See Peter Hünermann, "Der Text: Werden—Gestalt—Bedeutung. Eine Hermeneutische Reflexion," in *Herders Theologischer Kommentar zum Zweiten Vatikanischen Konzil*, ed. Hans-Jochen Hilberath and Peter Hünermann, 5 vols. (Freiburg i.B.: Herder, 2004–2005), 5:5–101, esp. 11–17 and 85–87.

[36] See Dossetti, *Chiesa eucaristica*, 35; Giuseppe Dossetti, *Il Vaticano II. Frammenti di una riflessione*, ed. Francesco Margiotta Broglio (Bologna: Il Mulino, 1996).

Catholic Church of Vatican II.[37] The crisis with the Lefebvrists of 2009 (and the discussions that followed between Rome and their leaders about the possibility of their readmission into the Catholic Church) should also tell something to the specialists of the liturgical reform of Vatican II and to the faithful attending Mass in the conciliar rite, whose theological content is inextricably tied to the rest of the council teachings. The significance of the particular moment of "reception" of Vatican II that became visible in 2009, at the dawn of the twenty-first century, also deserves some further discussion from the point of view of the connections between the liturgical reform of Vatican II and the whole meaning of the council.

---

[37] See also Peter Hünermann, "Zur theologischen Arbeit am Beginn der dritten Millenniums," in *Das Zweite Vatikanische Konzil und die Zeichen der Zeit heute,* ed. Peter Hünermann (Freiburg i.B.: Herder, 2006), 569–93.

Conclusion

In his speech at the end of the first session of the council in December 1962, Pope John XXIII expressed his satisfaction with the firstfruit of Vatican II, the debate on the liturgical *schema*:

> It was no accident that the first *schema* to be considered was the one dealing with the sacred liturgy, which has to do with man's relationship with God. This relationship is of the utmost importance and must be based on the solid foundation of revelation and apostolic teaching, so as to contribute to man's spiritual good and to do so with a broadness of vision that avoids the superficiality and haste that often characterize human relationships.[1]

One year later the liturgical reform was formally approved on November 22, 1963, and promulgated on December 4, 1963, after a show of impressive unanimity among the council fathers. It was the first document "produced" by Vatican II, the first sign that the council was soon coming to the local Churches and parishes of Catholics around the world. Thanks to this mandate coming from the floor of St. Peter's, the "liturgy of Vatican II" has changed the Church as nothing else coming from the council has changed it.

In this sense, the success of the liturgical reform is beyond dispute. What is not beyond dispute, as it is evident from the state of the conversation going on in the Catholic Church today, is whether the liturgical reform has been beneficial for the life of the Catholic Church. Much of this debate happens outside of the proper mechanisms of reception of a conciliar teaching. Belligerent Catholic bloggers were not part of Congar's imagination when he published his famous article "Quod omnes tangit, ab omnibus tractari et adprobari debet" about the theological fact of "reception" in the Church.[2] In light of the principle of reception, the daily or weekly event of the Catholic

---

[1] *Acta Synodalia*, vol. 1, bk. 4, 645.

[2] See Yves Congar, "Quod omnes tangit ab omnibus tractari et approbari debet," *Revue historique de droit français et étranger* 35 (1958): 210–59.

faithful and clergy celebrating Mass in the conciliar rite is a form of plebiscite for the liturgy of Vatican II.

It is certainly true that the liturgical reform of Vatican II can be read as the "autobiography of Catholicism" of our time.[3] That does not mean that the liturgical reform has been perfect or that it is not in need of improvements and implementations. It means that it is a history in which the Catholic Church has found itself in the last five decades more than in any other written document or statement. All that said, it is impressive to see that different liturgists agree on the list of items that nostalgic revisionists would like to change for the future of the liturgy of the Catholic Church in the Roman Rite:[4] among these, liturgical orientation, language, liturgical music, concelebration, and universal prayer. It seems, indeed, that the elements that have been fully received by the Christian people since Vatican II are the same elements that the vociferous ideologues of the "new liturgical reform" or of the "reform of the reform" want to put in reversal. Here, it is not a matter of "different receptions" of Vatican II; it is a matter of acknowledging reception as an important mechanism for theological discernment in a Church that prizes—often acritically—the hierarchical principle.

To the ones who say that the reception of the liturgical reform is one of the major criteria for understanding the legitimacy of that reform, the nostalgic advocates of the preconciliar rite reply by saying that the liturgical reform of Vatican II destroyed the sense of beauty and solemnity of the Mass of Pius V. But this allegation, widely accepted and seldom disputed, is far from being respectful of the history of the liturgy as lived experience of the Christian people. What is true, on the contrary, is that the decision of Vatican II to open—prudently, but not as a concession nor as an exception—Catholic liturgy to the vernacular languages was the key passage in the history of the liturgical constitution between the preparatory phase in 1960 and the fall of 1963. That is why now the reaction against the liturgical reform seems to be so focused on the issue of language and translations.

---

[3] See Alberto Melloni, "Sacrosanctum Concilium 1963–2003. Lo spessore storico della riforma liturgica e la ricezione del Vaticano II," *Rivista liturgica* 90, no. 6 (2003): 915–30.

[4] See Paul De Clerck, "La réforme liturgique: ce qui reste à faire," *Questions liturgiques* 91, nos. 1–2 (2010): 64–75; John Baldovin, *Reforming the Liturgy: A Response to the Critics* (Collegeville, MN: Liturgical Press, 2008), 105–34. See also Ansgar J. Chupungco, *What, Then, Is Liturgy? Musings and Memoir* (Collegeville, MN: Liturgical Press, 2010), 9–24.

One simple fact is now forgotten: that Latin had become a "sacred language" for the Roman Rite of Catholic liturgy only in the post-Trent period—a "sacralization" that had nothing to do with more ancient times, when Latin had become for the Church of the West the unifying idiom understandable for most Christians. A "resacralization" of Latin as the true liturgical language now, in the twenty-first century, would make even less sense than it did in the seventeenth and eighteenth centuries.

Whoever is nostalgic for the artistic beauty of Catholic liturgy should keep in mind that Vatican II and the liturgical reform happened after a general separation between "religious performance" and art in the Western world. There is surely much to do in order to avoid the reduction and dispersion of the religious rites to arid promotional and self-expressive events. But all that goes beyond the Catholic Church—and goes much beyond Vatican II. Contemporary art and Catholicism seem to be at odds, and in this fight Catholicism seems to have lost its inspirational force.[5] As we all know, nostalgia seeks no cure. An expert in the culture of early modern Catholicism, John O'Malley, notes in the conclusion to his book devoted to the "four cultures of the West":

> Christian Churches even in the post-baroque, indeed post-modern, era do not labor under that last disability. They know they use symbols, and they know they engage in rituals. [. . .] Even with all these changes culture four [art] is still culture four, powerfully present among us and creative, lifting us (we know not how or why) to another world.[6]

W. H. Auden said, "False enchantment can all too easily last a life-time." One of the paradoxes of the liturgical reform is that Vatican II had, in a world conquered by a "disenchantment" masterfully explained by Charles Taylor,[7] to reform liturgy, that is, part of "the culture of enchantment"[8] appropriated by Christian theology and praxis in the course of history of its inculturation. The problem with the

[5] See Gerhard Larcher, *Annäherungsversuche von Kunst und Glaube. Ein fundamentaltheologisches Skizzenbuch* (Münster: LIT, 2006); Italian translation: *Estetica della fede. Un abbozzo teologico-fondamentale*, trans. Marcello Neri (Milano: Glossa, 2011).

[6] John W. O'Malley, *Four Cultures of the West* (Cambridge, MA: Harvard University Press, Belknap Press, 2004), 232–33.

[7] See Charles Taylor, *A Secular Age* (Cambridge, MA: Harvard University Press, Belknap Press, 2007).

[8] O'Malley, *Four Cultures of the West*, 180–81.

current attempts to undermine the liturgical reform of Vatican II is that they are the fruit of a fascination with a world that does not exist anymore, and this is not Vatican II's fault. The nostalgia for the old rite usually discards globalization of Catholicism as a theologically irrelevant fact, or as a mistake, or as a thing that happened only after 1965, and not as a constitutive element of Christianity and Catholicism in their relationship with culture since its very origins.

In order to understand the importance of the liturgical reform, it is crucial to look at it in the context not only of the history of Vatican II but also in the context of the other conciliar documents that have received crucial inputs from the liturgical constitution. Both these hermeneutical principles are a necessary step in assessing the *status quaestionis* of the liturgical reform. Vatican II inquired deeply, just as Trent did before, about the didactic and pastoral nature of the liturgy. The liturgical innovations of Vatican II were made for the pastoral needs of the faithful. They were conducted with great attention to fidelity to the early liturgical traditions of the Church, in accordance with the principles repeatedly affirmed in the acts of ecclesiastical authority. That is why the liturgical reform of Vatican II is the most important reform of Catholicism in the last five centuries.[9] What has been recently described in harsh terms as "an order of worship deliberately manufactured to express the modernizing, antiquarianist and ecumenical preoccupations of the apostles of the aggiornamento"[10] was the major reform of Vatican II and a success. Whether the advocates of the "reform of the reform" like it or not, pastorally and theologically the reception of the liturgical reform of Vatican II is a settled question.

It is time to rediscover the liturgical reform in the sense of remembering the deep theological implications of *Sacrosanctum Concilium*, not only because the spontaneous connections that Catholics were able to make thirty or forty years ago between the liturgical reform and the rest of the council teachings are not so spontaneous anymore, but also because the liturgical reform has now become the symbol of the council itself. For one thing, many theologians seem to forget that the Bible became once again *the book* of Catholics thanks to the litur-

---

[9] See Arnaud Join-Lambert, "Richesses de Vatican II à (re)découvrir," *Questions Liturgiques* 91, nos. 1–2 (2010): 52–53.

[10] Geoffrey Hull, *The Banished Heart: Origins of Heteropraxis in the Catholic Church* (London and New York: T&T Clark, 2010), 35.

gical reform and that, without the liturgical reform, *Dei Verbum* would largely be a dead letter. That is why the rejection of the liturgical reform is not driven by the rejection of the "abuses" of the postconciliar years; it seems more and more the forefront of an overall rejection of the theology of Vatican II.[11] *Sacrosanctum Concilium* is at the crossroads of the whole corpus of Vatican II: between God's revelation and personal conscience, between ecclesiology of the local Church and Church as "sacrament" and people of God.[12]

Times have changed. Now the call to a "new liturgical movement" often heard within Catholicism means just and only a call to cast doubts and to reverse the liturgical reform of Vatican II. Fifty years from the event of Vatican II, "going back to the liturgical movement" does not mean anything but a return to the preconciliar mentality, with the nostalgia nourished by the desperation of those who no longer have any confidence in the future. These calls for a nostalgic "new liturgical movement" are nothing more than "a radical negation of every possible movement in the field of ritual and the emergence of a stagnation for a Church that is lifeless and without children."[13] At the twenty-fifth anniversary of the liturgical constitution, John Paul II reminded the Church of the importance of the liturgical reform: "These are all reasons for holding fast to the teaching of the Constitution *Sacrosanctum Concilium* and to the reforms which it has made possible: 'the liturgical renewal is the most visible fruit of the whole work of the Council' [Final Report of the Extraordinary Assembly of the Synod of Bishops, December 7, 1985]. For many people the message of the Second Vatican Council has been experienced principally through the liturgical reform."[14]

Rediscovering the historical context of the liturgical constitution can help many Catholics avoid the temptation to rewrite the history of

---

[11] See Daniele Menozzi, "Opposition to the Council," in *The Reception of Vatican II*, ed. Giuseppe Alberigo, Jean-Pierre Jossua, and Joseph A. Komonchak (Washington, DC: The Catholic University of America Press, 1987), 325–48.

[12] See Christoph Theobald, *La réception du concile Vatican II. I. Accéder à la source* (Paris: Cerf, 2009), esp. 431.

[13] Marco Gallo and Andrea Grillo, "Il tempo giusto per leggere 'Il movimento liturgico' di Bernard Botte," preface to Bernard Botte, *Il movimento liturgico. Testimonianza e ricordi* (Cantalupa: Effatà, 2009), 13; English translation: *From Silence to Participation: An Insider's View of Liturgical Renewal*, trans. John Sullivan (Washington, DC: Pastoral Press, 1988).

[14] John Paul II, apostolic letter *Vicesimus quintus annus* (1988), no. 12.

Vatican II and its liturgical reform through a deletion of the history of the liturgical movement and of its long pre–Vatican II work. Those who accuse Vatican II of having improvised a liturgical reform must be reminded that the liturgical question was born in Europe at the beginning of the nineteenth century, after the French Revolution. Only between Pius X and Pius XII the official teaching of the Church accepted the idea of the necessity of some changes. Now, thinking of going back fifty or sixty years would be the attempt to go back to a golden age that never existed. Even worse, it would be a serious wound to the process of reception of the council that needs, like every ecumenical council, a reception whose pace must be counted in generations, not in years or even in decades. Every historian of the Church and of its theology knows that the Council of Trent and its liturgy—the Mass of Pius V—became "canonical" only in the mid-seventeenth century, that is, almost one century after the conclusion of the Council of Trent. For us and for Vatican II, the beginning of the twenty-first century is at the exact same crossroads the Council of Trent was 450 years ago. Now, if we want to stay faithful to the deep intention of the Council of Trent, we need to change its language and style as *Sacrosanctum Concilium* changed it:

> Vatican II tried to do for its time what Trent had done for the Reformation crisis: identify the needs of the day [. . .], interpret them in the light of the Gospel, and determine how to meet them with two criteria at work: fidelity to the tradition and adequacy to the day. If in meeting this supreme pastoral responsibility, the Second Vatican Council found it necessary to depart from Trent's dogmatic formulas or practical decisions, even then it was still following the footsteps of the Council of Trent.[15]

The promulgation of *Sacrosanctum Concilium* on December 4, 1963, exactly four hundred years after the conclusion of the Council of Trent on December 4, 1563, "carried within itself the seeds of significant changes in piety, discourse, and attitudes toward church authority that were unforeseen and unwelcome by most of the council's strongest

---

[15] Joseph A. Komonchak, "The Council of Trent at the Second Vatican Council," in *From Trent to Vatican II: Historical and Theological Investigations*, ed. Raymond F. Bulman and Frederick J. Parrella (New York: Oxford University Press, 2006), 76–77.

supporters."[16] John Paul II, first as a bishop and later as the pope, thoroughly accepted the liturgical reform. John Paul II, who was also a council father, reminded the Church of the importance of the liturgical reform:

> The vast majority of the pastors and the Christian people have accepted the liturgical reform in a spirit of obedience and indeed joyful fervour. For this we should give thanks to God for that movement of the Holy Spirit in the Church which the liturgical renewal represents; for the fact that the table of the word of God is now abundantly furnished for all; for the immense effort undertaken throughout the world to provide the Christian people with translations of the Bible, the Missal and other liturgical books, for the increased participation of the faithful by prayer and song, gesture and silence, in the Eucharist and the other sacraments; for the ministries exercised by lay people and the responsibilities that they have assumed in virtue of the common priesthood into which they have been initiated through Baptism and Confirmation; for the radiant vitality of so many Christian communities, a vitality drawn from the wellspring of the Liturgy.[17]

Now, in the Church of the twenty-first century, rejecting the liturgical reform risks putting Roman Catholicism on the path "from the open Church to neo-exclusivism."[18] On the other hand, embracing the theology of the liturgical reform means understanding the Church under the sign of "sacramentality" and the Church as a sacrament, more than in an apologetic and juridical sense.[19]

Liturgy has always changed, not in years, but in generations, and we are in one of those moments of passage. The theological complex called Vatican II worked as a hub for the theological development and *ressourcement* that migrated from the early twentieth-century liturgical movement to the liturgical constitution, and then from the liturgical constitution to the Church of Vatican II. We are now part of this

---

[16] Mark S. Massa, *Catholics and American Culture: Fulton Sheen, Dorothy Day, and the Notre Dame Football Team* (New York: Herder and Herder, 1999), 166.

[17] John Paul II, apostolic letter *Vicesimus quintus annus* (1988), no. 12.

[18] See Gerard Mannion, *Ecclesiology and Postmodernity: Questions for the Church in Our Time* (Collegeville, MN: Liturgical Press, 2007), 43–74.

[19] See Salvador Pié-Ninot, *Eclesiologia. La sacramentalidad de la comunidad cristiana* (Salamanca: Sigueme, 2007); Italian edition: *Ecclesiologia. La sacramentalità della comunità cristiana* (Brescia: Morcelliana, 2008).

passage from Vatican II as a document—in a mostly linguistic and intellectual form—to a canonically accepted way of expressing Christian faith in the Catholic Church.

As the symbol of the council, the liturgical reform of Vatican II is becoming the *pierre d'attente*, the toothing-stone, necessary for some Catholic milieus to cast doubts not only on the results of the council but also on its very validity and legitimacy as an ecumenical council. *Sacrosanctum Concilium* rebuilt the vital connection between theology, liturgy, and the life of the Church: whoever wants to reverse the liturgical reform of Vatican II must also be ready to break a connection that has already become part of the *sensus fidelium*.

Bibliography

Archives

Vatican Secret Archives (ASV, Archivio Segreto Vaticano, Città del Vaticano), Archivio Concilio Vaticano II, index 1198, fonds 1350–1421 (Commissio de Liturgia).

Archive of John XXIII Foundation for Religious Studies in Bologna (Istituto per le scienze religiose—Fondazione per le scienze religiose Giovanni XXIII, Bologna), fond Pierre Duprey.

1. History of Vatican II

Acerbi, Antonio. *Due ecclesiologie. Ecclesiologia giuridica ed ecclesiologia di comunione nella Lumen gentium.* Bologna: EDB, 1975.

Acta et documenta Concilio Oecumenico Vaticano II apparando. Series I—Antepraeparatoria, Città del Vaticano: Typis Polyglottis Vaticanis, 1960–61; *Series II—Praeparatoria,* Città del Vaticano: Typis Polyglottis Vaticanis, 1964–94.

Acta Synodalia Sacrosancti Concilii Oecumenici Vaticani II. Città del Vaticano: Typis Polyglottis Vaticanis, 1970–99.

Alberigo, Giuseppe. *Transizione epocale. Studi sul Concilio Vaticano II.* Bologna: Il Mulino, 2009.

———. *A Brief History of Vatican II.* New York: Orbis, 2006. (Original Italian: *Breve storia del concilio Vaticano II.* Bologna: Il Mulino, 2005.)

Alberigo, Giuseppe, and Alberto Melloni, eds. *Verso il concilio Vaticano II (1960–1962). Passaggi e problemi della preparazione conciliare.* Bologna: Il Mulino, 1993.

Buonasorte, Nicla. *Tra Roma e Lefebvre: il tradizionalismo cattolico italiano e il Concilio Vaticano II.* Roma: Studium, 2003.

Burigana, Riccardo. *La Bibbia nel concilio. La redazione della costituzione "Dei Verbum" del Vaticano II.* Bologna: Il Mulino, 1998.

Carnets conciliare de l'évêque de Namur A.-M. Charue. Edited by Leo Declerck and Claude Soetens. Louvain-la-Neuve: Peeters, 2000.

Carnets conciliaires de Mgr Gérard Philips secrétaire adjoint de la Commission doctrinale. Edited by Karim Schelkens. Leuven: Peeters, 2006.

The Catholic Church and the Jewish People: Recent Reflections from Rome. Edited by Philip A. Cunningham, Norbert J. Hofmann, and Joseph Sievers. New York: Fordham University Press, 2007.

Congar, Yves. *Journal d'un théologien: 1946–1956*. Edited by Étienne Fouilloux. Paris: Cerf, 2001.

———. *Mon journal du concile*. Edited by Éric Mahieu. Paris: Cerf, 2002.

Edelby, Neophytos. *Il Vaticano II nel diario di un vescovo arabo*. Edited by Riccardo Cannelli. Cinisello Balsamo: San Paolo, 1996.

Faggioli, Massimo. *Breve storia dei movimenti cattolici*. Roma: Carocci, 2008. (Spanish translation: *Historia y evolución de los movimentos católicos. De León XIII a Benedicto XVI*. Madrid: PPC, 2011.)

———. *Vatican II: The Battle for Meaning*. Mahwah, NJ: Paulist Press, 2012.

———. *Il vescovo e il concilio. Modello episcopale e aggiornamento al Vaticano II*. Bologna: Il Mulino, 2005.

Herders Theologischer Kommentar zum Zweiten Vatikanischen Konzil. 5 vols. Edited by Hans Jochen Hilberath and Peter Hünermann. Freiburg i.B.: Herder, 2004–5.

History of Vatican II. 5 vols. Edited by Giuseppe Alberigo. English version edited by Joseph A. Komonchak. Maryknoll, NY: Orbis, 1995–2006.

Komonchak, Joseph A. "The Council of Trent at the Second Vatican Council." In *From Trent to Vatican II: Historical and Theological Investigations*, edited by Raymond F. Bulman and Frederick J. Parrella, 61–80. New York: Oxford University Press, 2006.

De Lubac, Henri. *Carnets du Concile*. Edited by Loïc Figoureux. Paris: Cerf, 2007.

Massa, Mark S. *The American Catholic Revolution: How the Sixties Changed the Church Forever*. New York: Oxford University Press, 2010.

Miccoli, Giovanni. *La Chiesa dell'anticoncilio. I tradizionalisti alla riconquista di Roma*. Roma-Bari: Laterza, 2011.

O'Malley, John W. *What Happened at Vatican II*. Cambridge, MA: Harvard University Press, Belknap Press, 2008.

Paiano, Maria. "Il rinnovamento della liturgia: dai movimenti alla chiesa universale." In *Verso il concilio Vaticano II (1960–1962). Passaggi e problemi della preparazione conciliare*, edited by Giuseppe Alberigo and Alberto Melloni, 67–140. Genova: Marietti, 1993.

Pulikkan, Paul. *Indian Church at Vatican II: A Historico-Theological Study of the Indian Participation in the Second Vatican Council*. Trichur, India: Maryamatha Publications, 2001.

Ruggieri, Giuseppe. "Appunti per una teologia in papa Roncalli." In *Papa Giovanni*, edited by Giuseppe Alberigo, 245–71. Bari: Laterza, 1987.

Schillebeeckx, Edward. *The Council Notes of Edward Schillebeeckx 1962–1963*. Edited by Karim Schelkens. Leuven: Peeters, 2011.

Turbanti, Giovanni. *Un concilio per il mondo moderno. La redazione della costituzione pastorale "Gaudium et spes" del Vaticano II*. Bologna: Il Mulino, 2000.

Unfinished Journey: The Church 40 Years after Vatican II. Edited by John Wilkins. London: Continuum, 2004.

Vatican II: Did Anything Happen? Edited by David G. Schultenover. New York and London: Continuum, 2007.

Vorgrimler, Herbert, ed. *Commentary on the Documents of Vatican II*. Translated by Lalit Adolphus, Kevin Smyth, and Richard Strachan. London: Burns & Oates; New York, Herder & Herder, 1967–69. (Original German: *Das Zweite Vatikanische Konzil. Konstitutionen, Dekrete und Erklärungen lateinisch und deutsch Kommentare—Lexikon für Theologie und Kirche*. 3 vols. Freiburg i.B.: Herder, 1966–68.)

Wagner, Johannes. *Mein Weg zur Liturgiereform, 1936–1986. Erinnerungen*. Freiburg i.B.: Herder, 1993.

2. The Liturgical Reform of Vatican II

The Active Participation Revisited—La participation active. 100 ans après Pie X et 40 ans après Vatican II. Edited by Jozef Lamberts. Leuven: Peeters, 2005.

Baldovin, John. *Reforming the Liturgy: A Response to the Critics*. Collegeville, MN: Liturgical Press, 2008.

Benedict XVI and the Sacred Liturgy. Edited by Neil J. Roy and Janet E. Rutherford. Dublin: Four Courts Press, 2010.

Bordeyne, Philippe, and Laurent Villemin, eds. *Vatican II et la théologie. Perspectives pour le XXIe siècle*. Paris: Cerf, 2006.

Botte, Bernard. *From Silence to Participation: An Insider's View of Liturgical Renewal*. Washington, DC: Pastoral Press, 1988. (Original French: *Le Mouvement liturgique: temoignage et souvenirs*. Paris, 1973. New Italian edition: *Il movimento liturgico. Testimonianza e ricordi*. Cantalupa: Effatà, 2009.)

Bovens, Paul. "Chronique inachevée des publications autour de la Lettre apostolique en forme de Motu proprio 'Summorum Pontificum' de Benoît XVI." *Ephemerides Theologicae Lovanienses* 84 (2008): 529–36.

Brovelli, Franco. *Per uno studio de "L'année liturgique" di P. Guéranger. Contributo alla storia del movimento liturgico*. Roma: CLV–Edizioni liturgiche, 1981.

Bugnini, Annibale. *The Reform of the Liturgy, 1948–1975*. Collegeville, MN: Liturgical Press, 1990. (Original Italian: *La riforma liturgica 1948–1975*. Roma: CLV–Edizioni liturgiche, 1983.)

Van Bühren, Ralf. *Kunst und Kirche im 20. Jahrhundert. Die Rezeption des Zweiten Vatikanischen Konzils*. Schoening: Paderborn, 2008.

The Church and the Liturgy. Glen Rock, NJ: Paulist Press, 1965.

Congar, Yves. "L'ecclesia ou communauté chrétienne, sujet intégral de l'action liturgique." In *La liturgie après Vatican II; bilans, études, prospective*, edited by Jean-Pierre Jossua and Yves Congar, 241–82. Paris: Cerf, 1967.

———. *At the Heart of Christian Worship: Liturgical Essays of Yves Congar*. Translated and edited by Paul Philibert. Collegeville, MN: Liturgical Press, 2010.

Cuva, Armando. "La notion de participation dans Sacrosanctum concilium." *La Maison-Dieu* 241 (2005): 137–49.

Daniélou, Jean. *L'oraison comme probléme politique*. Paris: Fayard, 1965.

De Clerck, Paul. "La Constitution Sacrosanctum Concilium. Réflexions sur sa réception dans le long terme." *Questions Liturgiques* 91 (2010): 142–55.

———. " 'Lex orandi, lex credendi'. Un principe heuristique." *La Maison-Dieu* 222, no. 2 (2000): 61–78.

———. "La liturgie a-t-elle besoin d'une réforme permanente?" *La Maison-Dieu* 260, no. 4 (2009): 211–26.

———. "La participation active. Perspective historico-liturgiques, de Pie X à Vatican II." In *The Active Participation Revisited—La participation active. 100 ans après Pie X et 40 ans après Vatican II*, edited by Jozef Lamberts, 13–31. Leuven: Peeters, 2005.

———. "Pierre-Marie Gy: souvenirs et témoignage d'un liturgiste au temps de Vatican II. Souvenirs et témoignage collectés par Paul De Clerck." *La Maison-Dieu* 261, no. 3 (2010): 127–60.

———. "La réforme liturgique: ce qui reste à faire." *Questions liturgiques* 91 (2010): 64–75.

Egender, Nicolas. "L'enjeu de la liturgie. Quarantième anniversaire de la Constitution sur la Liturgie." *Irénikon* 3 (2005): 342–71.

Eisenbach, Franziskus. *Die Gegenwart Jesu Christi im Gottesdienst: Systematische Studien zur Liturgiekonstitution des II. Vatikanischen Konzils*. Mainz: Matthias-Grünewald-Verlag, 1982.

Empereur, James L., and Christopher G. Kiesling. *The Liturgy That Does Justice*. Collegeville, MN: Liturgical Press, 1990.

Fernandez Menes, Juan Carlos. "Iglesia y liturgia, núcleos eclesiológicos de la constitución Sacrosanctum Concilium." *Studium Legionense* 46 (2005): 155–211.

Ferrone, Rita. *Liturgy:* Sacrosanctum Concilium. New York: Paulist Press, 2007.

Galavotti, Enrico. "Verso una nuova era liturgica. Appunti sul contributo di Cipriano Vagaggini al concilio Vaticano II." In *Teologia in un regime di simboli. Scritti in onore di Cipriano Vagaggini (1909–1999),* edited by Matteo Ferrari and Giordano Remondi, 56–93. Camaldoli: Edizioni Camaldoli, 2011.

Giampietro, Nicola. "Il motu proprio 'Sacram Liturgiam': una rilettura a quarant'anni dalla promulgazione (1964–2004)." *Ephemerides Liturgicae* 119 (2005): 133–50.

Grillo, Andrea. "40 anni prima e 40 anni dopo 'Sacrosanctum Concilium'. Una 'considerazione inattuale' sulla attualità del movimento liturgico." *Ecclesia Orans* 21 (2004): 269–300.

———. "Un bilancio del motu proprio 'Summorum pontificum'. Quattro paradossi e una intenzione dimenticata." *Concilium* 45, no. 2 (2009): 125–32.

———. "Ende der Liturgiereform? Das Motuproprio 'Summorum Pontificum.'" *Stimmen der Zeit* 225, no. 11 (2007): 730–40.

———. "Maschile e/o femminile. Un confronto 'prospettico' tra concilio di Trento e concilio Vaticano II." In *Anatemi di ieri, sfide di oggi. Contrappunti di genere nella rilettura del concilio di Trento,* edited by Antonio Autiero and Marinella Perroni, 199–212. Bologna: EDB, 2011.

———. *La nascita della liturgia nel XX secolo. Saggio sul rapporto tra movimento liturgico e (post-) modernità.* Assisi: Cittadella, 2003.

———. *Oltre Pio V. La Riforma liturgica nel conflitto di interpretazioni.* Brescia: Queriniana, 2007.

———. "Il pensiero di Cipriano Vagaggini, tra eredità tomista e confronto con la modernità. Profilo e fortuna di un grande liturgista." *Cipriano Vagaggini. L'intelligenza della liturgia. Rivista Liturgica* 3 (maggio–giugno 2009): 362–84.

———. "Dalla riforma necessaria alla riforma non sufficiente. Il movimento liturgico come 'effetto' del Concilio Vaticano II?" *Ecclesia Orans* 23 (2006): 281–96.

Gy, Pierre-Marie. "La liturgie de l'Église. La tradition vivante et Vatican II." *Revue de l'Institut Catholique de Paris* 50 (1994): 29–37.

————. "Souvenirs et témoignage d'un liturgiste au temps de Vatican II."
La Maison-Dieu 261, no. 1 (2010): 127–60.

Häussling, Angelus A. "Pascha-Mysterium. Kritisches zu einem Beitrag in
der dritten Auflage des Lexicon für Theologie und Kirche." *Archiv für
Liturgiewissenschaft* 41 (1999): 157–65.

Initiation Chretienne et la liturgie: hommage au Prof. Em. Dr. Jozef Lamberts. Edited
by Lambert Leussen. Leuven: Peeters, 2008.

Jackson, Pamela. *An Abundance of Graces: Reflections on* Sacrosanctum Concilium.
Chicago and Mundelein, IL: Hillenbrand Books, 2004.

Join-Lambert, Arnaud. "Richesses de Vatican II à (re)découvrir." *Questions
Liturgiques* 91 (2010): 42–63.

Jungmann, Josef A. *The Mass of the Roman Rite: Its Origins and Development.*
Translated by Francis A. Brunner; revised by Charles K. Riepe. 2 vols.
Westminster, MD: Christian Classics, 1959. (Originial German: *Missarum
sollemnia. Eine genetische erklärung der römischen Messe.* Wien: Herder,
1948; 2., durchgesehene. Augl., Wien: Herder, 1949.)

Kasper, Walter. *Die Liturgie der Kirche.* Walter Kasper Gesammelte Schriften, 10.
Freiburg i.B.: Herder, 2010.

Klöckener, Martin. "La dynamique du mouvement liturgique et de la réforme
liturgique. Points communs et différences théologiques et spirituelles."
La Maison-Dieu 260, no. 4 (2009): 69–109.

La liturgie après Vatican II; bilans, études, prospective. Edited by Jean-Pierre Jossua
and Yves Congar. Paris: Cerf, 1967.

Lamberts, Jozef. "L'évolution de la notion de 'participation active' dans le
Mouvement liturgique du XXe siècle." *La Maison-Dieu* 241 (2005): 77–120.

The Liturgy of Vatican II: A Symposium. Edited by William Baraúna. English
edition by Jovian Lang. Chicago: Franciscan Herald Press, 1966.

Malcherek, Reinhold. "Gemeinschaft von Gott und den Menschen. Überlegungen zur Liturgie als Gottmenschlicher Dialog nach dem Liturgiekonstitution des II. Vatikanischen Konzils." *Ecclesia Orans* 18 (2001):
237–68.

————. "Liturgie als personaler Begegnung. Liturgitheologische Reflexionen
im Licht von 'Sacrosanctum Concilium' und theologischer Entwürfe im
Umfeld des II. Vatikanischen Konzils." *Ecclesia Orans* 21 (2004): 365–87.

Manzanares, Julio. *Liturgia y descentralización en el Concilio Vaticano II. Las conferencias episcopales, eje de la reforma litúrgica conciliar.* Roma: Pontificia
Università Gregoriana Editrice, 1970.

Marini, Piero. *A Challenging Reform: Realizing the Vision of the Liturgical Renewal, 1963–1975*. Edited by Mark R. Francis, John R. Page, and Keith F. Pecklers. Collegeville, MN: Liturgical Press, 2007.

———. "Sacrosanctum Concilium 40 anni dopo. Tra consegne e impegni permanenti." *Rivista Liturgica* 91, no. 5 (2004): 771–80.

Marx, Paul B. *Virgil Michel and the Liturgical Movement*. Collegeville, MN: Liturgical Press, 1957.

Mattheeuws, Gino. "The International Liturgical Conferences (1951–1960). A Blueprint for the Liturgical Renewal of Vatican II." *Questions liturgiques* 78 (1997): 92–112.

Mazzolini, Sandra. "La lingua dell'altro come mezzo di propagazione della fede." In *Anatemi di ieri, sfide di oggi. Contrappunti di genere nella rilettura del concilio di Trento*, edited by Antonio Autiero and Marinella Perroni, 187–98. Bologna: EDB, 2011.

McManus, Frederick R. *The Revival of the Liturgy*. New York: Herder and Herder, 1963.

Metzger, Marcel. "L'attention aux traditions dans le mouvement liturgique occidental." In *Les mouvements liturgiques. Corrélations entre pratiques et recherches*, edited by Carlo Braga and Alessandro Pistoia, 255–76. Roma: CLV, 2004.

———. "La réforme liturgique du Concile Vatican II et les idéologies qui résistent." *Revue des Sciences Religieuses* 85, no. 1 (2011): 101–10.

Midili, Giuseppe. "La Sacrosanctum concilium, pietra miliare della riforma liturgica e ponte tra passato e futuro." *Ecclesia Orans* 25 (2008): 7–32.

Paiano, Maria. *Liturgia e società nel Novecento. Percorsi del movimento liturgico di fronte ai processi di secolarizzazione*. Roma: Edizioni di Storia e Letteratura, 2000.

Pecklers, Keith F. "La liturgia en el Concilio Vaticano II y su futuro en la Iglesia." *ITER: Revista de Teología* 18 (2007): 42–43, 393–410.

———. *The Unread Vision: The Liturgical Movement in the United States of America, 1926–1955*. Collegeville, MN: Liturgical Press, 1998.

———. *Worship: A Primer in Christian Ritual*. Collegeville, MN: Liturgical Press, 2003.

Pistoia, Alessandro. "La 'Sacrosanctum Concilium' dopo le commemorazioni del quarantennio: note a margine." *Ephemerides Liturgicae* 118 (2004): 403–16.

Poswick, R.-Ferdinand, and Lambert Vos. "Autour d'un centenaire (1909–2009). Les débuts du mouvement liturgique: Beauduin, Marmion, Festugière et . . . les autres." *Questions Liturgiques* 92, no. 1 (2011): 3–28.

Prétot, Patrick. "La Constitution sur la liturgie: une herméneutique de la tradition liturgique." In *Vatican II et la théologie. Perspectives pour le XXIe siècle*, edited by Philippe Bordeyne and Laurent Villemin, 17–34. Paris: Cerf, 2006.

———. "Liturgie et ecclésiologie à une époque d'individualisation." *La Maison-Dieu* 260, no. 4 (2009): 183–210.

———. "The Sacraments as 'Celebrations of the Church': Liturgy's Impact on Sacramental Theology." In *Sacraments: Revelation of the Humanity of God; Engaging the Fundamental Theology of Louis-Marie Chauvet*, edited by Philippe Bordeyne and Bruce T. Morrill, 25–41. Collegeville, MN: Liturgical Press, 2008.

Ratzinger, Joseph. "'Der Geist der Liturgie' oder: Die Treue zum Konzil. Antwort an Pater Gy." *Liturgisches Jahrbuch* 52 (2002): 111–15.

———. *Theologie der Liturgie. Gesammelte Schriften*, Band 11. Freiburg i.B.: Herder, 2008.

———. "The Theology of Liturgy." In *Looking Again at the Question of the Liturgy with Cardinal Ratzinger*, 18–32. Proceedings of the July 2001 Fontgombault Liturgical Conference. Saint Michael's Abbey Press, 2003.

Rother, Wolfgang F. "Liturgische Gegenreform(ation)? Vom Zweiten Vatikanischen Konzil zum Apostolischen Schreiben 'Summorum Pontificum.'" *Una-Voce-Korrespondenz* 38 (2008): 152–70.

Routhier, Gilles. "La liturgie aux prises avec un monde et une église en mutation." *La Maison-Dieu* 260, no. 4 (2009): 153–81.

Scardilli, Pietro Damiano. *I nuclei ecclesiologici nella costituzione liturgica del Vaticano II*. Roma: Pontificia Università Gregoriana, 2007.

Schmidt, Herman. *La Costituzione sulla Sacra Liturgia. Testo, Genesi, Commento, Documentazione*. Roma: Herder, 1966.

Schrott, Simon. "The Need for Discontinuity: Considerations on a Hermeneutic of Liturgical Reform according to *Sacrosanctum Concilium*." *Studia Liturgica* 41 (2011): 56–67.

Stubenrauch, Thomas. *Wer ist Träger der Liturgie? Zur Rezeption des II. Vatikanischen Konzils im Codex Iuris Canonici von 1983*. Trier: Paulinus, 2003.

Theobald, Christoph. *La réception du concile Vatican II, I. Accéder à la source*. Paris: Cerf, 2009.

Vagaggini, Cipriano. "La ecclesiologia di comunione come fondamento teologico principale della riforma liturgica nei suoi punti maggiori." In *Liturgia, opera divina e umana. Studi sulla riforma liturgica offerti a S.E. Mons. Annibale Bugnini in occasione del suo 70° compleanno*, edited by Pierre Jounel, Reiner Kaczynski, and Gottardo Pasqualetti, 59–131. Roma: CLV–Edizioni Liturgiche, 1982.

———. *Theological Dimensions of the Liturgy*. Collegeville, MN: Liturgical Press, 1959, 1976. (First Italian edition: *Il senso teologico della liturgia*. Roma: Edizioni Paoline, 1957.)

3. *Ressourcement*, Ecclesiology, and Reform

Congar, Yves. "Quod omnes tangit ab omnibus tractari et approbari debet." *Revue historique de droit français et étranger* 35 (1958): 210–59.

———. *Vraie et fausse réforme dans l'Église*. Paris: Cerf, 1950. (English translation: *True and False Reform in the Church*, translated by Paul Philibert. Collegeville, MN: Liturgical Press, 2011.)

Dejaifve, Georges. "L'ecclesiologia del concilio Vaticano II." In *L'ecclesiologia dal Vaticano I al Vaticano II*, 87–98. Brescia: La Scuola, 1973.

De Mey, Peter. "Church Renewal and Reform in the Documents of Vatican II. History, Theology, Terminology." *The Jurist* 1–2 (2011): 369–400.

Dossetti, Giuseppe. *Per una "chiesa eucaristica". Rilettura della portata dottrinale della Costituzione liturgica del Vaticano II. Lezioni del 1965*. Edited by Giuseppe Alberigo and Giuseppe Ruggieri. Bologna: Il Mulino, 2002.

Dulles, Avery. *Models of the Church*. New York: Doubleday, 1974.

L'épiscopat et l'Église universelle. Edited by Yves Congar and Bernard Dominique Dupuy. Paris: Cerf, 1962.

Exkommunikation oder Kommunikation? Der Weg der Kirche nach dem II. Vatikanum und die Pius-Brüder. Edited by Peter Hünermann. Freiburg i.B.: Herder, 2009.

Faggioli, Massimo. "Polis e liturgia nella chiesa conciliare." *Rivista di Pastorale Liturgica* 277, no. 6 (2009): 19–24.

Fouilloux, Étienne. *Les catholiques et l'unité chrétienne du XIXe au XXe siècle: itinéraires européens d'expression française*. Paris: Centurion, 1982.

———. *Éditer les Pères de l'Église au XXe siècle*. Paris: Cerf, 1995.

———. *Une Église en quête de liberté: la pensée catholique française entre modernisme et Vatican II (1914–1962)*. Paris: Desclée de Brouwer, 1998.

Frühmorgen, Franz. *Bischof und Bistum—Bischof und Presbyterium. Eine liturgiewissenschaftliche Studie zu den Artikeln 41 und 42 der Liturgiekonstitution des Zweiten Vatikanums*. Regensburg: Pustet, 1994.

Gaillardetz, Richard R. *Ecclesiology for a Global Church: A People Called and Sent*. Maryknoll, NY: Orbis, 2008.

Gianotti, Daniele. *I Padri della Chiesa al Concilio Vaticano II. La teologia patristica nella Lumen Gentium*. Bologna: EDB, 2010.

Haquin, André. *Dom Lambert Beauduin et le renouveau liturgique*. Gembloux: J. Duculot, 1970.

Isaac, Jules. *Jésus et Israël*. Paris: Albin Michel, 1948.

Ladner, Gerhart B. *The Idea of Reform: Its Impact on Christian Thought and Action in the Age of the Fathers*. Cambridge, MA: Harvard University Press, 1959.

Laplanche, François. *La crise de l'origine: la science catholique des Évangiles et l'histoire au XXe siècle*. Paris: Albin Michel, 2006.

Liturgie lieu théologique. Edited by Paul De Clerck. Paris: Beauchesne, 1999.

Loonbeek, Raymond, and Jacques Mortiau. *Un pionnier, Dom Lambert Beauduin (1873–1960). Liturgie et unité des chrétiens*. 2 vols. Louvain-la-Neuve: Collège Erasme, 2001.

———. *Dom Lambert Beauduin visionnaire et précurseur (1873–1960). Un moine au coeur libre*. Paris: Cerf, 2005.

Mannion, Gerard. *Ecclesiology and Postmodernity: Questions for the Church in Our Time*. Collegeville, MN: Liturgical Press, 2007.

Melloni, Alberto. "Contesti, fatti e reazioni attorno alla Veterum Sapientia di Giovanni XXIII." *Rivista Liturgica* 89, no. 3 (2002): 391–407.

———. "Da *Nostra aetate* ad Assisi '86. Cornici e fatti di una ricezione creativa del concilio Vaticano II." *Convivium Assisense* 9, no. 1 (2007): 63–89.

———. "Sacrosanctum Concilium 1963–2003. Lo spessore storico della riforma liturgica e la ricezione del Vaticano II." *Rivista liturgica* 90, no. 6 (2003): 915–30.

Montagnes, Bernard. *The Story of Father Marie-Joseph Lagrange: Founder of Modern Catholic Bible Study*. New York: Paulist Press, 2006. (Original edition: *Marie-Joseph Lagrange. Une biographie critique*. Paris: Cerf, 2005.)

Mortari, Luciana. *Consacrazione episcopale e collegialità*. Firenze: Vallecchi, 1969.

O'Malley, John W. *Four Cultures of the West*. Cambridge, MA: Harvard University Press, Belknap Press, 2004.

———. *Trent and All That: Renaming Catholicism in the Early Modern Era.* Cambridge, MA: Harvard University Press, 2000.

Les Pères et la naissance de l'ecclésiologie. Edited by Marie-Anne Vannier. Paris: Cerf, 2009.

Pié-Ninot, Salvador. *Eclesiologia. La sacramentalidad de la comunidad cristiana.* Salamanca: Sigueme, 2007. (Italian edition: *Ecclesiologia. La sacramentalità della comunità cristiana.* Brescia: Morcelliana, 2008.)

Prodi, Paolo. *Il paradigma tridentino. Un'epoca della storia della Chiesa.* Brescia: Morcelliana, 2010.

Prusak, Bernard P. *The Church Unfinished: Ecclesiology through the Centuries.* New York: Paulist Press, 2004.

Ressourcement: A Movement for Renewal in Twentieth-Century Catholic Theology. Edited by Gabriel Flynn and Paul D. Murray. Oxford: Oxford University Press, 2012.

Tillard, Jean Marie R. *L'Église locale. Ecclésiologie de communion et catholicité.* Paris: Cerf, 1995.

Vatican II et la théologie. Perspectives pour le XXIe siècle. Edited by Philippe Bordeyne and Laurent Villemin. Paris, Cerf: 2006.

Villemin, Laurent. "L'autorité des conférences épiscopales en matière de liturgie. Interprétations initiales et réinterprétations récentes." In *L'autorité et les autorités. L'herméneutique théologique de Vatican II,* edited by Gilles Routhier and Guy Jobin, 151–65. Paris: Cerf, 2010.

———. "Principes ecclésiologiques de la réforme liturgique de Vatican II." *Lumière et Vie* 279 (juillet–septembre 2008): 71–79.

Index of Names

Index of Subjects

active participation, 20, 43, 60, 74–75, 103–5, 119, 131
aesthetics, 3, 43, 71, 98, 126
aggiornamento, 2, 31, 44, 48, 61, 66–67, 120, 126, 155

Christendom, 42, 53, 102, 106, 116
Code of Canon Law (1917), 70, 74, 77
Code of Canon Law (1983), 7
Cold War devotions, 53
Constantine Era, 38, 73, 100, 154
Council of Trent, Tridentinism, 8, 23, 26, 45, 51, 53–54, 66, 76, 78, 82–83, 94, 101, 121, 125–27, 135–36, 139–40, 146, 163–66

Eastern Churches, Eastern traditions, 35, 57, 85, 126, 133, 140
Ecclesia Dei (John Paul II; 1988; *motu proprio*), 8, 150
ecumenism, 17, 30–37, 49, 97, 100, 107–11, 137, 142, 149, 155
episcopal
    collegiality, 8, 86, 89, 103, 152, 155
    conferences, 65, 73, 80, 90, 130, 144, 152
eucharistic ecclesiology, 6, 15, 18, 71

fathers of the Church, 22, 29, 47, 49–51

historicity, ix

inculturation, cultures, ix, 38, 40, 43, 55, 68, 82, 92, 118, 120, 130, 144, 163

Jews, Judaism, 50, 100, 112–15, 157

lex orandi, lex credendi, 7, 87, 90–92, 96, 152, 154, 156
liturgical
    movement, 9, 11, 23, 27–29, 33, 38, 74–75, 81, 94, 100, 112, 115, 119, 123
    pluralism, rites, 26, 32, 34, 63, 67, 104

missions, evangelization, 38–41
Mediator Dei (Pius XII; 1947; encyclical), 5, 28–29, 40, 43, 60, 69, 70, 89
Mirae Caritatis (Leo XIII; 1902; encyclical), 45
Mystici Corporis (Pius XII; 1943; encyclical), 59–60, 62, 76

neoscholasticism, 25, 27, 55

rapprochement, 17–18, 94–99, 102–8, 113–18, 154
reception of the liturgical reform, 3, 91, 161, 168
reform
    in the Church, 2, 12
    movements, 4, 20–21, 24–25, 28, 97, 109
    of the liturgical reform, 3, 9, 17, 19, 23, 71, 121, 144, 162, 165
ressourcement, 11, 16–18, 20–57, 67, 71–72, 75–77, 81, 98, 113, 117, 120, 123, 137–38, 142, 154, 167

Scripture, 15, 37, 49–50, 69, 92, 100, 103, 108, 113–14, 118, 124, 138–39, 143, 151–52, 156, 164, 167

secularization, secularism, 4, 12, 23–24, 56, 78, 110, 138, 157
Summorum Pontificum (Benedict XVI; 2007; *motu proprio*), 1, 86, 143–44

Thomism, 38
Traditio Apostolica, 51
traditionalism, 23
Tra le sollecitudini (Pius X; 1903; *motu proprio*), 10

Uniatism, 36

Vatican Council
　First, 72, 80
　Second:
　　Ad Gentes (1965; decree), 42, 88, 101
　　Apostolicam Actuositatem (1965; decree), 42, 62, 88
　　Christus Dominus (1965; decree), 62–63, 88, 104
　　Dei Verbum (1965; constitution), 33, 50, 54–55, 92, 101, 113–14, 124, 138, 149, 165
　　Dignitatis Humanae (1965; declaration), 92, 156
　　Gaudet Mater Ecclesia (1962; opening speech), 54, 93

Gaudium et Spes (1965; constitution), 17, 43, 62–63, 94–95, 124, 156
Gravissimum Educationis (1965; declaration), 88
Humanae Salutis (1961; apostolic constitution), 93
Lumen Gentium (1964; constitution), 5–6, 8, 16–17, 40, 45–46, 54–55, 61–63, 70–73, 79–80, 83–85, 88–89, 91–92, 94, 103–4, 124
Message to the World (1962), 98–99, 116
Nostra Aetate (1965; declaration), 17, 92, 95, 147, 149, 156–57
Optatam Totius (1965; decree), 88
Orientalium Ecclesiarum (1964; decree), 88
Presbyterorum Ordinis (1965; decree), 42, 88
Unitatis Redintegratio (1964; decree), 17, 62, 71, 92, 95
vernacular language and Latin, 20, 41, 46, 56, 60, 127, 129–30, 133–36, 138–39, 142, 162
Vicesimus quintus annus (John Paul II; 1988; apostolic letter), 142

188

Meet the Pug

Pugs are recognized by the American Kennel Club as members of the Toy group.

- Pugs were first known in China, where they were companions to Buddhist monks.

- The name Pug, a European slang word for "dear one," was used to describe Marmoset monkeys that were kept as pets in the eighteenth century. With their big eyes, round faces, and impish ways, the monkeys resembled the little dogs. Soon the dogs were being called pug dogs, and the name stuck.

- Pugs were specifically bred to be companion dogs. They are known to be social dogs, not "one-person" dogs, and will gladly share the company of any family member or friend.

- Pugs combine cocky confidence with a friendly, sensitive nature.

- Pugs typically weigh between 14 and 18 pounds.

- The coat of the Pug is velvety soft and can be silver, apricot-fawn, or black. Pugs are short-coated and naturally clean; compared to many other breeds, Pugs require little grooming.

- Pugs have hearty appetites. In fact, many Pugs are convinced that more of just about anything is better.

- Pugs relish playtime and daily exercise.

Consulting Editor
IAN DUNBAR PH.D., MRCVS

Featuring Photographs by
MARY BLOOM

Howell Book House
An Imprint of Macmillan General Reference USA
A Pearson Education Macmillan Company
1633 Broadway
New York, NY 10019

Macmillan Publishing books may be purchased for
business or sales promotional use. For information
please write: Special Markets Department,
Macmillan Publishing USA, 1633 Broadway,
New York, NY 10019.

Library of Congress Cataloging-in-Publication
Data
            The essential Pug.
                p.   cm.
        Includes bibliographical references and index.
        ISBN 1-58245-025-0
        1. Pug.   I. Howell Book House.
        SF429.P9E87   1999   98-46322
        636.76—dc21
                        CIP

Manufactured in the United States of America
10 9 8 7 6 5 4 3

Series Director: Michele Matrisciani
Production Team: Carrie Allen, Heather Pope, and
    Christy Wagner
Book Design: Paul Costello
Photography:
    Courtesy of Diana Robinson: 80
    All other photos by Mary Bloom

ARE YOU READY?!

☐ Have you prepared your home
and your family for your new
pet?

☐ Have you gotten the proper
supplies you'll need to care for
your dog?

☐ Have you found a veterinarian
that you (and your dog) are
comfortable with?

☐ Have you thought about how
you want your dog to behave?

☐ Have you arranged your schedule to accommodate your dog's
needs for exercise and attention?

*No matter what stage you're at with
your dog—still thinking about getting one, or he's already part of the
family—this Essential guide will
provide you with the practical information you need to understand and
care for your canine companion. Of
course you're ready—you have this
book!*

THE ESSENTIAL

Pug

The Pug's Senses

SIGHT

Pugs can detect movement at a greater distance than we can, but they can't see as well up close. They can also see better in less light, but can't distinguish many colors.

SOUND

Pugs can hear about four times better than we can, and they can hear high-pitched sounds especially well.

TASTE

Pugs have fewer taste buds than we do, so they're likelier to try anything—and usually do, which is why it's important for their owners to monitor their food intake. Dogs are omnivorous, which means they eat meat as well as vegetables.

TOUCH

Pugs are social animals and love to be petted, groomed, and played with.

SMELL

A Pug's nose, like that of other dogs, is his greatest sensory organ. A dog's sense of smell is so great he can follow a trail that's weeks old. Because the Pug's nose is pushed in, his sense of smell isn't as great as his longer-muzzled cousins, but he'll still find lingering crumbs as well as the next dog!

CHAPTER ONE

Getting to Know Your Pug

For thousands of years, the Pug has been bred for the sole purpose of being a companion. He does not track, hunt, retrieve, point or herd. He loves. And he is happiest when he is loved in return. Few today will argue with the statement that the Pug is the companion par excellence.

Pugs are marvelously adaptive and are anxious to discover and share your mood. They love to run loose (always in an enclosed area), to snooze in front of the fireplace or romp in the snow.

THE MULTI-TALENTED PUG

From rough play in the backyard or a tramp in the woods, to a gentle guardian of an infant or a patient listener to one's problems, the Pug can be all things to all people. His fondness for children of all ages and his reliability as a companion to man are legendary.

As you walk through your home, you will hear the "click, click, click" of your Pug's toenails as he follows close at your heels, wondering what you will do next: go to the kitchen for a little snack, sit in your favorite armchair to watch TV or read a book or go for a walk to see what's new in the neighborhood. Any one of these events (or a dozen others)

will send your Pug into an active explosion of joy.

Arguably, your Pug could be called a guard dog for he will certainly give voice when a stranger is approaching, but will seldom bark for no reason at all.

PUGS ARE SOCIAL DOGS

Pugs are not "one-person" dogs. They know who is a member of their family and gladly share the company of any family member or friend. They may, however, display

The Pug has been bred for the sole purpose of being a companion.

Pugs feel most secure and comfortable when they have a set routine.

some partiality toward the one who puts down the food dish.

PUGS LIKE ROUTINE

Pugs like routine. If you take them for a walk each morning, they will come to expect this every day. If they receive some daily grooming, they will look forward to it.

A Pug wants to know what is expected of him. Will he share your or your child's bed at night, or will he sleep in his very own place in the kitchen or laundry room? Is he supposed to bark at strangers or simply go to the front door as a stranger approaches the house? At what hour can he expect dinner? Will he beg at the family's dinner table or take a snooze while his humans eat? These are a few of the things your Pug will want to know for, above all, he wishes to please his people. The way to make your Pug happiest is to train him well so he knows what to expect and when to expect it. Establish a schedule and stick to it. This will make your Pug comfortable and secure that all his needs are being met by the people he loves and trusts.

Pugs love to be close to their favorite family members.

3

PUGS NEED ATTENTION

The worst thing that can happen to a Pug is to be ignored. Once they get used to your routines, they will want to be near you to share in them as much as possible. Your Pug will want to be with you whether you are resting, walking, driving or washing dishes. Of course, your Pug cannot share many of your activities, but he will soon learn which he can and which he can't.

GROOMING REQUIREMENTS

If Pugs are kept clean by frequent brushing and occasional bathing, they are largely free from doggy odors. Any bad odors they emit are probably caused by either flatulence or bad breath. Flatulence could mean that they are not being fed the right food. Bad breath is most often the result of tartar collecting on the teeth and is a sign that a good cleaning by your veterinarian is in order. Teeth should be checked by your vet at least every six months,

Pugs require regular grooming to keep them looking and feeling their best.

4

and failure to do so will result not only in unpleasant breath, but also premature loss of teeth and the discomfort of dental abscesses.

Although the Pug is a short-coated breed, the length and density of the coat will vary considerably from dog to dog. Most fawn Pugs have double coats: a layer of very soft undercoat, under a layer of longer and harsher coat. Puppies in particular will normally have a very dense undercoat; and, as they mature, much of this will be shed. Older dogs also shed, sometimes seasonally, sometimes more often. If

the outer coat sheds, this is often a sign of some other health problem and, if severe, calls for a check-up by your vet. Black Pugs are usually (but not always) single-coated, lacking the soft undercoat. For that reason, they shed less than the fawns.

PUGS SNORE

As in any other breed with a short muzzle, Pugs tend to emit a variety of noises when they doze or sleep. This can vary from a slight snuffling to a good, hearty snore. The test of a true Pug lover is how he reacts to this snoring. Some people find it annoying, but the Pug lover is comforted by the sound, knowing that as long as the snoring is regular, everything is all right.

PUGS NEED EXERCISE

A Pug is by nature both an active dog and a "lounge lizard"—whichever you teach him to be. Either way, he should engage in daily exercise to remain in good health. A daily walk of about a mile or so is one way to accomplish this, and at least a portion of this should be at a brisk pace.

Pugs need exercise to stay in good health.

5

If you have two or more Pugs and an enclosure around your property, chances are the Pugs will exercise each other—and few things are more fun to watch than two or more Pugs chasing each other at full tilt, mouths open, ears flying and tails trying to catch up with the rest of the dogs' bodies.

Quite obviously, the degree of exercise will be governed by the weather to some extent. In temperatures over 80 or 85 degrees, exercise must be modified; likewise, when the temperature drops below 45 degrees, your Pug should not be left outside for extended periods of time,

CHARACTERISTICS OF THE PUG

good with children

very social

tends to snore loudly

does not require intense exercise

adaptable

cannot tolerate extreme heat

Unlike people, dogs do not perspire over their entire body, but are cooled by panting and through the pads of their feet. Hence, they are more susceptible to heat stroke than people are. Because Pugs are bracycephalic, or short muzzled, they can overheat even more easily. If you live in a hot climate, exercise your Pug in the early morning or evening. Never leave your Pug in the car on a hot day, even with the windows down. A stationary car can become too hot very quickly, and it's just not worth risking your Pug's life for a ride.

even if you have provided him with a sweater. When left outside, a Pug should always have water and, in hot weather, available shade.

CHAPTER TWO

Homecoming

Before bringing home your new family member, do a little planning to help make the transition easier. The first decision to make is where the puppy will live. Will she have access to the entire house or be limited to certain rooms? A similar consideration applies to the yard. It is simpler to control a puppy's activities and to housetrain the puppy if she is confined to definite areas. If doors do not exist where needed, baby gates make satisfactory temporary barriers.

A dog crate is an excellent investment and is an invaluable aid in raising a puppy. It provides a safe, quiet place where a dog can sleep. If it's used properly, a crate helps with housetraining. However, long periods of uninterrupted stays are not recommended—especially for young puppies. Unless you have someone at home or can have someone come in a few times a day to let her out to relieve herself and socialize with her for a while, a *small* crate is not advisable. Never lock a young puppy in a small crate for an entire day!

A dog crate will provide your Pug with a safe place to rest or play.

Make sure your Pug will have company and companionship during the day. If the members of your family are not at home during the day, try to come home at lunchtime, let your puppy out and spend some time with her. If this isn't possible, try to get a neighbor or friend who lives close by to come spend time with the puppy. Your Pug thrives on human attention and guidance, and a puppy left alone most of the day will find ways to get your attention, most of them not so cute and many downright destructive.

ACCESSORIES

The breeder should tell you what your puppy has been eating. Buy some of this food and have it on hand when your puppy arrives. Keep the puppy on the food and feeding schedule of the breeder, especially for the first few days. If you want to switch foods after that, introduce the new one slowly, gradually adding more and more to the old until it has been entirely replaced.

Your puppy will need a close-fitting nylon or cotton-webbed collar. This collar should be adjustable so that it can be used for the first couple of months. A properly fit collar is tight enough that it will not slip over the head, yet an adult finger fits easily under it. A puppy should never wear a choke chain or any other adult training collar.

Pug puppies need human companionship and shouldn't be left alone for long periods of time.

In addition to a collar, you'll need a 4-to-6-foot-long leash. One made of nylon or cotton-webbed material is a fine and inexpensive first leash. It does not need to be more than $1/2$ an inch in width. It is important to make sure that the clip is of excellent quality and cannot become unclasped on its own. You will need one or two leads for walking the dog, as well as a collar or harness. If you live in a cold climate, a sweater or jacket for excursions with your Pug would be appropriate. Get a somewhat larger size than you immediately need to allow for growth.

Excessive chewing can be partially resolved by providing a puppy with her own chew toys. Small-size dog biscuits are good for the teeth and also act as an amusing toy. Do not buy chew toys composed of compressed particles, as these particles disintegrate when chewed and can get stuck in the puppy's throat. Hard rubber or plastic toys are also good for chewing, as are large rawhide bones. Avoid the smaller chewsticks, as they can splinter and choke the puppy. Anything given to a dog must be large enough that it cannot be swallowed.

The final starter items a puppy will need are a water bowl and food

PUPPY ESSENTIALS

To prepare yourself and your family for your puppy's homecoming, and to be sure your pup has what she needs, you should obtain the following:

Food and Water Bowls: One for each. We recommend stainless steel or heavy crockery—something solid but easy to clean.

Bed and/or Crate Pad: Something soft, washable and big enough for your soon-to-be-adult dog.

Crate: Make housetraining easier and provide a safe, secure den for your dog with a crate—it only looks like a cage to you!

Toys: As much fun to buy as they are for your pup to play with. Don't overwhelm your puppy with too many toys, though, especially the first few days she's home. And be sure to include something hollow you can stuff with goodies, like a Kong.

I.D. Tag: Inscribed with your name and phone number.

Collar: An adjustable buckle collar is best. Remember, your pup's going to grow fast!

Leash: Style is nice, but durability and your comfort while holding it count, too. You can't go wrong with leather for most dogs.

Grooming Supplies: The proper brushes, special shampoo, toenail clippers, a toothbrush and doggy toothpaste.

dish. You can select a smaller food dish for your puppy and then get a bigger one when your dog matures. Bowls are available in plastic, stainless steel and even ceramic. Stainless steel is probably the best choice, as it is practically indestructible. Nonspill dishes are available for the dog that likes to play in her water.

Identification

You will have to provide your puppy with some means of identification.

The first option is a common identification tag attached to the puppy's collar, bearing your name and phone number. This is the first thing someone who finds your Pug will look for, and the information on it is straightforward and accessible. However, puppies can easily slip out of collars, and tags can fall off, so it is important to have a more permanent method of identification as well.

A microchip can also be used to identify your dog. A veterinarian can inject a tiny microchip encoded with your Pug's information under her skin. Many animal shelters and vet's offices have the scanner to read the chip, and it cannot get lost or be removed. However, until the scanners (expensive pieces of equipment) are more widely available, it is preferable to choose another form of identification as well.

The third method is a tattoo of some identifying number (your Social Security number, your dog's AKC number) placed on the inside of your dog's hind leg. A tattoo is easily noticed and located, and it requires no sophisticated machinery to read. Anyone finding a lost dog with a tattoo will inform a vet or local animal shelter who will know what to do.

The single best preventive measure one can take to ensure that a dog is not lost or stolen is to provide her with a completely fenced yard. If you have a fence, it should be carefully inspected to insure there are no holes or gaps in it, and no places

IDENTIFY YOUR DOG

It is a terrible thing to think about, but your dog could somehow, someday, get lost or stolen. For safety's sake, every dog should wear a buckle collar with an identification tag. A tag is the first thing a stranger will look for on a lost dog. Inscribe the tag with your dog's name and your name and phone number.

There are two ways to permanently identify your dog. The first is a tattoo, placed on the inside of your dog's thigh. The tattoo should be your Social Security number or your dog's AKC registration number. The second is a microchip, a rice-sized pellet that is inserted under the dog's skin at the base of the neck, between the shoulder blades. When a scanner is passed over the dog, it will beep, notifying the person that the dog has a chip. The scanner will then show a code, identifying the dog.

11

Chew toys are an excellent diversion for a teething puppy.

Providing your Pug with a fenced-in yard is the best way to keep her from being lost or stolen.

where a vigorous and mischievous puppy could escape by digging an escape path under the fence.

PUPPY-PROOFING

Outside

If you do not have a fenced yard, it would be useful to provide at least an outside kennel area where the puppy could safely relieve herself. Failing that, the youngster should be walked outdoors on a lead several times a day, taking care at first that the lead is sufficiently tight around her neck so that she cannot slip out of it.

Inside

You will also need to puppy-proof your home. Curious puppies will get into everything everywhere. Even if you generally keep your Pug close to you or in her indoor or outdoor enclosure, there will be times when she wants to explore and you cannot watch her. Make sure your home has been puppy-proofed so you can be reasonably confident she won't do serious damage to herself or your home.

Securely stow away all household cleaners and other poisonous products such as antifreeze, which, unfortunately, has a taste dogs seem to love. Keep all electrical cords out of reach, and secure electrical outlets.

Make sure you have removed poisonous plants from your house and garden. Puppies put everything into their mouths, and you need to make sure there's nothing dangerous they can get into. Inside, dangerous plants include poinsettia, ivy and philodendron. Outside, holly, hydrangea and azalea are among the plants of which your puppy should steer clear. The bulbs and root systems of daffodils, tulips and others are also poisonous.

THE ALL-IMPORTANT ROUTINE

Most puppies do best if their lives follow a schedule. They need definite and regular periods of time for playing, eating and sleeping. Puppies

HOUSEHOLD DANGERS

Curious puppies and inquisitive dogs get into trouble not because they are bad, but simply because they want to investigate the world around them. It's our job to protect our dogs from harmful substances, like the following:

In the Garage

antifreeze

garden supplies, like snail and slug bait, pesticides, fertilizers, mouse and rat poisons

In the House

cleaners, especially pine oil

perfumes, colognes, aftershaves

medications, vitamins

office and craft supplies

electric cords

chicken or turkey bones

chocolate, onions

some house and garden plants, like ivy, oleander and poinsettia

13

like to start their day early. This is a good time to take a walk or play some games of fetch. After breakfast, most are ready for a nap. How often this pattern is repeated will depend on one's daily routine. Sometimes it is easier for a working

Puppy-proofing will protect your Pug from indoor and outdoor hazards.

Puppies need a daily routine of scheduled time for playing, eating and sleeping.

person or family to stick with a regular schedule than it is for someone who is home all of the time.

Most dogs reach their peaks of activity and need the least amount of rest from 6 months to 3 years of age. As they mature, they spend increasingly longer periods of time sleeping. It is important to make an effort to ensure that a Pug receives sufficient exercise each day to keep her in proper weight and fitness throughout her life. Puppies need short periods of exercise, but, due to the fact that their bodies are developing, should never be exercised to excess. Walking is more suitable for Pugs than running.

CHAPTER THREE

To Good Health

The strongest body and soundest genetic background will not help a dog lead a healthy life unless he receives regular attention

from his owner. Dogs are susceptible to infection, parasites and diseases for which they have no natural immunity. It is up to us to take preventative measures to make sure that none of these interferes with our dog's health. It may help to think of the upkeep of a dog's health in relation to the calendar. Certain things need to be done on a weekly, monthly and annual basis.

PREVENTIVE HEALTH CARE

Weekly grooming can be the single best monitor of a dog's overall health. The actual condition of the

Run your hands regularly over your dog to feel for any unusual bumps or scratches.

Regular attention and preventative measures will help your Pug lead a long, healthy life.

coat and skin and the "feel" of the body can indicate good health or potential problems. Grooming will help you discover small lumps on or under the skin in the early stages before they become large enough to be seen without close examination.

You may spot fleas and ticks when brushing the coat and examining the skin. Besides harboring diseases and parasites, fleas can make daily life a nightmare for some dogs. Some Pugs are allergic to even a couple of fleas on their bodies. They scratch, chew and destroy their coat and skin because of fleas.

Flea Control

Flea control is never a simple endeavor. Dogs bring fleas inside, where they lay eggs in the carpeting and furniture—anywhere your dog goes in the house. Consequently, real control is a matter of not only treating the dog, but also the other environments the flea inhabits. The yard can be sprayed; and in the house, sprays and flea bombs can be used, but there are more choices for the dog's flea eradication. Flea sprays are effective for one to two weeks. Dips applied to the dog's coat following a bath have equal periods of effectiveness. The disadvantage to both of these is that some dogs may have problems with the chemicals.

Flea collars prevent the fleas from traveling to your dog's head, where it's moister and more hospitable. The problem with collars is that dog owners often tend to leave flea collars on their dogs long after they've ceased to be effective. Again, some dogs may have problems with flea collars, and children should never be allowed to handle them.

Some owners opt for a product that works from the inside out. One such option is a pill (prescribed by a

FLEAS AND TICKS

There are so many safe, effective products available now to combat fleas and ticks that—thankfully—they are less of a problem. Prevention is key, however. Ask your veterinarian about starting your puppy on a flea/tick repellant right away. With this, regular grooming and environmental controls, your dog and your home should stay pest-free. Without this attention, you risk infesting your dog and your home, and you're in for an ugly and costly battle to clear up the problem.

veterinarian) that you give to the dog on a regular basis. The chemicals in the pill course through the dog's bloodstream, and when a flea bites, the blood kills the flea.

Another available option is a product that comes in capsule form. The liquid in the capsule is applied near the dog's shoulders, close to the skin where it disperses itself over the skin and coat to protect against fleas and ticks. Ask your veterinarian about this nontoxic, long-lasting tick and flea preventative.

Ticks

As you examine your dog, check also for ticks that may have lodged in his skin, particularly around the ears or in the hair at the base of the ear, the armpits or around the genitals. If you find a tick, which is a small insect about the size of a pencil eraser when engorged with blood, smear it with petroleum jelly. As the tick suffocates, it will back out and you can then grab it with tweezers and kill it. If the tick doesn't back out, grab it with tweezers and gently pull it out, twisting very gently. Don't just grab and pull or the tick's head may remain in the skin, causing an infection or abscess for which veterinary treatment may be required.

A word of caution: Don't use your fingers or fingernails to pull out ticks. Ticks can carry a number of diseases, including Lyme disease, Rocky Mountain spotted fever and others, all of which can be very serious.

Proper Ear Care

Another weekly job is cleaning the ears. Many times an ear problem is evident if a dog scratches his ears or shakes his head frequently. Clean ears are less likely to develop problems, and if something does occur, it will be spotted early when it can be treated easily. If a dog's ears are very dirty and seem to need cleaning on a daily basis, it is a good indication that something else is going on in the ears besides ordinary dirt and the normal accumulation of earwax. A visit to the veterinarian may indicate a situation that needs special attention.

Brushing Teeth

Regular brushing of the teeth often does not seem necessary when a dog is young and spends much of his time chewing; the teeth always seem to be immaculately clean. As a dog ages, it becomes more important to brush the teeth daily.

Use tweezers to remove ticks from your dog.

18

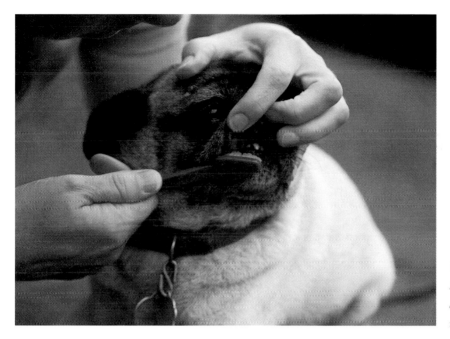

Check your dog's teeth frequently and brush them regularly.

To help prolong the health of your dog's mouth, he should have his teeth cleaned twice a year at a veterinary clinic. Observing the mouth regularly, checking for the formation of abnormalities or broken teeth, can lead to early detection of oral cancer or infection.

Keeping Nails Trimmed

The nails on all feet should be kept short enough that they do not touch the ground when the dog walks.

Dogs with long nails can have difficulty walking on hard or slick surfaces. This can be especially true of older dogs. As nails grow longer, the only way the foot can compensate and retain balance is for the toes themselves to spread apart, causing the foot itself to become flattened and splayed.

Nails that are allowed to become long are also more prone to splitting. This is painful to the dog and usually requires surgical removal of the remainder of the nail for proper healing to occur.

Keeping Eyes Clear

A Pug's eyes sometimes need special attention. A small amount of matter in the corner of the eye is normal, as is a bit of "tearing."

Pugs with eyelashes that turn inward and rub against the eye itself often exhibit more tearing than normal due to the irritation to the eyes. These eyelashes can be surgically removed if it appears to be a problem, but are often ignored.

Excessive tearing can be an indication that a tear duct is blocked. This, too, can be corrected by a simple surgical procedure. Eye discharge that is thicker and mucous-like in consistency is often a sign of an eye infection or an actual injury to the eye. This can be verified by a veterinarian, who will provide a topical ointment to place in the corner of the eye. Most minor eye injuries heal quickly if proper action is taken.

VACCINES

All dogs need yearly vaccinations to protect them from common deadly diseases. The DHL vaccine, which protects a dog from distemper, hepatitis and leptospirosis, is given for the first time at about 7 weeks of age, followed by one or two boosters several weeks apart. After this, a dog should be vaccinated every year throughout his life.

Since the mid-1970s, parvovirus and coronavirus have been the cause of death for thousands of dogs. Puppies and older dogs are most frequently affected by these illnesses. Fortunately, vaccines for these are now routinely given on a yearly basis in combination with the DHL shot.

Kennel cough, though rarely dangerous in a healthy dog that receives proper treatment, can be annoying. It can be picked up anywhere that large numbers of dogs congregate, such as veterinary clinics, grooming shops, boarding kennels, obedience classes and dog shows. The Bordatella vaccine, given twice a year, will protect a dog from getting most strains of kennel cough. It is often not routinely given, so it may be necessary to request it.

INTERNAL PARASITES

While the exterior part of a dog's body hosts fleas and ticks, the inside of the body is commonly inhabited by a variety of parasites. Most of these are in the worm family. Tapeworms, roundworms, whipworms, hookworms and heartworms all plague dogs. There are also several types of protozoa, mainly *coccidia* and *giardia*, that cause problems.

The common tapeworm is acquired by the dog eating infected fleas or lice. Normally, one is not aware that a healthy dog even has tapeworms. The only clues may be a dull coat, a loss of weight despite a good appetite or occasional gastrointestinal problems. Confirmation is by the presence of worm segments in the stool. These appear as small, pinkish-white, flattened rectangular-shaped pieces. When dry, they look like rice. If segments are not present, diagnosis can be made by the discovery of eggs when a stool sample is examined under a microscope. Ridding a dog temporarily of tapeworm is easy with a worming medicine prescribed by a veterinarian. Over-the-counter wormers are not effective for tapeworms and may be dangerous. Long-term tapeworm control is not possible unless the flea situation is also handled.

Ascarids are the most common roundworm (nematode) found in dogs. Adult dogs that have

YOUR PUPPY'S VACCINES

Vaccines are given to prevent your dog from getting infectious diseases like canine distemper or rabies. Vaccines are the ultimate preventive medicine: They're given before your dog ever gets the disease so as to protect him from the disease. That's why it is necessary for your dog to be vaccinated routinely. Puppy vaccines start at 8 weeks of age for the five-in-one DHLPP vaccine and are given every three to four weeks until the puppy is 16 months old. Your veterinarian will put your puppy on a proper schedule and will remind you when to bring in your dog for shots.

roundworms rarely exhibit any symptoms that would indicate the worm is in their body. These worms are cylindrical in shape and may be as long as 4 to 5 inches. They do pose a real danger to puppies, where they are usually passed from the mother through the uterus to the unborn puppies.

It is wise to assume that all puppies have roundworms. In heavy infestations they will actually appear in the puppy stools, though their presence is best diagnosed by a stool sample. Treatment is easy and can begin as early as 2 weeks of age and is administered every two weeks

All puppies should be checked for roundworms.

thereafter until eggs no longer appear in a stool sample or dead worms are not found in the stool following treatment. Severely infected puppies can die from roundworm infestation. Again, the worming medication should be obtained through a veterinarian.

Hookworm is usually found in warmer climates and infestation is generally the result of ingestion of larvae from the ground or penetration of the skin by larvae. Hookworms can cause anemia, diarrhea and emaciation. As these worms are very tiny and not visible to the eye, diagnosis of infection must be made by a veterinarian.

Whipworms live in the large intestine and cause few if any symptoms. Dogs usually become infected when they ingest larvae in contaminated soil. Again, diagnosis and treatment should all be done by a veterinarian. One of the easiest ways to control these parasites is by picking up stools on a daily basis. This will help prevent the soil from becoming infested.

The protozoa can be trickier to diagnose and treat. Coccidiosis and giardia are the most common, and primarily affect young puppies. They are generally associated with over-crowded, unsanitary conditions and can be acquired from the mother (if she is a carrier), the premises themselves (soil) or even water, especially rural puddles and streams.

The most common symptom of protozoan infection is mucous-like, blood-tinged feces. It is only with freshly collected samples that diagnosis of this condition can be made. With coccidiosis, besides diarrhea, the puppies will appear listless and lose their appetites. Puppies often harbor the protozoa and show no symptoms unless placed under stress. Consequently, many times a puppy will not become ill until he goes to his new home. Once diagnosed, treatment is quick and effective and the puppy returns to normal almost immediately.

Heartworm

The most serious of the common internal parasites is the heartworm. A dog that is bitten by a mosquito infected with the heartworm *microfilaria* (larvae) will develop worms that are 6 to 12 inches long. As these worms mature they take up residence in the dog's heart.

Regular vaccinations, preventative medications and proper care will help keep your Pug healthy.

ADVANTAGES OF SPAY/NEUTER

The greatest advantage of spaying (for females) or neutering (for males) your dog is that you are guaranteed that your dog will not produce puppies. There are too many puppies already available for too few homes. There are other advantages as well.

Advantages of Spaying

No messy heats.

No "suitors" howling at your windows or waiting in your yard.

No risk of pyometra (disease of the uterus) and decreased incidences of mammary cancer.

Advantages of Neutering

Decreased incidences of fighting, but does not affect the dog's personality.

Decreased roaming in search of bitches in season.

Decreased incidences of many urogenital diseases.

The symptoms of heartworm may include coughing, tiring easily, difficulty breathing and weight loss. Heart failure and liver disease may eventually result. Verification of heartworm infection is done by drawing blood and screening for the microfilaria.

In areas where heartworm is a risk, it is best to place a dog on a preventative, usually a pill given once a month.

At least once a year a dog should have a full veterinary examination. The overall condition of the dog can be observed and a blood sample collected for a complete yearly screening. This way, the dog's thyroid function can be tested, and the dog's organs can be monitored. If there are any problems, this form of testing can spot trouble areas while they are easily treatable.

Proper care, regular vaccinations, periodic stool checks and preventative medications for heartworm will all help ensure your dog's health.

SPAYING/NEUTERING

Spaying a female dog or neutering a male is another way to make sure they lead long and healthy lives. Females spayed at a young age have almost no risk of developing mammary tumors or reproductive problems. Neutering a male is an excellent solution to dog aggression and also removes the chances of testicular cancer.

Female Pugs usually experience their first heat cycle somewhere between 6 months and 1 year of age. Unless they are spayed, they will continue to come into heat on a regular cycle. The length of time between heats varies, with anything from every six months to once a year being normal.

There is absolutely no benefit to a female having a first season before being spayed, nor in letting her have a litter. The decision to breed any dog should never be taken lightly. The obvious considerations are whether the dog is a good physical specimen of the breed and has a sound temperament. There are genetic problems that are common to Pugs, such as mange, entropion and knee problems (luxated patella). Responsible breeders screen for possible problems prior to making breeding decisions.

Finding suitable homes for puppies is another serious consideration. Due to the Pug's popularity as a breed, many people are attracted to Pugs and seek puppies without realizing the drawbacks of the breed.

Owning a dog is a lifetime commitment to that animal. There are so many unwanted dogs—and yes, even unwanted Pugs—that people must be absolutely sure that they are not just adding to the pet over-population problem. When breeding a litter of puppies, it is more likely that you will lose more money than you will make when time, effort, equipment and veterinary costs are factored in.

COMMON PROBLEMS

Not Eating or Vomiting

One of the surest signs that a Pug may be ill is if he does not eat. That is why it is important to know your dog's eating habits. For most dogs, one missed meal under normal conditions is not cause for alarm, but

Get to know your Pug's eating habits—if he starts missing meals he may be ill.

PREVENTIVE CARE PAYS

Using common sense, paying attention to your dog and working with your veterinarian, you can minimize health risks and problems. Use vet-recommended flea, tick and heartworm preventive medications; feed a nutritious diet appropriate for your dog's size, age and activity level; give your dog sufficient exercise and regular grooming; train and socialize your dog; keep current on your dog's shots; and enjoy all the years you have with your friend.

more than that and it is time to take your dog to the veterinarian to search for reasons. The vital signs should be checked and gums examined. Normally, a dog's gums are pink; if your Pug is ill, they will be pale and gray.

There are many reasons why dogs vomit, and many of them are not cause for alarm. You should be concerned, however, when your dog vomits frequently over the period of a day. If the vomiting is associated with diarrhea, elevated temperature and lethargy, the cause is most likely a virus. The dog should receive supportive veterinary treatment if recovery is to proceed quickly. Vomiting that is not associated with other symptoms is often an

indication of an intestinal blockage. Rocks, toys and clothing will lodge in a dog's intestine, preventing the normal passage of digested foods and liquids.

If a blockage is suspected, the first thing to do is to take an x-ray of the stomach and intestinal region. Sometimes objects will pass on their own, but usually surgical removal of the object is necessary.

Diarrhea

Diarrhea is characterized as very loose, watery stools that a dog has difficulty controlling. It can be caused by anything as simple as changing diet, eating too much food, eating rich human food or having internal parasites.

First try to locate the source of the problem and remove it from the dog's access. Immediate relief is usually available by giving the dog an intestinal relief medication such as Kaopectate or Pepto-Bismol. Use the same amount per weight as for humans. Take the dog off his food for a day to allow the intestines to rest, then feed meals of cooked rice with bland ingredients added. Gradually introduce the dog's regular food back into his diet.

If diarrhea is bloody or has a more offensive odor than might be expected and is combined with vomiting and fever, it is most likely a virus that requires immediate veterinary attention. If worms are suspected as the cause, a stool sample should be examined by a veterinarian and treatment to rid the dog of the parasite should follow when the dog is back to normal. If allergies are suspected, a series of tests can be given to find the specific cause. This is especially likely if, after recovery no other evidence of a cause exists, a dog returns to his former diet the diarrhea recurs.

Dehydration

To test your dog for dehydration, take some skin between your thumb and forefinger and lift the skin upward gently. If the skin does not go back to its original position quickly, the Pug may be suffering from dehydration. Consult your veterinarian immediately.

Poisoning

Vomiting, breathing with difficulty, diarrhea, cries of pain and abnormal body or breath odor are all signs

POISON ALERT

If your dog has ingested a potentially poisonous substance, waste no time. Call the National Animal Poison Control Center hot line:

(800) 548-2423 ($30 per case) or

(900) 680-0000 ($20 first five minutes; $2.95 each additional minute)

that your pet may have ingested a poisonous substance. Poisons can also be inhaled, absorbed through the skin or injected into the skin, as in the case of a snakebite. Poisons require professional help without delay! Call the National Animal Poison Control Center hot line at (900) 680-0000. The call will be charged to your phone—$20.00 for the first five minutes and $2.95 for each additional minute.

Some of the many household substances harmful to your dog.

27

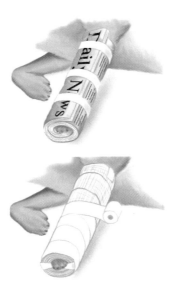

Make a temporary splint by wrapping the leg in firm casing, then bandaging it.

Broken Bones

If your dog breaks a bone, immobilize the limb very carefully, and seek veterinary help right away. If you suspect a spinal injury, place the dog on a board very slowly and carefully tie him securely to the board before immediately transporting him to the veterinarian.

Scratches and Cuts

Minor skin irritations, such as scratches, can usually be cured by using an over-the-counter antibiotic cream or ointment. For minor skin problems, many ointments suitable for a baby work well on a Pug.

Heatstroke

Heatstroke can quickly lead to death. *Never* leave your dog in a car, even with the windows open, even on a cloudy day with the car under the shade of a tree. Heat builds up quickly; your dog could die in a matter of minutes. Do not leave your Pug outside on a hot day, especially if no shade or water is provided.

Heatstroke symptoms include collapse, high fever, diarrhea, vomiting, excessive panting and grayish lips. If you notice these symptoms, you need to cool the animal immediately. Try to reduce the body temperature with towels soaked in cold water; massage the body and legs very gently. Fanning the dog may help. If the dog will drink cool water, let him. If he will not drink, wipe the inside of his mouth with cool water. Get the dog to the nearest veterinary hospital. Do not delay!

Bee Stings

Bee stings are painful and may cause an allergic reaction. Symptoms may be swelling around the bite and difficulty breathing. Severe allergic reaction could lead to death. If a stinger is present, remove it. Clean the bitten area thoroughly with alcohol; apply a cold compress to reduce swelling and itching, and then apply an anti-inflammatory ointment or cream medication. Seek medical help.

Applying abdominal thrusts can save a choking dog.

Choking

Puppies are curious creatures and will naturally chew anything they can get into their mouths, be it a bone, a twig, stones, tiny toys, string or any number of things. These can get caught in the teeth or, worse, lodged in the throat and may finally rest in the stomach or intestines. Symptoms may be drooling, pawing at the mouth, gagging, difficulty breathing, blue tongue or mouth, difficulty swallowing and bloody vomit. If the foreign object can be seen and you can remove it with your pinky finger easily, do so. Use a sweeping motion, being careful not to push the object farther down the dog's throat. If you can't remove it using your pinky, use the Heimlich maneuver. Place your dog on his side and, using both hands palms down, apply quick thrusts to the abdomen, just below the dog's last rib. If your dog won't lie down, grasp either side of the end of the rib cage

and squeeze in short thrusts. Make a sharp enough movement to cause the air in the lungs to force the object out. If the cause cannot be found or removed, then professional help is needed.

Bleeding

For open wounds, try to stop the bleeding by applying pressure to the wound for 5 minutes using a sterile bandage. If bleeding has not stopped after this time, continue the pressure. Do not remove the pad if it sticks to the wound because more serious injury could result. Just place a new sterile bandage over the first, and apply a little more pressure to stop the bleeding. This procedure will usually be successful. Take the dog to the medical center for treatment, especially if the bleeding cannot be quickly controlled.

If bleeding cannot be stopped with pressure, try pressing on the

29

WHEN TO CALL THE VETERINARIAN

In any emergency situation, you should call your veterinarian immediately. Try to stay calm when you call, and give the vet or the assistant as much information as possible before you leave for the clinic. That way, the staff will be able to take immediate, specific action when you arrive. Emergencies include:

- Bleeding or deep wounds
- Hyperthermia (overheating)
- Shock
- Dehydration
- Abdominal pain
- Burns
- Fits
- Unconsciousness
- Broken bones
- Paralysis

Call your veterinarian if you suspect any health troubles.

upper inside of the front leg for bleeding of that limb; for the rear limbs, press on the upper inside of the rear leg; for tail bleeding, press on the underside of the tail at its

base. Do not attempt to stop the bleeding with a tourniquet unless the bleeding is profuse and cannot be stopped any other way. A tourniquet must be tight; consequently, it cannot be left on for a long time because it will stop the circulation. It could be more dangerous than the bleeding!

Burns

Do not put creams or oils on a burn. Cool water can be used to carefully wash the burn area. Transport the dog to the veterinary clinic immediately.

COMMON PUG PROBLEMS

Although Pugs are subject to all the ailments of the canine species, there are a few common ailments of which every Pug owner should be aware. These are: (1) mange, (2) entropion and (3) knee problems (luxated patella). Chances are fairly good that your Pug will have or acquire one or more of these.

Mange

Mange comes in two forms. In Pugs, the most common form and

the easiest to deal with is demodectic mange (also known as red or
puppy mange). It usually occurs
between the ages of 4 and 10
months, but it can occur as late as
18 months. Mange is a mite. It is
normally present on most dogs, but
it is kept in check by the dog's
immune system. Any traumatic
event, such as cutting teeth, an air-
plane trip, the first season or "heat"
(in the female) or even a loud noise,
can lower the natural immunity and
cause the mites to multiply and
become virulent. Spots of hair loss
will occur that, if unattended, will be
followed by skin eruptions and secondary bacterial infections.

At its onset, your Pug may look
a bit "moth-eaten," with small spots
of thin hair or no hair at all. It is
important to catch this condition
early and get your puppy to the veterinary clinic at once for a confirm-
ing diagnosis and treatment.
Although some cases will clear up
by themselves, most vets recommend "dipping" weekly over a period of three to six weeks.

If caught early, the effects of the
mite infestation are minimal, often
almost undetectable, but if noticed
late, it can be a serious danger to
your Pug. The good news is that,

once it has occurred, it seldom
returns.

Sarcoptic mange, which is transmittable to humans, is a much more
serious problem but happily is quite
unusual in Pugs. Demodectic mange
is not transmittable to humans.

Entropion

The second common problem to
which Pugs are heir is entropion, a
condition in which eyelashes rub
against the surface of the eye,
causing irritation that, if left

*Pugs are prone
to mange,
entropion and
knee problems.*

untreated, can lead to blindness. This problem is shared by just about all flat-nosed breeds and is one result of the short muzzle.

Symptoms of entropion are squinting, excessive tear production and staining of the hair below the eyes. If left untreated, the formation of spots of pigment on the eye's surface (pigmentosis) will impair vision. As with other health problems, early detection is important. The condition can be corrected by a minor surgical procedure or can be alleviated or retarded by treating the eyes with a solution of olive oil and cyclosporin (which your veterinarian must prescribe).

Patella Luxation

The third problem, luxation of the patella (kneecap), has been turning up with some frequency in Pugs, although not nearly as frequently as in larger, heavier breeds. The dog's stifle (knee) is protected by a small bone called a patella, similar to the human kneecap. If, at the point where the upper leg bone (femur) joins the lower leg bone, the femur slips out of place and does not make normal contact at the stifle, then the dog has a luxated patella (trick knee).

This can be a "sometime" situation, which corrects itself, or a permanent condition. As time goes by, the "sometime" slippage will become permanent unless corrected. This condition can be painful and a nuisance. Corrective surgery is a fairly simple procedure.

Pug Dog Encephalitis

This is a "breed-specific" disease found only in Pugs. So far, this is the *only* disease found exclusively in Pugs. Other breeds may have encephalitis, but the nature of this disease is unique to Pugs.

Encephalitis is basically an inflammation of the brain; meningitis is an inflammation of the brain's coverings (meninges). Pug encephalitis usually involves both the brain and its outer membranes. The causes of this inflammation are numerous and some are unknown. Bacteria, viruses, fungi and other organisms have been identified. It can be caused by the immune system making a "mistake," by either failing to react to the infecting agent or by mistaking the brain for a foreign agent.

Symptoms include seizures, circling, pressing the head against a firm object (probably indicating headache), weakness on one side of the body, faulty eyesight and sometimes neck pain. Ordinary tests usually come back normal, although there is sometimes a rise in the white blood cells of the spinal fluid. These symptoms become progressively worse; however, a temporary improvement may occur spontaneously or as a result of medicating with prednisone.

There are no known cases in which a Pug has survived this disease. As with any new disease, it will take years for veterinary researchers to gather enough data to understand PDE, and much depends on the cooperation of Pug owners everywhere. If this happens to your Pug, it is very important that you ask your vet to contact his or her veterinary college and request guidance on what should be done. You must also notify your Pug's breeder.

Hemivertibrae

Hemivertibrae simply means "half of a vertebrae." This appears to be an inherited defect. As a dog's skeleton matures, one or more of the vertebra

does not form correctly, which may result in curvature of the spine and compression of the spinal cord. This in turn causes loss of feeling and/or a loss of control of the rear limbs. The unfortunate thing about HV is that it is undetectable until a puppy is 6 to 8 months old and has gone to its new home. While any vertebrae in the spinal column can be affected by HV, it affects the dog only if it occurs in those vertebrae at the base of the neck.

As there is no known way to predict whether a puppy will develop HV, and there is no generally accepted method of treatment, the only preventive measures that can be taken are to provide the Pug's breeder with the dog's medical history, and to rely on his/her integrity in not repeating a breeding that produced the affected Pug. This, of course, offers the owner little consolation.

TAKING YOUR PUG'S TEMPERATURE

Learn to take your pet's temperature. An elevated or depressed temperature may spell the difference between your dog just being "off his

33

WHAT'S WRONG WITH MY DOG?

We've listed some common conditions of health problems and their possible causes. If any of the following conditions appear serious or persist for more than 24 hours, make an appointment to see your veterinarian immediately.

CONDITIONS	POSSIBLE CAUSES
DIARRHEA	Intestinal upset, typically caused by eating something bad or overeating. Can also be a viral infection, a bad case of nerves or anxiety or a parasite infection. If you see blood in the feces, get to the vet right away.
VOMITING/RETCHING	Dogs regurgitate fairly regularly (bitches for their young), whenever something upsets their stomach, or even out of excitement or anxiety. Often dogs eat grass, which, because it's indigestible in its pure form, irritates their stomachs and causes them to vomit. Getting a good look at *what* your dog vomited can better indicate what's causing it.
COUGHING	Obstruction in the throat; virus (kennel cough); roundworm infestation; congestive heart failure.
RUNNY NOSE	Because dogs don't catch colds like people, a runny nose is a sign of congestion or irritation.
LOSS OF APPETITE	Because most dogs are hearty and regular eaters, a loss of appetite can be your first and most accurate sign of a serious problem.
LOSS OF ENERGY (LETHARGY)	Any number of things could be slowing down your dog, from an infection to internal tumors to overexercise—even overeating.

feed" for a day or the presence of some infection, which could be best treated early.

Ask someone to restrain the front end of your dog while you focus your attention on the other end. Grasp the base of the tail firmly, and with the other hand carefully insert a well-lubricated (with petroleum jelly) rectal thermometer into

CONDITIONS	POSSIBLE CAUSES
STINKY BREATH	Imagine if you never brushed your teeth! Foul-smelling breath indicates plaque and tartar buildup that could possibly have caused infection. Start brushing your dog's teeth.
LIMPING	This could be caused by something as simple as a hurt or bruised pad, to something as complicated as hip dysplasia, torn ligaments or broken bones.
CONSTANT ITCHING	Probably due to fleas, mites or an allergic reaction to food or environment (your vet will need to help you determine what your dog's allergic to).
RED, INFLAMED, ITCHY SPOTS	Often referred to as "hot spots," these are particularly common on coated breeds. They're caused by a bacterial infection that gets aggravated as the dog licks and bites at the spot.
BALD SPOTS	These are the result of excessive itching or biting at the skin so that the hair follicles are damaged; excessively dry skin; mange; calluses; and even infections. You need to determine what the underlying cause is.
STINKY EARS/HEAD SHAKING	Take a look under your dog's ear flap. Do you see brown, waxy buildup? Clean the ears with something soft and a special cleaner, and don't use cotton swabs or go too deep into the ear canal.
UNUSUAL LUMPS	Could be fatty tissue, could be something serious (infection, trauma, tumor). Don't wait to find out.

35

the anus. Holding your pet in this fashion should keep him fairly well immobilized. Be sure the thermometer you use is strong enough for this purpose; human oral-type thermometers are too fragile. The average temperature of the dog is approximately 101 degrees Fahrenheit, but there may be normal variation of a degree or so either way; so taking your pet's temperature before he is sick is a good way of establishing your dog's "baseline."

MEDICATING YOUR PUG

If your vet sends you home with medication for your pet for whatever reason, have him or her demonstrate how to administer it.

If you have to give your dog a pill, put him on a table to get him closer to your eye level and immobilize him somewhat. With one hand, grasp the upper part of the muzzle and open his mouth. If you intentionally put your dog's lips between his teeth and your fingers, he will be more reluctant to close his mouth before you are ready. With your other hand, place the pill as far back on his tongue as possible, taking care not to let it fall off to the side,

where it may be bitten or expelled rather than swallowed. Close your dog's mouth and hold his muzzle upright while stroking his throat to encourage swallowing. Keep doing this until you are sure he has swallowed. If your pet spits the pill out, keep at it until you succeed. You have to get the point across that you don't enjoy this any more than he does, but it has to be done!

Liquid medications are pretty rare these days, and if you can't add it to the feed, ask your vet for a syringe (minus the needle). This is a much more controlled method of administering liquids than spoons, but the principle is the same. Here you want to keep your dog's mouth closed, only opening the lips at the corner of his mouth. You then inject or pour the liquid in as you tilt the head back slightly. And you keep the muzzle closed until your dog swallows.

CHAPTER FOUR

Positively Nutritious

Because the normal, healthy Pug is firmly convinced that more of just about anything is better, you must be particularly careful about what you feed Pugsy.

The nutritional needs of a dog change throughout her lifetime. It is necessary to be aware of these changes not only for proper initial growth to occur, but also so your dog can lead a healthy life for many years.

Before bringing your puppy home, ask the breeder for the puppy's feeding schedule and information about what and how much she is used to eating. Maintain this regimen for at least the first few days before gradually changing to a schedule that is more in line with your family's lifestyle. The breeder may supply you with a small quantity of the food the puppy has been eating. Use this or have your own

Puppies and adolescent dogs require a high intake of protein, calories and nutrients to fuel their rapidly developing bodies.

supply of the same food ready when you bring your puppy home.

After the puppy has been with you for three days and has become acclimated to her new environment, you can begin a gradual food change. Add much more new food to the usual food each day until it has entirely replaced the previous diet.

LIFE-STAGE FEEDING

Puppies and adolescent dogs require a much higher intake of protein, calories and nutrients than adult dogs due to the demands of their rapidly developing bodies.

Most commercial brands of dry kibble meet these requirements and are well balanced for proper growth. The majority of puppy foods now available are so carefully planned that it is unwise to add anything other than water to them.

The major ingredients of most dry dog foods are chicken, beef or lamb by-products; and corn, wheat or rice. The higher the meat content, the higher the protein percentage, palatability and digestibility of the food. Protein percentages in puppy food are usually between 25 and 30 percent. There are many advantages of dry foods over semimoist and canned dog foods for puppies and normal, healthy adult Pugs.

It is best to feed meals that are primarily dry food because the chewing action involved in eating a dry food is better for teeth and gum health. Dry food is also less expensive than canned food of equal quality.

Dogs whose diets are based on canned or soft foods have a greater likelihood of developing calcium deposits and gum disease. Canned or semimoist foods do serve certain functions, however. As a supplement to dry dog food, in small portions, canned or semimoist foods can be useful to stimulate appetites and aid in weight gain. But unless very special conditions exist, they are not the best way for a dog to meet her food needs.

A FEEDING SCHEDULE

By the time you bring your puppy home, she will probably be at the stage where three meals will suffice. Your new puppy should be fed morning, midday and evening. Fresh water should be available to her at all times. A good plan to follow is to divide the amount recommended by

GROWTH STAGE FOODS

Once upon a time, there was puppy food and there was adult dog food. Now there are foods for puppies, young adults/active dogs, less active dogs and senior citizens. What's the difference between these foods? They vary by the amounts of nutrients they provide for the dog's growth stage/activity level.

Less active dogs don't need as much protein or fat as growing, active dogs; senior dogs don't need some of the nutrients vital to puppies. By feeding a high-quality food that's appropriate for your dog's age and activity level, you're benefiting your dog and yourself. Feed too much protein to a couch potato and she'll have energy to spare, which means a few more trips around the block will be needed to burn it off. Feed an adult diet to a puppy, and risk growth and development abnormalities that could affect her for a lifetime.

39

FOOD ALLERGIES

If your puppy or dog seems to itch all the time for no apparent reason, she could be allergic to one or more ingredients in her food. This is not uncommon, and it's why many foods contain lamb and rice instead of beef, wheat or soy. Have your dog tested by your veterinarian, and be patient while you strive to identify and eliminate the allergens from your dog's food (or environment).

To Supplement or Not to Supplement?

If you're feeding your dog a diet that's correct for her developmental stage and she's alert, healthy looking and neither over- nor under-weight, you don't need to add supplements. These include table scraps as well as vitamins and minerals. In fact, unless you are a nutrition expert, using food supplements can actually hurt a growing puppy. For example, mixing too much calcium into your dog's food can lead to musculoskeletal disorders. Educating yourself about the quantity of vitamins and minerals your dog needs to be healthy will help you determine what needs to be supplemented. If you have any concerns about the nutritional quality of the food you're feeding, discuss them with your veterinarian.

the veterinarian by three. If the puppy is finishing all three of these portions throughout the day and the appearance of the body indicates proper growth, then stay with those amounts. If the puppy looks like she is gaining weight excessively, then reduce the amount that is given. The same applies for the puppy that leaves quantities of food uneaten, yet is at a good weight and energy level otherwise. Obviously if a puppy is eating her rations and appears thin, her food intake should be increased. This is something that can only be accomplished by observation and good judgment.

From 6 months to 1 year of age the puppy should remain on puppy food, but the feedings should

Feeding your Pug dry food helps keep her teeth and gums healthy.

Like humans, Pugs require good nutrition and exercise throughout their lifetime to remain healthy.

decrease to twice a day. By the time a dog reaches 1 year of age she should be switched to an adult maintenance diet. The number of feedings can remain at twice a day, though it is easier for most owners to feed a large meal once a day.

Puppies and dogs should have a place of their own where they can eat their meals without disturbance. A dog's crate can be an ideal place to feed a dog. Give the dog a definite period of time to eat her food rather than allowing her to nibble throughout the day. If the food has not been eaten within a 10-minute period, pick it up and do not feed again until the next mealtime. One of the best ways to spot health problems in dogs, and Pugs in particular because they tend to be good eaters, is by monitoring their food intake. Most Pugs that miss more than one meal under normal circumstances are not well.

Some owners like to add variety to their dogs' lives with human food. Scraps given regularly can lead to

A well-fed puppy has bright eyes, a shiny coat and lots of energy.

HOW MANY MEALS A DAY?

Individual dogs vary in how much they should eat to maintain a desired body weight—not too fat, but not too thin. Puppies need several meals a day, while older dogs may need only one. Determine how much food keeps your adult dog looking and feeling her best. Then decide how many meals you want to feed with that amount. Like us, most dogs love to eat, and offering two meals a day is more enjoyable for them. If you're worried about overfeeding, make sure you measure correctly and abstain from adding tidbits to the meals.

Whether you feed one or two meals, only leave your dog's food out for the amount of time it takes her to eat it—10 minutes, for example. Free-feeding (when food is available any time) and leisurely meals encourage picky eating. Don't worry if your dog doesn't finish all her dinner in the allotted time. She'll learn she should.

weight gain if the amount of the dog's regular food is not reduced. The risk of destroying the nutritional balance of the dog food also exists. Some human foods fed in large quantities can lead to gastrointestinal problems, which can result in loose stools and even diarrhea.

The amount of food an adult Pug should eat daily will vary according to the size of the dog, her activity level and how much time she spends outside.

Most Pug owners should consider placing their dog on a food that is very low in fat and protein content by the age of 8 or 9, unless the dog is still very active. A dog that is inactive either by choice or the owner's laziness has lower nutritional requirements. Another thing to keep in mind is that as dogs age, their kidneys can be destroyed if kept on a food with high protein content. Foods formulated for older dogs are low in fat and protein content.

Maintaining the proper weight and nutrition of an older Pug is probably more difficult than weight maintenance at any other stage of the Pug's life. A certain amount of body fat is necessary to protect her in the event of illness. Too much excess weight will make the dog even less active and more prone to physical problems. If a dog develops problems such as kidney failure, heart disease or an overly sensitive digestive tract, specially formulated foods that are commercially available might be necessary.

The physical appearance a Pug presents is as much a result of genetics as it is the food she eats. The owner that feeds a high quality food and keeps her in optimum weight for her size will be rewarded with a Pug whose health and fitness mirror her diet.

TYPES OF FOODS/TREATS

There are three types of commercially available dog food—dry, canned and semimoist—and a huge assortment of treats (lucky dogs!) to feed your dog. Which should you choose?

Dry and canned foods contain similar ingredients. The primary difference between them is their moisture content. The moisture is not just water. It's blood and broth, too, the very things that dogs adore. So while canned food is more palatable, dry food is more economical, convenient and effective in controlling tartar buildup. Most owners feed a 25 percent canned/75 percent dry diet to give their dogs the benefit of both. Just be sure your dog is getting the nutrition she needs (you and your veterinarian can determine this).

Semimoist foods have the flavor dogs love and the convenience owners want. However, they tend to contain excessive amounts of artificial colors and preservatives.

Dog treats come in every size, shape and flavor imaginable, from organic cookies shaped like postmen to beefy chew sticks. Dogs seem to love them all, so enjoy the variety. Just be sure not to overindulge your dog. Factor treats into her regular meal sizes.

43

CHAPTER FIVE

Putting on the Dog

Pugs are short-coated and naturally clean little dogs. The Pug owner doesn't have to worry about huge grooming expenses.

Unfortunately, some Pug owners seem to think this means little or no care is needed. It is true that, compared with a Poodle or Yorkshire Terrier, the Pug requires little coat care. But there are a number of things the Pug owner must do to keep his or her Pug healthy, comfortable and happy.

COAT CARE

The Pug's coat should be quite short and have a sheen or glisten to it. It should not shed excessively. A Pug's coat is a good barometer of his overall condition. While a daily brushing should take care of normal shedding, excessive shedding might

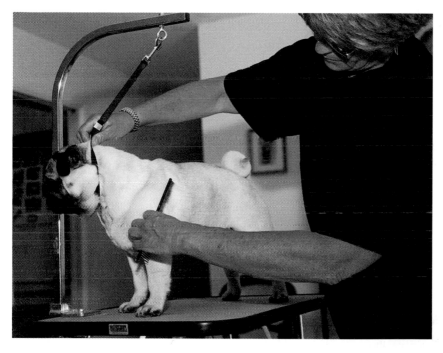

Pugs need regular grooming to keep them looking and feeling their best.

Daily brushing will take care of your Pug's shedding.

mean that the dog has some sort of problem, because the coat is one of the first things affected when a dog begins to have a health problem. If the excessive shedding does not lessen after brushing or stripping, it is a good idea to have your Pug examined by a veterinarian.

Shedding

So now you know it: Pugs shed. Some books say they don't, but they do. This is true more for the

GROOMING TOOLS

pin brush	scissors
slicker brush	nail clippers
flea comb	tooth-cleaning equipment
towel	shampoo
mat rake	conditioner
grooming glove	clippers

While grooming your Pug, check the skin folds on top of the nose for dirt or sores.

46

double-coated fawns than for the blacks, but all Pugs shed. Some may do it seasonally, some fairly steadily.

When a dog is shedding, the fawn owner is advised not to wear dark clothing, and the owner of a black Pug should not wear light-colored clothing. A Pug's hair tends to cling to clothing and requires a good, stiff clothes brush or some sort of sticky device to remove it.

If the shedding is heavy, one should use a slicker brush (available at most pet stores). This brush has fine steel teeth mounted in a rubber base, and is quite efficient in removing loose hair.

Brushing

The effects of shedding are minimized by taking a few minutes each day to brush the coat with an ordinary bristle (not nylon) hairbrush to remove loose hair and stimulate the follicles to produce the natural oils that give the coat its sheen. With sufficient encouragement, your pug will soon get used to the brushing and, in fact, will look forward to it.

You will probably want to have a small table or cabinet top, covered with a bath mat to keep your dog from slipping, on which to place the dog while brushing him. After you have finished his daily brushing, and while he is still on the table, make a careful study of his coat to reveal any sores and flea or tick infestations.

NOSE

Next, examine your Pug's head. Start by placing your thumb between his eyes just above his nose fold and push the skin back so that the entire top of the nose can be seen. Food will sometimes become lodged under the nose fold. As this area is usually moist, sores may develop there. Gently clean under the nose fold with a cotton ball or a piece of old toweling, and then rub a small quantity of petroleum jelly on the skin and nose.

EARS

Check each ear, holding the flap upright. Gently insert a cotton swab (not very far) and clean out any accumulated matter lodged there. Use a different end of the swab for each ear. If there is a dark brown, putrid-smelling substance, your Pug probably has an ear infection and needs to be seen by a veterinarian.

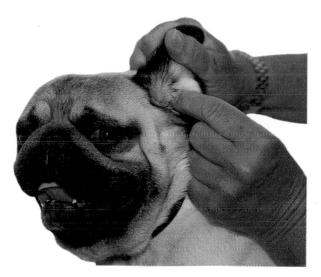

47

EYES

At this point, inspect the dog's eyes. Because Pugs are prone to eye injury, from minor scratches to more serious puncture wounds, care should be taken to detect excessive tearing or staining under the eye, and to see if the eye color has changed. An eye wound will usually look light blue. If this discoloration is noted, get your Pug to the veterinarian immediately!

Ears should be cleaned regularly and carefully.

MOUTH

Before leaving the head area, push back his lips far enough to inspect

A well-groomed Pug looks healthy and clean.

will look forward to it. The Pug is a naturally clean little dog and a bath about once a month should suffice, unless, of course, he has gotten into something that should be cleaned up immediately.

Shampoo

The bath products sold by your vet are usually quite good, as are those found in pet supply stores. Even if there is no sign of a flea or tick infestation, it is advisable to use a shampoo with antiflea/tick medication.

A laundry tub is the best place for a bath, as you will likely have some mopping up to do afterward. Attach a removable hose with a spray head to the tub faucet. Before placing Pugsy in the tub, put a drop of mineral oil in each of his eyes so that if shampoo gets into an eye, it won't sting. Before placing him in the tub and wetting him down, check the water's temperature; it should be warm but not hot. Wet his coat thoroughly before applying the shampoo, then follow the directions on the bottle. Be prepared to get a good soaking yourself if, or when, Pugsy decides to shake, as he

the teeth down to the gums. If tartar accumulation is evident or if gums are either bleeding or very pale, a trip to the vet's office is called for.

BATH

A dog's first bath is likely to go quite easily with lots of patience and as much hand feeding as possible, particularly with a young puppy. In time, he will come to enjoy all the attention that goes with bathing and probably will unless you keep a hand on him at all times.

Start to lather around the neck and head, being careful to avoid the eyes, then work down the body, legs and tail, being sure to reach all the "tight" places like under the legs, around the testicles and anal area and the base of the tail. Then rinse thoroughly, until the rinse water is clear.

Drying

Before removing him from the tub, let him drip for a minute and squeeze as much moisture as you can from the coat. Then give him a good toweling; most Pugs love to be toweled, the rougher the better.

If the weather is good or the house warm, and if you have

QUICK AND PAINLESS NAIL CLIPPING

This is possible if you make a habit out of handling your dog's feet and giving your dog treats when you do. When it's time to clip nails, go through the same routine, but take your clippers and snip off just the ends of the nail—clip too far down and you'll cut into the "quick," the nerve center, hurting your dog and causing the nail to bleed. Clip two nails a session while you're getting your dog used to the procedure, and you'll soon be doing all four feet quickly and easily.

49

toweled him thoroughly, it will do no harm to leave him loose in the laundry room or outside until he is completely dry. Otherwise, dry him with a hair dryer while he is on the grooming table.

CHAPTER SIX

Measuring Up

which judges compare actual dogs and breeders strive to produce dogs. At a dog show, the dog that wins is the one that comes closest, in the judge's opinion, to the standard for its breed.

In 1885, an American standard for the Pug was composed. This standard describes the ideal Pug. No animal actually lives up to the standard in every way, but breeders keep trying to come as close to this description as possible.

The Pug standard is closely copied from the standard previously written by the Kennel Club in England. Since 1885, a few additions have been made by the Pug

WHAT IS A BREED STANDARD?

A breed standard—a detailed description of an individual breed—is meant to portray the *ideal* specimen of that breed. This includes ideal structure, temperament, gait and type—all aspects of the dog. Because the standard describes an ideal specimen, it isn't based on any particular dog. It is a concept against

Dog Club of America and approved by the American Kennel Club (AKC), but the original standard is basically unchanged.

This chapter attempts to explicate the appearance and personality of the breed, according to the AKC standard. It is important to keep in mind when reading the standard and trying to match one's own Pug to it that the standard describes an *ideal* Pug, and some sections are geared toward a show interpretation.

What follow are descriptions of the ideal Pug. Excerpts from the breed standard appear in italics, and are followed by an explanation of their statements.

THE OFFICIAL STANDARD FOR THE PUG

The following is the standard approved by the American Kennel Club in 1991.

General Appearance

Symmetry and general appearance are decidedly square and cobby.

A Pug is square. Not literally, of course, but when you look at a Pug from any angle you should get an impression of squareness. The

THE AMERICAN KENNEL CLUB

Familiarly referred to as "the AKC," the American Kennel Club is a nonprofit organization devoted to the advancement of purebred dogs. The AKC maintains a registry of recognized breeds and adopts and enforces rules for dog events including shows, obedience trials, field trials, hunting tests, lure coursing, herding, earthdog trials, agility and the Canine Good Citizen program. It is a club of clubs, established in 1884 and composed, today, of over 500 autonomous dog clubs throughout the United States. Each club is represented by a delegate; the delegates make up the legislative body of the AKC, voting on rules and electing directors. The American Kennel Club maintains the Stud Book, the record of every dog ever registered with the AKC, and publishes a variety of materials on purebred dogs, including a monthly magazine, books and numerous educational pamphlets. For more information, contact the AKC at the address listed in Chapter 9, "Resources."

51

height at the shoulders should be about the same distance as the length from the front of his chest to the rear.

Size, Proportion, Substance

The Pug should be multum in parvo *and this condensation of form . . . is*

52

In a dog show, a Pug is judged on how closely he conforms to the breed standard.

shown by compactness of form, well knit proportions and hardness of developed muscle.

Multum in parvo is a Latin phrase every Pug owner should know. Translated freely, it means that there is a great deal in a little package— a compact, well-proportioned little dog with a big heart.

Head

The head is large, massive, round. The eyes are dark in color, very large, bold and prominent.

The Pug's crowning glory is its head; it should be round when viewed in profile, square when viewed from the front. Velvety black ears fall to about eye level. The large, round, dark eyes look at you in a soft, pleading, quizzical way, but come alive with excitement during playtime. The muzzle is broad, to match the breadth of the skull and, when his mouth is closed, you should see neither teeth nor tongue. Best of all are the wrinkles around the face, covering his brow and looping over his black nose, contributing so much to his characteristic expression.

Neck, Topline, Body

The neck is strong and thick with enough length to carry the head proudly. The short back is level from the withers to the high tail set. The body is cobby, wide in chest and well ribbed up.

This is self-explanatory when you look at a correct Pug. The "withers" are the shoulders, and "cobby" means compact.

Forequarters

The legs are very strong, straight, of moderate length, and are set well under. The shoulders are moderately laid back.

Standing in front of the Pug, you should see straight, sturdy legs coming down from broad shoulders and chest, forming a square. You do not want to see a bowed front and feet turned outward like a Bulldog.

At the side of the Pug is a broad, strong neck curving slightly just behind the skull and merging smoothly into the shoulders. The legs should be directly under the shoulders and the full, rounded

WHAT IS A BREED STANDARD?

A breed standard—a detailed description of an individual breed—is meant to portray the ideal specimen of that breed. This includes ideal structure, temperament, gait, type—all aspects of the dog. Because the standard describes an ideal specimen, it isn't based on any particular dog. It is a concept against which judges compare actual dogs and breeders strive to produce dogs. At a dog show, the dog that wins is the one that comes closest, in the judge's opinion, to the standard for its breed. Breed standards are written by the breed parent clubs, the national organizations formed to oversee the well-being of the breed. They are voted on and approved by the members of the parent clubs.

The Pug's crowning glory is his head.

The Pug's large, round eyes look at you in a quizzical way.

chest should protrude well forward of the legs. The topline, from shoulders to tail, should be straight and level, the tail set high and curled tightly over either hip. The rear legs should look strong, and when viewed from the side, be moderately bent and parallel to each other when viewed from the rear. The buttocks should be broad, emphasizing the dog's squareness, even when viewed from above.

Coat

The coat is fine, smooth, short and glossy, neither hard nor woolly.

In either color—black or fawn—the Pug's coat should be short and should feel smooth and soft to the touch, not hard or coarse.

Color

The colors are silver, apricot-fawn or black. The silver or apricot-fawn colors should be decided so as to make the contrast complete between the color and the trace and the mask.

Pugs usually come in one of two colors: black and fawn. Black Pugs should have a shiny, jet-black coat and very dark eyes. Occasionally, you will see a white mark or blaze on the chest or paws. This is considered a "mismark" and is inherited from a strain of black Pugs originating in China. Although it is not preferable, it does not affect the overall beauty of the dog. Fawns also will occasionally have a white mark but, as it more easily blends into the lighter coat, it is much less apparent. Except for color, there should be no difference between black and fawn Pugs. Fawns do outnumber blacks to a considerable degree, perhaps as much as 10 to 1.

One factor that may account for the popularity of the fawn over the black Pug is the fawn's markings. Its muzzle is—or should be—jet black, as should be its ears, the moles on its checks and its nails. Most desirable also is a darkened spot centered on the forehead known as a thumbmark or diamond. The line between the black muzzle and the lighter colored upper face should be quite distinct.

The chin and muzzle of most Pugs will begin graying anywhere between 2 and 6 years of age.

The standard also mentions a silver coat, a color that has become quite rare in the United States, though perhaps less so elsewhere. A silver coat has been compared to the

Black Pugs are not uncommon, though fawn Pugs outnumber them by 10 to 1.

color of moonlight, in contrast to the sunlike color of the true fawn. Silver is devoid of any brightness. There is a tendency to confuse silver with smutty fawn.

LOOSE SKIN

Pugs generally have loose skin that sometimes forms rolls of flesh around the throat, over the shoulders and down the back. These rolls usually become more pronounced with advancing age. The standard makes no mention of this phenomenon; some people like it, some don't.

We have now described what a Pug looks like standing still—which rarely happens. So, how should they look while in motion?

The rolls of skin that form along the neck and throat are a distinctive feature of the Pug, though the standard makes no mention of them.

Gait

Viewed from the front, the forelegs should be carried well forward, showing no weaknesses in the pasterns, the paws landing squarely with the central toes straight ahead.

As you watch a Pug move toward you, his legs should swing forward freely with each one moving in a straight line, not swinging out or tending to cross while moving. When he is moving away from you, again the legs should move parallel to one another, along the same line as the front legs, and should not swing out or in. As his trot picks up and he moves faster, there is a tendency for the legs to move toward a center line, and this is quite proper.

Of course, it is not at all unusual for a Pug—especially a puppy—to move at full gallop, with ears and tail streaming behind. This exhibits the Pug's enthusiasm at its best, high spirits, the sheer joy of being alive, the excitement of rough play.

Temperament

This is an even-tempered breed, exhibiting stability, playfulness, great charm, dignity and an outgoing loving disposition.

This description of the Pug's temperament sums up the breed's all-around appeal. What does the Pug Dog Club of America have to say about the breed?

No other dog can equal the Pug in his virtues as a family pet. He appeals to Mother because of his natural cleanliness, intelligence and the fact that he is a "Toy." He appeals to Father because he is a husky, sturdy dog with very little upkeep, needing no professional grooming. Children adore Pugs, and Pugs adore children. They are not too delicate for fun and games. Older people and shut-ins find them perfect as companions because their greatest need is to be by your side and accepted into your way of life. . . . A Pug is anxious to please, anxious to learn, and anxious to love. The Pug's biggest requirement is that you love him back. . . . The Pug's place is in the Toy Group. It is the largest breed in that Group. It is not so much a Toy because of his size, but rather because of his

nature. You can see by the breed's history that for many centuries these dogs have been bred to be companions and pleasures to their owners.

A pet Pug may not live up to all the requirements of the standard. And yet with the right temperament, attitude and good nature, he will be a joy to you and your family.

Pugs are the largest breed in the Toy Group.

CHAPTER SEVEN

A Matter of Fact

The history of many breeds can be precisely traced back to an original homeland or even to an original breeder. The Pug is an exception; the early "history" of this unusual, short-faced dog is more conjecture than established fact.

AN ANCIENT BREED

Over the years, many people have theorized that the Pug is descended from the Mastiff or from the Bulldog. However, it is now generally accepted that the Pug is as close to an original breed as possible. Descriptions of the Pug from China date back as far as 1000 B.C.

In that era, Pugs were the house pets of emperors and nobility. One Chinese ruler was said to have named a Pug as his viceroy, while another endowed his favorite Pug with a high literary title. It is a known fact that Pug-like dogs were given as gifts of great value to Japanese rulers, and several were presented to Russia's first ambassador to China. Beginning in the late sixteenth century, when trade was established with Europe, Portuguese, Dutch, Spanish and English sailors brought some Pugs back to their home countries.

THE PUG IN EUROPE

It was in the Netherlands that the Pug first gained wide popularity in the West. Legend has it that during the Spanish attempt to gain control over Holland, the Spanish troops launched a surprise attack on the Dutch camp, whose army was headed by William the Silent of the House of Orange. William's Pug was the first to alert his master to the attack, before any sentinel, and was credited with saving William's life. After that incident, the Pug became the honored pet of the Dutch ruling house. In 1688 when William of Orange became king of England, his retinue arrived in London with a large assemblage of Pugs.

Bette displays the Pug's winning charm.

Other early Pugs in Europe are known through the paintings of England's William Hogarth, and Spain's Francisco Goya. Hogarth pictured one Pug as quite small and black, definitely identifiable as the true Pug we know today. He also portrayed a larger Pug with a longer muzzle and long legs, indicating the probability of cross-breeding with another unidentified breed. Goya's famous painting of the Duchess of Alba portrays a fawn-colored Pug that would be quite proper by today's standard.

Early in the nineteenth century, the popularity of the Pug seems to have faded. At the same time, dog

WHERE DID DOGS COME FROM?

It can be argued that dogs were right there at man's side from the beginning of time. As soon as human beings began to document their existence, the dog was among their drawings and inscriptions. Dogs were not just friends, they served a purpose: There were dogs to hunt birds, pull sleds, herd sheep, burrow after rats—even sit in laps! What your dog was originally bred to do influences the way he behaves. The American Kennel Club recognizes over 140 breeds, and there are hundreds more distinct breeds around the world. To make sense of the breeds, they are grouped according to their size or function. The AKC has seven groups:

1. Sporting
2. Working
3. Herding
4. Hounds
5. Terriers
6. Toys
7. Non Sporting

Can you name a breed from each group? Here's some help: (1) Golden Retriever, (2) Doberman Pinscher, (3) Collie, (4) Beagle, (5) Scottish Terrier, (6) Maltese and (7) Dalmatian. All modern domestic dogs (*Canis familiaris*) are related, however different they look, and are all descended from *Canis lupus*, the gray wolf.

fanciers began to experiment with cross-breeding in order to establish or reinforce desirable characteristics in their breeds. For example, Pugs were supposedly interbred with Bulldogs in an effort to shorten the Bulldog's muzzle. The French are believed to have crossed Pugs with Bulldogs to reduce the latter's size, resulting in the French Bulldog. Almost surely, the Pug was bred into the Brussels Griffon. Other, often indiscriminate, cross-breeding did much damage to the breed and resulted in a large number of ugly, nondescript dogs that are depicted in nineteenth-century paintings and engravings, barely recognizable as Pugs.

Pugs have not always been held in high esteem. Toward the end of the eighteenth century, the breed's popularity reached a low ebb. One author in 1804 wrote: "In the whole catalogue of the canine species, there is not one of less utility, or possessing less the powers of attraction than the Pug dog, applicable to no sport, appropriated to no useful purpose, susceptible of no predominant passion, and in no way whatever remarkable for any extra eminence, he has continued from era to era for what alone he might have been originally intended, the patient follower of a ruminating philosopher, or the adulating and consolatory companion of an old maid."

In rebuttal, another author wrote: "No doubt the habit of many old ladies of giving Pugs no exercise, and at the same time cramming them with food until their goggles popped (and Pugs will never stop eating so long as anything edible is within reach) contributed to the unfair impression that all dogs of this breed were fat, immobile, pop-eyed, snorting slugs . . . " Today there is little contention that the Pug is a companion dog par excellence.

It should be noted that, even after the popularity of the Pugs declined sharply between 1800 and 1850, a number of devoted breeders continued to rear them and make every effort to improve the breed and halt the trend toward mongrelization. With the introduction of Pug imports from China in the latter half of the century, the fortunes of the breed began a sharp upswing. In fact, it could truly be said that the history of the Pug we know today really began at this point, as dog shows were begun and breeders began to keep better records.

THE BLACK PUG

Although black Pugs existed in England concurrently with the fawns, they were generally not held in favor and, in fact, were often "culled" from the litter and the less said about them, the better. In his 1730 painting, *The House of Cards*, the painter Hogarth depicted a black Pug, so we know that some of them escaped.

Queen Victoria was also known to have owned a black Pug, one heavily marked with white, indicating that it was probably of Chinese origin. But it was not until 1886 that blacks were taken seriously and placed in competition with the fawns. For this, we must thank the well-born English Lady Brassey, a lover of Pugs and an inveterate world traveler. While yachting in Chinese waters in 1876, she acquired and brought back to England several black Pugs, who made a considerable impact on the gene pool in that country. Furthermore, Lady Brassey had the temerity

61

Twentieth-century Pugs have been influenced by imports of Pugs from China in the late nineteenth century.

to exhibit her Chinese blacks at a dog show in 1886, where they gained instant popularity, leading to the creation of several kennels specializing in blacks, as well as to interbreeding with fawns, a practice still in existence.

THE CHINESE INFLUENCE

The Pugs that we know today are most likely the descendants of fresh blood brought into England from China in the mid- to late 1800s. At this point the written and graphic record of the breed begins to have some historical accuracy.

In 1860, British troops sacked the Imperial Palace in Beijing. This event brought fresh imports of Pugs, Pekingese and, to a lesser extent, Japanese Chins (until recently known as Japanese Spaniels) to the West.

About this time, the Chinese Empress Tsu Hsi brought the art and science of breeding to an all-time high, complete with detailed breeding records. The records clearly distinguish between the longer-legged, short-coated Lo-sze (Pug) and the short-legged, long-coated Pekingese. The following description was written by Wang Hou-Chun, one of the imperial kennel supervisors:

One of the most important characteristics of the Chinese Lo-sze is, in addition to universal shortness of coat, elasticity of skin existing to a greater degree than with the "Pekingese." The point most sought after by Chinese breeders was the "Prince" mark, formed by the wrinkles on the forehead with a vertical bar in imitation of the Chinese character for Prince . The button, or white blaze on the forehead, was also encouraged in the Lo-sze dog, but was not of the same importance as the wrinkles. Other points, such as compactness of body, flatness of face, squareness of jaw and soundness of bone, are similar to those of the "Pekingese," except as regards the ears, which were small and likened to a dried half-apricot set with the outer face on the side of the head and pointing slightly backward. The "horn-ear" [which we can equate to the modern Pug's "rose" ear] is also admissible. The legs are but slightly bent at the elbow. The tail is docked . . . with a view to symmetrical form. The curly tail, however, is known to have existed, and the double curl was also known.

Although we are unable to date this description of a Pug, it most certainly preceded the first British standard for the Pug (1883), and may well be the first defining description of the breed. Tail docking was never practiced in the West.

PUGS IN THE UNITED STATES

The date that Pugs arrived in the United States is a matter of conjecture; few records exist prior to 1879, when some 24 of them were exhibited in New York.

While they were quite popular in the early years of this century, the Pug's popularity waned severely during and after World War I, but began a slow but steady revival when, in 1931, the Pug Dog Club of America was established and became a member of the American

63

Pugs have been adored by their owners for centuries.

Kennel Club. However, it was not until 1953 that we find any written record of the PDC's activities. From then on, the breed has increased steadily in popularity.

WHY THE NAME "PUG"?

In America, the Pug's popularity has increased steadily since the 1950s.

Why do we call them Pugs? In the Far East, they were variously known as Lao-tze, Foo dogs and Pai dogs. In German-speaking countries, they were know as Mopshonden, Mops or Mopsi. The French know them as Carlin, and the Italians call them Carlini. Only the English-speaking countries call them Pugs.

Some say the word derives from the Latin *pugnus*, meaning "fist," because the Pug's head, viewed from the side, resembles a clenched fist. A more likely origin was the English use of the word "pug" in past centuries as a term of endearment. It was often applied to pet monkeys during the nineteenth century, when most ladies of quality had such pets upon whom they most likely lavished more love and care than on their own children. A lady might even refer fondly to her husband as "my dear Pug." The dogs, with their somewhat monkeylike expressions, were thus referred to not as "Pugs," but as "Pug dogs," thus distinguishing them from monkeys and husbands. In course of time, the dogs became known simply as "Pugs."

FAMOUS PUGS

As mentioned earlier, the House of Orange had a great affection for Pugs, as one of them reportedly saved the life of William of Orange. When, in 1688, William's grandson,

William III, mounted the British throne with his wife, Mary, the couple brought with them quite a few Pugs, leading to that breed's great popularity in England. One even appeared in a formal portrait of George III.

Another famous (or infamous) Pug was Fortune, whose beautiful owner, the Empress Josephine, kept him with her at all times—including her wedding night! When Napoléon approached his bride, he discovered that she was sharing her bed with Fortune. Fortune welcomed this intruder by taking a piece out of his leg.

In more recent times, Pugs have been owned by such notable persons as the Duke and Duchess of Windsor and the famous film actress, Sylvia Sidney.

THE PUG TODAY

Today, the Pug is renowned as a superb companion. He is a recognized charmer in the print media and on television, and a companion to famous faces all over the world. But the Pug's achievements do not stop there.

Pugs may have gotten their name from the Latin word pugnus, *meaning "fist," because that's what their heads look like.*

FAMOUS OWNERS OF THE PUG

Sammy Davis, Jr.

Andy Warhol

Lena Horne

Duke and Duchess of Windsor

Prince Ranier and Princess Grace of Monaco

The Pug may appear to be the ultimate loafer, but he can excel in obedience.

PUGS IN OBEDIENCE

Though the Pug has a reputation for being stubborn, he is also a loyal, curious and intelligent dog. These latter traits serve the Pug well in obedience training and competition. Although, admittedly, the Pug is a rarer breed in the obedience ring than, for example, a German Shepherd, many Pugs have proven their worth in obedience events.

Whether or not you intend to compete in organized activities, obedience training is helpful for every Pug and should be started informally when your Pug is a puppy. Start with easy exercises, offer lots of praise and positive reinforcement, and you will soon find your Pug wants to be a part of this fun activity.

THERAPY PUGS

Obedience training will make your Pug better behaved and more responsive in every kind of situation. This will be especially useful if you plan to try other activities with your Pug, like therapy work. All over the country, organizations have been established to bring the love, affection and attention that pets offer to those who need it most. People who cannot keep pets with them because they live in an institutional environment, such as a nursing home, benefit from visits by therapy animals. A Pug's easy-going temperament, friendly nature and huggable, unintimidating size make him a perfect candidate for this kind of work.

66

CHAPTER EIGHT

On Good Behavior

by Ian Dunbar, Ph.D., MRCVS

Training is the jewel in the crown—the most important aspect of doggy husbandry. There is no more important variable influencing dog behavior and temperament than the dog's education: A well-trained, well-behaved and good-natured puppydog is always a joy to live with, but an untrained and uncivilized dog can be a perpetual nightmare. Moreover, deny the dog an education and she will not have the opportunity to fulfill her own canine potential; neither will she have the ability to communicate effectively with her human companions.

BASIC TRAINING FOR OWNERS

Ideally, basic owner training should begin well before you select your dog. Find out all you can about your chosen breed first, then master rudimentary training and handling skills. If you already have your puppydog, owner training is a dire emergency—the clock is ticking! Especially for puppies, the first few weeks at home are the most important and influential days in the dog's life. Indeed, the cause of most adolescent and adult problems may be traced back to the initial days the pup explores her new home. This is the time to establish the *status quo*—to teach the puppydog how you would like her to behave and so prevent otherwise quite predictable problems.

In addition to consulting breeders and breed books such as this one (which understandably have a positive breed bias), seek out as many pet owners with your breed as you can find. Good points are obvious. What you want to find out are the breed-specific problems, so you can nip them in the bud. In particular, you should talk to owners with adolescent dogs and

Training your puppy is an opportunity to help her reach her own canine potential.

Luckily, modern psychological training methods are easy, efficient, effective and, above all, considerably dog-friendly and user-friendly. Doggy education is as simple as it is enjoyable. But before you can have a good time play-training with your new dog, you have to learn what to do and how to do it. There is no bigger variable influencing the success of dog training than the owner's experience and expertise. Before you embark on the dog's education, you must first educate yourself.

make a list of all anticipated problems. Most important, test drive at least half a dozen adolescent and adult dogs of your breed yourself. An 8-week-old puppy is deceptively easy to handle, but she will acquire adult size, speed and strength in just four months, so you should learn now what to prepare for.

Puppy and pet dog training classes offer a convenient venue to locate pet owners and observe dogs in action. For a list of suitable trainers in your area, contact the Association of Pet Dog Trainers (see Chapter 9). You may also begin your basic owner training by observing other owners in class. Watch as many classes and test drive as many dogs as possible. Select an upbeat, dog-friendly, people-friendly, fun-and-games, puppydog pet training class to learn the ropes. Also, watch training videos and read training books. You must find out what to do and how to do it *before* you have to do it.

PRINCIPLES OF TRAINING

Most people think training comprises teaching the dog to do things such as sit, speak and roll over, but even a 4-week-old pup knows how

The first few weeks at home are the time to teach your puppy how you would like her to behave.

The first step in training is teaching your dog human words that correspond with her behavior and activities.

to do these things already. Instead, the first step in training involves teaching the dog human words for each dog behavior and activity and for each aspect of the dog's environment. That way you, the owner, can more easily participate in the dog's domestic education by directing her to perform specific actions appropriately, that is, at the right time, in the right place and so on. Training opens communication channels, enabling an educated dog to at least understand her owner's requests.

In addition to teaching a dog what we want her to do, it is also necessary to teach her why she

should do what we ask. Indeed, 95 percent of training revolves around motivating the dog to want to do what we want. Dogs often understand what their owners want; they just don't see the point of doing it—especially when the owner's repetitively boring and seemingly senseless instructions are totally at odds with much more pressing and exciting doggy distractions. It is not so much the dog that is being stubborn or dominant; rather, it is the owner who has failed to acknowledge the dog's needs and feelings and to approach training from the dog's point of view.

The Meaning of Instructions

The secret to successful training is learning how to use training lures to predict or prompt specific behaviors—to coax the dog to do what you want when you want. Any highly valued object (such as a treat or toy) may be used as a lure, which the dog will follow with her eyes and nose. Moving the lure in specific ways entices the dog to move her nose, head and entire body in specific ways. In fact, by learning the art of manipulating various lures, it is possible to teach the dog to assume virtually any body position and perform any action. Once you have control over the expression of the dog's behaviors and can elicit any body position or behavior at will, you can easily teach the dog to perform on request.

Tell your dog what you want her to do, use a lure to entice her to respond correctly, then profusely praise and maybe reward her once she performs the desired action. For example, verbally request "Fido, sit!" while you move a squeaky toy upward and backward over the dog's muzzle (lure-movement and hand signal), smile knowingly as she looks

up (to follow the lure) and sits down (as a result of canine anatomical engineering), then praise her to distraction ("Gooood Fido!"). Squeak the toy, offer a training treat and give your dog and yourself a pat on the back.

Being able to elicit desired responses over and over enables the owner to reward the dog over and over. Consequently, the dog begins to think training is fun. For example, the more the dog is rewarded for sitting, the more she enjoys sitting. Eventually the dog comes to realize that, whereas most sitting is appreciated, sitting immediately upon request usually prompts especially enthusiastic praise and a slew of high-level rewards. The dog begins to sit on cue much of the time, showing that she is starting to grasp the meaning of the owner's verbal request and hand signal.

Why Comply?

Most dogs enjoy initial lure-reward training and are only too happy to comply with their owners' wishes. Unfortunately, repetitive drilling without appreciative feedback tends to diminish the dog's enthusiasm until she eventually fails to see the

OWNING A PARTY ANIMAL

It's a fact: The more of the world your puppy is exposed to, the more comfortable she'll be in it. Once your puppy's had her shots, start taking her everywhere with you. Encourage friendly interaction with strangers, expose her to different environments (towns, fields, beaches) and most important, enroll her in a puppy class where she'll get to play with other puppies. These simple, fun, shared activities will develop your pup into a confident socialite; reliable around other people and dogs.

point of complying anymore. Moreover, as the dog approaches adolescence she becomes more easily distracted as she develops other interests. Lengthy sessions with repetitive exercises tend to bore and demotivate both parties. If it's not fun, the owner doesn't do it and neither does the dog.

Integrate training into your dog's life: The greater number of training sessions each day and the shorter they are, the more willingly compliant your dog will become. Make sure to have a short (just a few seconds) training interlude before every enjoyable canine activity. For example, ask your dog to sit to greet people, to sit before you throw her

Frisbee and to sit for her supper. Really, sitting is no different from a canine "Please." Also, include numerous short training interludes during every enjoyable canine pastime, for example, when playing with the dog or when she is running in the park. In this fashion, doggy distractions may be effectively converted into rewards for training. Just as all games have rules, fun becomes training . . . and training becomes fun.

Eventually, rewards actually become unnecessary to continue motivating your dog. If trained with consideration and kindness, performing the desired behaviors will become self-rewarding and, in a sense, your dog will motivate herself. Just as it is not necessary to reward a human companion during an enjoyable walk in the park, or following a game of tennis, it is hardly necessary to reward our best friend—the dog—for walking by our side or while playing fetch. Human company during enjoyable activities is reward enough for most dogs.

Even though your dog has become self-motivating, it's still good to praise and pet her a lot and offer rewards once in a while, especially for a good job well done. And if for no other reason, praising and rewarding others is good for the human heart.

TRAINER'S TOOLS

Many training books extol the virtues of a vast array of training paraphernalia and electronic and metallic gizmos, most of which are designed for canine restraint, correction and punishment, rather than for actual facilitation of doggy education. In reality, most effective training tools are not found in stores; they come from within ourselves. In addition to a willing dog, all you really need is a functional human brain, gentle hands, a loving heart and a good attitude.

In terms of equipment, all dogs do require a quality buckle collar to sport dog tags and to attach the leash (for safety and to comply with local leash laws). Hollow chew toys (like Kongs or sterilized longbones) and a dog bed or collapsible crate are musts for housetraining. Three additional tools are required:

1. specific lures (training treats and toys) to predict and prompt specific desired behaviors;

2. rewards (praise, affection, training treats and toys) to reinforce

for the dog what a lot of fun it all is; and

3. knowledge—how to convert the dog's favorite activities and games (potential distractions to training) into "life-rewards," which may be employed to facilitate training.

The most powerful of these is knowledge. Education is the key! Watch training classes, participate in training classes, watch videos, read books, enjoy play-training with your dog and then your dog will say "Please," and your dog will say "Thank you!"

HOUSETRAINING

If dogs were left to their own devices, certainly they would chew, dig and bark for entertainment and then no doubt highlight a few areas of their living space with sprinkles of urine, in much the same way we decorate by hanging pictures. Consequently, when we ask a dog to live with us, we must teach her *where* she may dig, *where* she may perform her toilet duties, *what* she may chew and *when* she may bark. After all, when left at home alone for many hours, we cannot expect the dog to amuse herself by completing crosswords or watching the soaps on TV!

Also, it would be decidedly unfair to keep the house rules a secret from the dog, and then get angry and punish the poor critter for inevitably transgressing rules she did not even know existed. Remember: Without adequate education and guidance, the dog will be forced to establish her own rules—doggy rules—and most probably will be at odds with the owner's view of domestic living.

Since most problems develop during the first few days the dog is at home, prospective dog owners must be certain they are quite clear about the principles of housetraining *before* they get a dog. Early misbehaviors quickly become established as the *status quo*—becoming firmly entrenched as hard-to-break bad habits, which set the precedent for years to come. Make sure to teach your dog good habits right from the start. Good habits are just as hard to break as bad ones!

Ideally, when a new dog comes home, try to arrange for someone to be present as much as possible during the first few days (for adult dogs) or weeks for puppies. With only a little forethought, it is surprisingly easy to find a puppy sitter, such as a retired person, who would be willing to eat from your refrigerator and watch your television while keeping an eye on the newcomer to encourage the dog to play with chew toys and to ensure she goes outside on a regular basis.

Potty Training

To teach the dog where to relieve herself:

1. never let her make a single mistake;

2. let her know where you want her to go; and

3. handsomely reward her for doing so: "GOOOOOOOD DOG!!!" liver treat, liver treat, liver treat!

Preventing Mistakes

A single mistake is a training disaster, since it heralds many more in future weeks. And each time the dog soils the house, this further reinforces the dog's unfortunate preference for an indoor, carpeted toilet. Do not let an unhousetrained dog have full run of the house.

When you are away from home, or cannot pay full attention, confine the dog to an area where elimination is appropriate, such as an outdoor run or, better still, a small, comfortable indoor kennel with access to an outdoor run. When confined in this manner, most dogs will naturally housetrain themselves.

If that's not possible, confine the dog to an area, such as a utility room, kitchen, basement or garage, where elimination may not be desired in the long run but as an interim measure it is certainly preferable to doing it all around the house. Use newspaper to cover the floor of the dog's day room. The newspaper may be used to soak up the urine and to wrap up and dispose of the feces. Once your dog develops a preferred spot for eliminating, it is only necessary to cover that part of the floor with newspaper. The smaller papered area may then be moved (only a little each day) toward the door to the outside. Thus the dog will develop the tendency to go to the door when she needs to relieve herself.

Never confine an unhousetrained dog to a crate for long periods. Doing so would force the dog to soil the crate and ruin its usefulness as an aid for housetraining (see the following discussion).

Teaching Where

In order to teach your dog where you would like her to do her business, you have to be there to direct the proceedings—an obvious, yet often neglected, fact of life. In order to be there to teach the dog where to go, you need to know *when* she needs to go. Indeed, the success of housetraining depends on the owner's ability to predict these times. Certainly, a regular feeding schedule will facilitate prediction somewhat, but there is nothing like "loading the deck" and influencing the timing of the outcome yourself!

Whenever you are at home, make sure the dog is under constant supervision and/or confined to a small area. If already well trained, simply instruct the dog to lie down in her bed or basket. Alternatively, confine the dog to a crate (doggy den) or tie-down (a short, 18-inch lead that can be clipped to an eye hook in the baseboard near her bed). Short-term close confinement strongly inhibits urination and defecation, since the dog does not want to soil her sleeping area. Thus,

HOUSETRAINING 1-2-3

1. Prevent Mistakes. When you can't supervise your puppy, confine her in a single room or in her crate (but don't leave her for too long!). Puppy-proof the area by laying down newspapers so that if she does make a mistake, it won't matter.

2. Teach Where. Take your puppy to the spot you want her to use every hour.

3. When she goes, praise her profusely and give her three favorite treats.

when you release the puppydog each hour, she will definitely need to urinate immediately and defecate every third or fourth hour. Keep the dog confined to her doggy den and take her to her intended toilet area each hour, every hour and on the hour. When taking your dog outside, instruct her to sit quietly before opening the door—she will soon learn to sit by the door when she needs to go out!

Teaching Why

Being able to predict when the dog needs to go enables the owner to be on the spot to praise and reward the dog. Each hour, hurry the dog to the intended toilet area in the yard, issue the appropriate instruction ("Go pee!" or "Go poop!"), then give the dog 3 to 4 minutes to produce. Praise and offer a couple of training treats when successful. The treats are important because many people fail to praise their dogs with feeling . . . and housetraining is hardly the time for understatement. So either loosen up and enthusiastically praise that dog: "Wuzzzer-wuzzer-wuzzer, hooooser good wuffer den? Hoooo went pee for Daddy?" Or say "Good dog!" as best you can and offer the treats for effect.

Following elimination is an ideal time for a spot of play-training in the yard or house. Also, an empty dog may be allowed greater freedom around the house for the next half hour or so, just as long as you keep an eye out to make sure she does not get into other kinds of mischief. If you are preoccupied and cannot pay full attention, confine the dog to her doggy den once more to enjoy a peaceful snooze or to play with her many chew toys.

If your dog does not eliminate within the allotted time outside—no biggie! Back to her doggy den, and then try again after another hour.

As I own large dogs, I always feel more relaxed walking an empty dog, knowing that I will not need to finish our stroll weighted down with bags of feces!

Beware of falling into the trap of walking the dog to get her to eliminate. The good ol' dog walk is such an enormous highlight in the dog's life that it represents the single biggest potential reward in domestic dogdom. However, when in a hurry, or during inclement weather, many owners abruptly terminate the walk the moment the dog has done her business. This, in effect, severely punishes the dog for doing the right thing, in the right place at the right time. Consequently, many dogs become strongly inhibited from eliminating outdoors because they know it will signal an abrupt end to an otherwise thoroughly enjoyable walk.

Instead, instruct the dog to relieve herself in the yard prior to going for a walk. If you follow the above instructions, most dogs soon learn to eliminate on cue. As soon as the dog eliminates, praise (and offer a treat or two)—"Good dog! Let's go walkies!" Use the walk as a reward for eliminating in the yard. If the dog does not go, put her back in

her doggy den and think about a walk later on. You will find with a "No feces—no walk" policy, your dog will become one of the fastest defecators in the business.

If you do not have a backyard, instruct the dog to eliminate right outside your front door prior to the walk. Not only will this facilitate clean up and disposal of the feces in your own trash can but, also, the walk may again be used as a colossal reward.

CHEWING AND BARKING

Short-term close confinement also teaches the dog that occasional quiet moments are a reality of domestic living. Your puppydog is extremely impressionable during her first few weeks at home. Regular confinement at this time soon exerts a calming influence over the dog's personality. Remember, once the dog is housetrained and calmer, there will be a whole lifetime ahead for the dog to enjoy full run of the house and garden. On the other hand, by letting the newcomer have unrestricted access to the entire household and allowing her to run willy-nilly, she will most certainly develop a bunch of behavior problems in short order, no doubt necessitating confinement later in life. It would not be fair to remedially restrain and confine a dog you have trained, through neglect, to run free.

When confining the dog, make sure she always has an impressive array of suitable chew toys. Kongs and sterilized longbones (both readily available from pet stores) make the best chew toys, since they are hollow and may be stuffed with treats to heighten the dog's interest. For example, by stuffing the little hole at the top of a Kong with a small piece of freeze-dried liver, the dog will not want to leave it alone.

Remember, treats do not have to be junk food and they certainly should not represent extra calories. Rather, treats should be part of each dog's regular daily diet: Some food may be served in the dog's bowl for breakfast and dinner, some food may be used as training treats, and some food may be used for stuffing chew toys. I regularly stuff my dogs' many Kongs with different shaped biscuits and kibble. The kibble seems to fall out fairly easily, as do the oval-shaped biscuits, thus rewarding the dog instantaneously for checking out the chew toys. The bone-shaped

biscuits fall out after a while, rewarding the dog for worrying at the chew toy. But the triangular biscuits never come out. They remain inside the Kong as lures, maintaining the dog's fascination with her chew toy. To further focus the dog's interest, I always make sure to flavor the triangular biscuits by rubbing them with a little cheese or freeze-dried liver.

If stuffed chew toys are reserved especially for times the dog is confined, the puppydog will soon learn to enjoy quiet moments in her doggy den and she will quickly develop a chew-toy habit—a good habit! This is a simple autoshaping process; all the owner has to do is set up the situation and the dog all but trains herself—easy and effective. Even when the dog is given run of the house, her first inclination will be to indulge her rewarding chew-toy habit rather than destroy less-attractive household articles, such as curtains, carpets, chairs and compact discs. Similarly, a chew-toy chewer will be less inclined to scratch and chew herself excessively. Also, if the dog busies herself as a recreational chewer, she will be less inclined to develop into a recreational barker or digger when left at home alone.

Stuff a number of chew toys whenever the dog is left confined and remove the extra-special-tasting treats when you return. Your dog will now amuse herself with her chew toys before falling asleep and then resume playing with her chew toys when she expects you to return. Since most owner-absent misbehavior happens right after you leave and right before your expected return, your puppydog will now be conveniently preoccupied with her chew toys at these times.

COME

Most puppies will happily approach virtually anyone, whether called or not; that is, until they collide with adolescence and develop other more important doggy interests, such as sniffing a multiplicity of exquisite odors on the grass. Your mission, Mr./Ms. Owner, is to teach and reward the pup for coming reliably, willingly and happily when called—and you have just three months to get it done. Unless adequately reinforced, your puppy's tendency to approach people will self-destruct by adolescence.

Call your dog ("Fido, come!"), open your arms (and maybe squat

down) as a welcoming signal, waggle a treat or toy as a lure and reward the puppydog when she comes running. Do not wait to praise the dog until she reaches you—she may come 95 percent of the way and then run off after some distraction. Instead, praise the dog's first step toward you and continue praising enthusiastically for every step she takes in your direction.

When the rapidly approaching puppy dog is three lengths away from impact, instruct her to sit ("Fido, sit!") and hold the lure in front of you in an outstretched hand to prevent her from hitting you mid-chest and knocking you flat on your back! As Fido decelerates to nose the lure, move the treat upwards and backwards just over her muzzle with an upwards motion of your extended arm (palm-upwards). As the dog looks up to follow the lure, she will sit down (if she jumps up, you are holding the lure too high). Praise the dog for sitting. Move backwards and call her again. Repeat this many times over, always praising when Fido comes and sits; on occasion, reward her.

For the first couple of trials, use a training treat both as a lure to entice the dog to come and sit and as a reward for doing so. Thereafter, try to use different items as lures and rewards. For example, lure the dog with a Kong or Frisbee but reward her with a food treat. Or lure the dog with a food treat but pat her and throw a tennis ball as a reward. After just a few repetitions, dispense with the lures and rewards; the dog will begin to respond willingly to your verbal requests and hand signals just for the prospect of praise from your heart and affection from your hands.

Instruct every family member, friend and visitor how to get the dog to come and sit. Invite people over for a series of pooch parties; do not keep the pup a secret—let other people enjoy this puppy, and let the pup enjoy other people. Puppydog parties are not only fun, they easily attract a lot of people to help you train your dog. Unless you teach your dog how to meet people, that is, to sit for greetings, no doubt the dog will resort to jumping up. Then you and the visitors will get annoyed, and the dog will be punished. This is not fair. Send out those invitations for puppy parties and teach your dog to be mannerly and socially acceptable.

Even though your dog quickly masters obedient recalls in the house, her reliability may falter when playing in the backyard or local park. Ironically, it is the owner who has unintentionally trained the dog not to respond in these instances. By allowing the dog to play and run around and otherwise have a good time, but then to call the dog to put her on leash to take

To teach come, call your dog, open your arms as a welcoming signal, wave a toy or a treat and praise for every step in your direction.

her home, the dog quickly learns playing is fun but training is a drag. Thus, playing in the park becomes a severe distraction, which works against training. Bad news!

Instead, whether playing with the dog off leash or on leash, request her to come at frequent intervals—say, every minute or so. On most occasions, praise and pet the dog for a few seconds while she is sitting, then tell her to go play again. For especially fast recalls, offer a couple of training treats and take the time to praise and pet the dog enthusiastically before releasing her. The dog will learn that coming when called is not necessarily the end of the play session, and neither is it the end of the world; rather, it signals an enjoyable, quality time-out with the owner before resuming play once more. In fact, playing in the park now becomes a very effective life-reward, which works to facilitate training by reinforcing each obedient and timely recall. Good news!

SIT AND DOWN

Teaching the dog a variety of body positions is easy for owner and dog, impressive for spectators and extremely useful for all. Using lure-reward techniques, it is possible to train several positions at once to verbal commands or hand signals (which impress the socks off onlookers).

Sit and down—the two control commands—prevent or resolve nearly a hundred behavior problems. For example, if the dog happily and obediently sits or lies down when requested, she cannot jump on visitors, dash out the front door, run around and chase her tail, pester other dogs, harass cats or annoy family, friends or strangers. Additionally, "Sit" or "Down" are the best emergency commands for off-leash control.

It is easier to teach and maintain a reliable sit than maintain a reliable recall. Sit is the purest and simplest of commands—either the dog is sitting or she is not. If there is any change of circumstances or potential danger in the park, for example, simply instruct the dog to sit. If she sits, you have a number of options: Allow the dog to resume playing when she is safe, walk up and put the dog on leash or call the dog. The dog will be much more likely to come when called if she has already acknowledged her compliance by sitting. If the dog does not sit in the park—train her to!

Stand and rollover-stay are the two positions for examining the dog. Your veterinarian will love you to distraction if you take a little time to teach the dog to stand still and roll over and play possum. Also, your vet bills will be smaller because it will take the veterinarian less time to examine your dog. The rollover-stay is an especially useful command and is really just a variation of the down-stay: Whereas the dog lies prone in

Keep training sessions short, fun and fre-quent, especially for puppies.

the traditional down, she lies supine in the rollover-stay.

As with teaching come and sit, the training techniques to teach the dog to assume all other body positions on cue are user-friendly and dog-friendly. Simply give the appropriate request, lure the dog into the desired body position using a training treat or toy and then praise (and maybe reward) the dog as soon as she complies. Try not to touch the dog to get her to respond. If you teach the dog by guid-ing her into position, the dog will quickly learn that rump-pressure means sit, for example, but as yet you still have no control over your dog if she is just six feet away. It will still be necessary to teach the dog to sit on request. So do not make training a time-consuming two-step process; instead, teach the dog to sit to a verbal request or hand signal from the outset. Once the dog sits willingly when requested, by all means use your hands to pet the dog when she does so.

To teach down when the dog is already sitting, say "Fido, down!" hold the lure in one hand (palm down) and lower that hand to the floor between the dog's forepaws. As the dog lowers her head to follow the lure, slowly move the lure away from the dog just a fraction (in front of her paws). The dog will lie down as she stretches her nose forward to follow the lure. Praise the dog when she does so. If the dog stands up, you pulled the lure away too far and too quickly.

When teaching the dog to lie down from the standing position, say "Down" and lower the lure to the floor as before. Once the dog has lowered her forequarters and assumed a play bow, gently and slowly move the lure toward the dog between her forelegs. Praise the dog as soon as her rear end plops down.

After just a couple of trials it will be possible to alternate sits and downs and have the dog energetically perform doggy push-ups. Praise the dog a lot, and after half a dozen or so push-ups reward the dog with a training treat or toy. You will notice the more energetically you move your arm—upwards (palm up) to get the dog to sit, and downwards (palm down) to get the dog to lie down—the more energetically the dog responds to your requests. Now try training the dog in silence and you will notice she has also learned to respond to hand signals. Yeah! Not too shabby for the first session.

FINDING A TRAINER

Have fun with your dog, take a training class! But don't just sign on any dotted line, find a trainer whose approach and style you like and whose students (and their dogs) are really learning. Ask to visit a class to observe a trainer in action. For the names of trainer near you, ask your veterinarian, your pet supply store, your dog-owning neighbors or call 1-800-PET-DOGS (the Association of Pet Dog Trainers).

RELEVANCY TRAINING

Once you have taught the dog what you expect her to do when requested to come, sit and down, the time is right to teach the dog why she should comply with your wishes. The secret is to have many (many) extremely short training interludes (two to five seconds each) at numerous (numerous) times during the course of the dog's day. Especially work with the dog immediately before the dog's good times and during the dog's good times. For example, ask your dog to sit and/or lie down each time before opening doors, serving meals, offering treats and tummy rubs.

83

Toys that Earn Their Keep

To entertain even the most distracted of dogs, while you're home or away, have a selection of the following toys on hand: hollow chew toys (like Kongs, sterilized hollow longbones and cubes or balls that can be stuffed with kibble). Smear peanut butter or honey on the inside of the hollow toy or bone and stuff the bone with kibble and your dog will think of nothing else but working the object to get at the food. Great to take your dog's mind off the fact that you've left the house.

Similarly, request the dog to sit many times during play or on walks, and in no time at all the dog will be only too pleased to follow your instructions because she has learned that a compliant response heralds all sorts of goodies. Basically all you are trying to teach the dog is how to say please: "Please throw the tennis ball. Please may I snuggle on the couch."

Remember, it is important to keep training interludes short and to have many short sessions each and every day. The shortest (and most useful) session comprises asking the dog to sit and then go play during a play session. When trained this way, your dog will soon associate training with good times. In fact, the dog may

be unable to distinguish between training and good times and, indeed, there should be no distinction. The warped concept that training involves forcing the dog to comply and/or dominating her will is totally at odds with the picture of a truly well-trained dog. In reality, enjoying a game of training with a dog is no different from enjoying a game of backgammon or tennis with a friend; and walking with a dog should be no different from strolling with a spouse, or with buddies on the golf course.

Walk by Your Side

Many people attempt to teach a dog to heel by putting her on a leash and physically correcting the dog when she makes mistakes. There are a number of things seriously wrong with this approach, the first being that most people do not want precision heeling; rather, they simply want the dog to follow or walk by their side. Second, when physically restrained during "training," even though the dog may grudgingly mope by your side when "hand-cuffed" on leash, let's see what happens when she is off leash. History! The dog is in the next county because she never enjoyed walking with you on leash and you have no control over her off leash. So let's just teach the dog off leash from the outset to want to walk with us. Third, if the dog has not been trained to heel, it is a trifle hasty to think about punishing the poor dog for making mistakes and breaking heeling rules she didn't even know existed. This is simply not fair!

Let's teach the dog to enjoy following us and to want to walk by our side off leash. Then it will be easier to teach high-precision off-leash heeling patterns if desired. Before going on outdoor walks, it is necessary to teach the dog not to pull. Then it becomes easy to teach on-leash walking and heeling because the dog already wants to walk with you, she is familiar with the desired walking and heeling positions and she knows not to pull.

FOLLOWING

Start by training your dog to follow you. Many puppies will follow if you simply walk away from them and maybe click your fingers or chuckle. Adult dogs may require additional enticement to stimulate them to follow, such as a training lure or, at the very least, a lively trainer. To teach the dog to follow: (1) keep walking and (2) walk away from the dog. If the dog attempts to lead or lag, change pace; slow down if the dog forges too far ahead, but speed up if she lags too far behind. Say "Steady!" or "Easy!" each time before you slow down and "Quickly!" or "Hustle!" each time before you speed up, and the dog will learn to change pace on cue. If the dog lags or leads too far, or if she wanders right or left, simply walk quickly in the opposite direction and maybe even run away from the dog and hide.

Practicing is a lot of fun. Indoors, entice the dog to follow upstairs, into a bedroom, into the bathroom, downstairs, around the living room couch, zigzagging between dining room chairs and into the kitchen for dinner.

Remember, following has a lot to do with attitude—your attitude! Most probably your dog will not want to follow Mr. Grumpy Troll with the personality of wilted lettuce. Lighten up—walk with a jaunty step, whistle a happy tune, sing, skip and tell jokes to your dog and she will be right there by your side.

BY YOUR SIDE

It is smart to train the dog to walk close on one side or the other—either side will do, your choice. When walking, it is generally bad news to have the dog suddenly cut in front of you. In fact, I train my dogs to walk "By my side" and "Other side"—both very useful instructions. It is possible to position the dog fairly accurately by looking to the appropriate side and clicking your fingers or slapping your thigh on that side. A precise positioning may be attained by holding a training lure, such as a chew toy, tennis ball or food treat. Stop and stand still several times throughout the walk, just as you would when window shopping or meeting a friend. Use the lure to make sure the dog slows down and stays close whenever you stop.

Pugs, like all dogs, will need to have their abundant energy and curiosity reigned in by training.

When teaching the dog to heel, we generally want her to sit in heel position when we stop. Teach heel position at the standstill and the dog will learn that the default heel position is sitting by your side (left or right—your choice, unless you wish to compete in obedience trials, in which case the dog must heel on the left).

Several times a day, stand up and call your dog to come and sit in heel position—"Fido, heel!" For example, instruct the dog to come to heel each time there are commercials on TV or each time you turn a page of a novel, and the dog will get it in a single evening.

NO PULLING ON LEASH

You can start teaching your dog not to pull on leash anywhere—in front of the television or outdoors—but regardless of location, you must not take a single step with tension in the leash. For a reason known only to dogs, even just a couple of paces of pulling on leash is intrinsically motivating and diabolically rewarding. Instead, attach the leash to the dog's collar, grasp the other end firmly with both hands held close to your chest, and stand still—do not budge an inch.

Stand still and wait for the dog to stop pulling, and to sit and/or lie down. All dogs stop pulling and sit eventually. Most take only a couple of minutes; the all-time record is 22 $^1/_2$ minutes. Time how long it takes. Gently praise the dog when she stops pulling, and as soon as she sits, enthusiastically praise the dog and take just one step forwards, then immediately stand still. This single step usually demonstrates the ballistic reinforcing nature of pulling on leash; most dogs explode to the end of the leash, so be prepared for the strain. Stand firm and wait for the dog to sit again. Repeat this half a dozen times and you will probably notice a progressive reduction in the force of the dog's one-step explosions and a radical reduction in the time it takes for the dog to sit each time.

As the dog learns "Sit we go" and "Pull we stop," she will begin to

Your dog will quickly learn that the appearance of a leash means the arrival of a long-awaited trip outdoors.

walk forward calmly with each single step and automatically sit when you stop. Now try two steps before you stop. Wooooooo! Scary! When the dog has mastered two steps at a time, try for three. After each success, progressively increase the number of steps in the sequence: try four steps and then six, eight, ten and twenty steps before stopping. Congratulations! You are now walking the dog on leash.

CHAPTER NINE

Resources

BOOKS

About Pugs

Brown, Ellen S. *The Complete Pug*. New York: Howell Book House, 1997.

Hutchinson, Robert. *For the Love of Pugs*. San Francisco: BrownTrout, 1998.

Thomas, Shirley. *The New Pug*. New York: Howell Book House, 1994.

About Health Care

American Kennel Club. *American Kennel Club Dog Care and Training*. New York: Howell Book House, 1991.

Carlson, Delbert, DVM, and James Giffen, MD. *Dog Owner's Home Veterinary Handbook*. New York: Howell Book House, 1992.

DeBitetto, James, DVM, and Sarah Hodgson. *You & Your Puppy*. New York: Howell Book House, 1995.

Drs. Race Foster and Marty Smith. *Right from the Start*. New York: Howell Book House, 1998.

Lane, Marion, *The Humane Society of the United States Complete Guide to Dog Care*. New York: Little, Brown & Co., 1998.

McGinnis, Terri. *The Well Dog Book*. New York: Random House, 1991.

Schwartz, Stephanie, DVM. *First Aid for Dogs: An Owner's Guide to a Happy, Healthy Pet*. New York: Howell Book House, 1998.

Volhard, Wendy and Kerry L. Brown, *The Holistic Guide for a Healthy Dog*. New York: Howell Book House, 1995.

About Training

Ammen, Amy. *Training in No Time*. New York: Howell Book House, 1995.

Benjamin, Carol Lea. *Mother Knows Best*. New York: Howell Book House, 1985.

Bohnenkamp, Gwen. *Manners for the Modern Dog*. San Francisco: Perfect Paws, 1990.

Dunbar, Ian, Ph. D., MRCVS. *Dr. Dunbar's Good Little Book*. James & Kenneth Publishers, 2140 Shattuck Ave. #2406, Berkeley, CA 94704. (510) 658-8588. Order from Publisher.

Evans, Job Michael. *People, Pooches and Problems*. New York: Howell Book House, 1991.

Palika, Liz. *All Dogs Need Some Training.* New York: Howell Book House, 1997.

Volhard, Jack and Melissa Bartlett. *What All Good Dogs Should Know: The Sensible Way to Train.* New York: Howell Book House, 1991.

About Activities

Hall, Lynn. *Dog Showing for Beginners.* New York: Howell Book House, 1994.

O'Neil, Jackie. *All About Agility.* New York: Howell Book House, 1998.

Simmons-Moake, Jane. *Agility Training, The Fun Sport for All Dogs.* New York: Howell Book House, 1991.

Vanacore, Connie. *Dog Showing: An Owner's Guide.* New York: Howell Book House, 1990.

Volhard, Jack and Wendy. *The Canine Good Citizen.* New York: Howell Book House, 1994.

MAGAZINES

The AKC GAZETTE, The Official Journal for the Sport of Purebred Dogs.
American Kennel Club
260 Madison Avenue
New York, NY 10016
www.akc.org

DOG & KENNEL
7-L Dundas Circle
Greensboro, NC 27407
(336) 292-4047
www.dogandkennel.com

DOG FANCY
Fancy Publications
3 Burroughs
Irvine, CA 92618
(714) 855-8822
http://dogfancy.com

DOG WORLD
Maclean Hunter Publishing Corp.
500 N. Dearborn, Ste. 1100
Chicago, IL 60610
(312) 396-0600
www.dogworldmag.com

PETLIFE: Your Companion Animal Magazine
Magnolia Media Group
1400 Two Tandy Center
Fort Worth, TX 76102
(800) 767-9377
www.petlifeweb.com

MORE INFORMATION ABOUT PUGS

National Breed Club

PUG DOG CLUB OF AMERICA

Corresponding Secretary:
  James P. Cavallaro
  1820 Shadowlawn St.
  Jacksonville, FL 32205

Breeder Contact:
  Mary Ann Hall
  15988 Kettington Rd.
  Chesterfield, MO 63017
  (314) 207-1508

Breed Rescue (if any):
  Maryann Johnson
  (320) 485-2876

The Club can send you information on all aspects of the breed including the names and addresses of breed clubs in your area, as well as obedience clubs. Inquire about membership.

The American Kennel Club

The American Kennel Club (AKC), devoted to the advancement of purebred dogs, is the oldest and largest registry organization in this country. Every breed recognized by the AKC has a national (parent) club. National clubs are a great source of information on your breed. The affiliated clubs hold AKC events and use AKC rules to hold performance events, dog shows, educational programs, health clinics and training classes. The AKC staff is divided between offices in New York City and Raleigh, North Carolina. The AKC has an excellent web site that provides information on the organization and all AKC-recognized breeds. The address is www.akc.org.

For registration and performance events information, or for customer service, contact:

THE AMERICAN KENNEL CLUB
5580 Centerview Dr., Suite 200
Raleigh, NC 27606
(919) 233-9767

The AKC's executive offices and the AKC Library (open to the public) are at this address:

THE AMERICAN KENNEL CLUB
260 Madison Ave.
New York, New York 10016
(212) 696-8200 (general information)
(212) 696-8246 (AKC Library)
www.akc.org

UNITED KENNEL CLUB
100 E. Kilgore Rd.
Kalamazoo, MI 49001-5598
(616) 343-9020
www.ukcdogs.com

AMERICAN RARE BREED ASSOCIATION
9921 Frank Tippett Rd.
Cheltenham, MD 20623
(301) 868-5718 (voice or fax)
www.arba.org

CANADIAN KENNEL CLUB
89 Skyway Ave., Ste. 100
Etobicoke, Ontario
Canada M9W 6R4
(416) 675-5511
www.ckc.ca

ORTHOPEDIC FOUNDATION FOR ANIMALS (OFA)
2300 E. Nifong Blvd.
Columbia, MO 65201-3856
(314) 442-0418
www.offa.org/

Trainers

Animal Behavior & Training Associates (ABTA)
9018 Balboa Blvd., Ste. 591
Northridge, CA 91325
(800) 795-3294
www.Good-dawg.com

Association of Pet Dog Trainers
(APDT)
(800) PET-DOGS
www.apdt.com

National Association of Dog Obedience
Instructors (NADOI)
729 Grapevine Highway, Ste. 369
Hurst, TX 76054-2085
www.kimberly.uidaho.edu/nadoi

Associations

Delta Society
P.O. Box 1080
Renton, WA 98507-1080
(Promotes the human/animal bond
through pet-assisted therapy and other
programs)
www.petsforum.com/
DELTASOCIETY/dsi400.htm

Dog Writers Association of America
(DWAA)
Sally Cooper, Secretary
222 Woodchuck Lane
Harwinton, CT 06791
www.dwaa.org

National Association for Search and
Rescue (NASAR)
4500 Southgate Place, Ste. 100
Chantilly, VA 20157
(703) 222-6277
www.nasar.org

Therapy Dogs International
6 Hilltop Rd.
Mendham, NJ 07945

OTHER USEFUL RESOURCES — WEB SITES

General Information— Links to Additional Sites, On-Line Shopping

www.k9web.com – resources for the dog
world
www.netpet.com – pet related products,
software and services
www.apapets.com – The American Pet
Association
www.dogandcatbooks.com – book cata-
log
www.dogbooks.com – on line bookshop
www.animal.discovery.com/ – cable
television channel on-line

Health

www.avma.org – American Veterinary
Medical Association (AVMA)
www.aplb.org – Association for Pet Loss
Bereavement (APLB)—contains an
index of national hotlines for on-line
and office counseling
www.netfopets.com/AskTheExperts.
html – veterinary questions answered
on-line

Breed Information

www.bestdogs.com/news/ – newsgroup
www.cheta.net/connect/canine/breeds/
– Canine Connections Breed
Information Index

91

INDEX

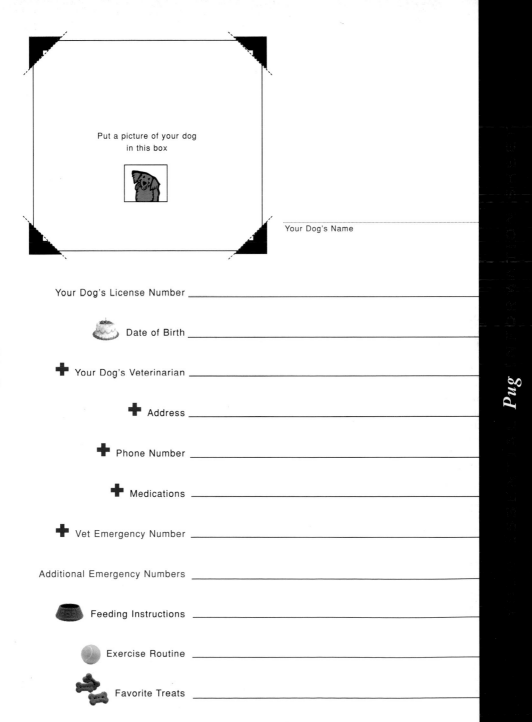

Put a picture of your dog
in this box

Your Dog's Name

Your Dog's License Number _____

Date of Birth _____

Your Dog's Veterinarian _____

Address _____

Phone Number _____

Medications _____

Vet Emergency Number _____

Additional Emergency Numbers _____

Feeding Instructions _____

Exercise Routine _____

Favorite Treats _____

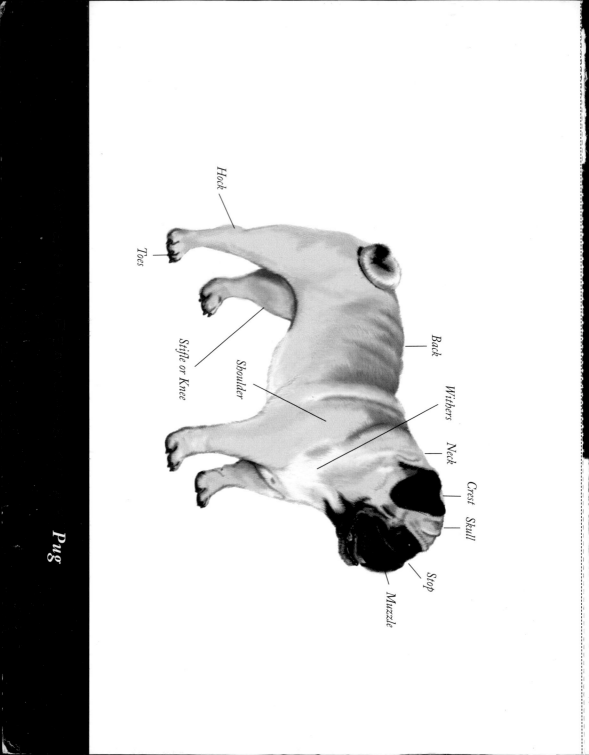

Pug

Hock

Toes

Stifle or Knee

Shoulder

Back

Withers

Neck

Crest Skull

Stop

Muzzle